Corporate Sigma

Optimizing the Health of Your Company with Systems Thinking

Corporate Sigma

Optimizing the Health of Your Company with Systems Thinking

Anwar El-Homsi
Jeff Slutsky

CRC Press
Taylor & Francis Group
Boca Raton   London   New York

CRC Press is an imprint of the
Taylor & Francis Group, an **informa** business

A PRODUCTIVITY PRESS BOOK

Productivity Press
Taylor & Francis Group
270 Madison Avenue
New York, NY 10016

Library of Congress Cataloging-in-Publication Data

El-Homsi, Anwar, 1951-
  Corporate sigma : optimizing the health of your company with systems thinking / Anwar El-Homsi, Jeff Slutsky.
      p. cm.
   Includes bibliographical references and index.
   ISBN 978-1-4398-0394-3 (hbk. : alk. paper)
   1. Total quality management. 2. System analysis. 3. Organizational effectiveness. 4. Business planning. I. Slutsky, Jeff, 1956- II. Title.

HD62.15.E42 2010
658.4'013--dc22   2009042135

Visit the Taylor & Francis Web site at
http://www.taylorandfrancis.com

and the Productivity Press Web site at
http://www.productivitypress.com

For Saadedine El-Homsi and Heather El-Homsi

Anwar El-Homsi

For Jason, Alison, and Jackie Greene and Mike Wolkoff

Jeff Slutsky

Contents

Foreword

I always wondered why some of my favorite teams had such exceptional talent at every position, as well as a great coach, and yet failed to win. It seemed that a bad break here or there brought about the defeat of my band of heroes — until I read *Corporate Sigma*. I discovered it is not the sum of the parts that carries the day in sports or in industry. Rather, it is the development of the organization from a systems thinking point of view that enables corporations or teams to achieve dynasty status — constantly winning despite increasingly complex environments, strong competitors, and wildly different regulatory changes, to name a few. In the turbulent world that we all live in, what the future holds is impossible to predict.

Developing an organization to interact with these changes, adding key capabilities where they count most, and ensuring health and vitality in all parts of the company are levers that great coaches and leaders pull. *Corporate Sigma* helps to isolate key functions and then to blend them from strategic and tactical points of view to achieve a system capable of learning, adapting, developing, and growing according to the winning vision you set for it. It is a comprehensive look at the tools you can use — as a coach, parent, or executive — to develop extraordinary competence in your people and systems to win and win big.

Michael D. Gowen
Executive Vice President
Global Business Operations and Process Excellence
Bausch & Lomb, Inc.

Acknowledgments

Writing a book is an adventure. To begin with, it is a toy and an amusement; then it becomes a mistress, and then it becomes a master, and then a tyrant. The last phase is that just as you are about to be reconciled to your servitude, you kill the monster, and fling him out to the public.

Winston Churchill
British politician

Writing is a form of therapy; sometimes I wonder how all those who do not write, compose, or paint can manage to escape the madness, the melancholia, the panic and fear which is inherent in a human condition.

Graham Greene
Author

The realization of this book was a result of team effort. We would like to express our thanks and gratitude to the entire team — Steven Paul, Susan Kadray, Leslie Henckler, and Mike Kraitsik — who have given constructive feedback and encouragement. We are truly blessed by their invaluable help and dedication.

For their practical assistance, we would like to thank Darius Kasinskas for his contribution to the Leadership Sigma section, Mark N. Scott for his contribution to the IT Sigma section, John Dubuc for his contribution to systems thinking, Francine Z. Schaefer and Matilda Lorenzo for their contribution to the human resources section, and especially to Heather El-Homsi and Chuck Hardy for their invaluable assistance throughout the process.

Writing this book has been a challenge as well as a learning process. We would like to give a special word of thanks to our families and friends, who inspired and stimulated us to take this challenge.

Introduction: Taking Charge

In the twenty-first century, the winners will be those who stay ahead of the change curve, constantly redefining their industries, creating a new market, blazing new trails, reinventing the competitive rules, and challenging the status quo.

Rowan Gibson
Author

For corporations, as for a newborn baby, there is a normal process of growth, learning, and maturation. The child is nurtured, cared for, educated, and routinely taken for health checkups. All vital signs are monitored, and when illness is detected, it is dealt with quickly. The doctor recommends a cure; if needed, an appropriate treatment or medication may be administered, and the child is monitored to prevent reoccurrence. These are the early years of our lives. As we age, through adolescence and into adulthood, the bond we have to our caretakers is weakened and we are left to navigate our future and our health concerns on our own. As adults, we find that some of us have done a good job maintaining the health of our bodies; the others fall ill. Some have adopted bad habits that cause internal organs to fail or operate at less-than-optimum levels. This is often the result when the health of the human body is not monitored and cared for properly.

Corporations, like people, have vital systems that must be monitored and cared for, and they, too, go through life cycles. In the early stages of a corporation's existence, much attention is paid to these vital systems to ensure success. Yet as time goes on, the young corporation grows, brings in "new blood," and forms habits. Employees often are referred to as the lifeblood of an organization, that is, the blood that flows through the organization and nurtures all of the corporation's vital organs. The collection of habits that are formed creates the corporate "culture." Like the human body, all of the functions of an organization must remain healthy to operate at optimum levels.

In *Corporate Sigma*, we show you how to monitor all of your company's vital organs, how to identify illness, and how to administer the appropriate medicine, when needed, to keep the corporation healthy.

We begin by looking at the brain of the organization, its leadership. We do not live in a stationary world; the world around us is constantly changing, with or without the influence of people. We operate today with open borders in a global marketplace. The speed of innovation and technology is relentless. Organizations today face uncertainty and many critical challenges. Some of these challenges are

- top-line growth,
- pricing,
- consistent execution of strategy by top management,
- speed to market,
- innovation,
- and productivity, to name a few.

Only those organizations that successfully address these challenges will survive and thrive. That means that organizational leadership, like the world, needs to adapt to change. Simply put, *what worked in the past will no longer work in the future.*

Every leader has the opportunity to shape the future of his or her organization. He or she can create the vision and the purpose to build a great company. Many leaders believe that their job is to predict the future and lead their organization there. However, we cannot predict the future. Most attempts to predict the future based on past performance only confuse the situation. Absent a crystal ball, what is the role of today's leaders?

One of the leader's roles is to be the "doctor," the one who not only recognizes and provides a cure for illnesses that arise but also recognizes what is good about the organization — the core values or strengths of the company — and then builds off these values to "create" the future. Today's leaders need to envision the possibilities, then create and shape a brighter future for the organization.

One of our objectives in writing *Corporate Sigma* is to guide leaders to identify where they should devote their efforts to build a lasting and visionary company. Our goal is to provide the road map for leaders to plot a course from where they are now to where they want to be. We also want to promote systems thinking, what Peter Drucker calls "the concept of the future," in which organizations can truly learn and realize their highest ambition. *Systems thinking* is the process of examining the whole rather than the parts. A system is a group of interacting, interdependent, related parts that form a complex and unified whole, which has a purpose. A system maintains its existence through the interaction of its parts.

In *Corporate Sigma*, we use the same concept and look at the corporation as a system and at each department (operation, research and development, IT, human resources, and so forth) as subsystems. Dr. Edward Deming, a quality management expert, stated that in an orchestra the players are not there to play solos as prima donnas, each one trying to catch the ear of the listener: they are there to support each other.

Our main purpose in writing *Corporate Sigma* is to aid you in assessing the health of the entire organization and to guide you in providing the appropriate medicine or cure to the challenges facing most companies today.

I.1 LACK OF ENGAGEMENT: THE VIRUS

According to Gallup research, approximately 70% of U.S. employees are not engaged with their work. Gallup statistics also show that unhappy workers cost the American business economy up to $350 billion annually in lost productivity. This disengagement is the result of employee dissatisfaction with their work, which is manifested in absenteeism, illness, and a variety of other big and small problems that occur when people are unhappy at work.

There are three types of employees. The first type is *engaged*. Engaged employees work with passion and feel a profound connection to their company. These employees are aware of what they need to do to add value and are willing to take that action. They drive innovation and productivity to move the organization forward. It is the goal of the organization to employ and retain all engaged employees.

The second type of employee is *not engaged*. These employees have essentially "checked out." They are sleepwalking through their workday and putting in their time, but not bringing energy or passion to their work. They are not efficient and cost the company money in the form of lost productivity.

The third type is the one we call *actively disengaged*. Employees in this category are not only unhappy at work, they are also very busy acting out their dissatisfaction. These employees undermine what the engaged employees accomplish. They pollute the air of the entire organization and are a form of cancer that needs to be removed.

Employee disengagement is a problem not only for the U.S. economy, it is also a global epidemic. Gallup reports that 61% of the British workforce, 67% of the Japanese workforce, and a whopping 82% of the workforce in

Singapore are not engaged. Other findings, according to the 2005 Gallup poll[1] include the following:

- Singapore's workforce ranks among the lowest engaged workforces in the world — disengaged employees cost Singapore $4.9 billion annually.
- Twenty percent of Australian workers are actively disengaged at work, which costs the economy an estimated $31.5 billion per year; the survey of 1500 Australian workers found that only 18% are engaged and providing their employers with high levels of productivity, profitability, and customer service.
- The percentage of engaged employees in organizations is less than 20% in Europe.
- The highest recorded levels of engaged employees are in Brazil (31%) and Mexico (40%). The lowest recorded levels are in Asia.

Furthermore, a recent Conference Board study indicated that more than half of all Americans workers are unhappy with their jobs.[2] Worker job unhappiness also extends to the United Kingdom, Sweden, the Netherlands, India, Japan, and Australia. New research shows that poor performance of disengaged employees can actually "infect" their coworkers and put a drag on an entire company's morale.

Not only does the current environment affect workers' morale, it also affects their health. Denise Kersten reports in a USAtoday.com article that a study conducted by Integra in 2000 found that more than 50% of respondents skip lunch due to job demands and 34% have difficulty sleeping due to job stress.[3] In addition to increases in work-related pain, the risk of heart attack increases by 33% on Monday morning. This has an impact on a company's bottom line. It seems that just the thought of going to work is stress sufficient enough to trigger a heart attack. The study seems to indicate that much of this was related to management not dealing with issues such as workplace verbal and physical abuse and nonperforming employees.

In the book *Good to Great*, Jim Collins emphasizes the importance of having the right people in the company. He recommends that leaders get the right people on the bus, get the wrong people off the bus, and place the right people in the right seats. He points out that by having the right people in the company, the problem of motivating and managing people will go away. He explains that the right people don't need to be tightly managed to be enthusiastic; they will be highly engaged and self-motivated, they will have the drive to produce the best results, and they will have the desire to be part of creating something great. Even if leaders have a great vision, without the right people to take them there, the effort is futile.

If U.S. businesses are to enjoy high productivity in today's global economy, active engagement of employees in their jobs is essential.

I.2 CAN YOU HEAR ME NOW?: THE SYMPTOMS

So how do you create a workforce of actively engaged employees? The first step is simple: *you listen*. Although it is true that some people just cannot be satisfied, the majority want to feel valued by the organization. We have not met a single worker who wanted to do a bad job; the fact is that most disengaged workers were not always that way. They likely started out as engaged or highly engaged but, over time and for a variety of reasons, became "unhealthy" or "ill," and ultimately disengaged. The illness may have been due to pollutants in the air, from feeling that they were treated unfairly, or because they felt their voices were not heard. As a result, these employees simply feel they are not valued by the company.

For whatever reason, the issue of disengaged employees must be addressed. Disengaged employees are unhealthy, and often their disease is contagious and likely to infect others in the organization. The first step to addressing this illness is to listen to your workforce. In recent years, we have met many people with many concerns. Some of these concerns are universal for any organization having this illness.

Here are some of the concerns we have heard:

- Why should I have any loyalty to the company when the company has no loyalty to me?
- As long as I show up, it doesn't matter how well I perform; promotions are based on who you know, not actual ability.
- Management doesn't care what we think; we're just numbers to them.
- Why should I work hard when nothing is done about those who waste time all day?
- Management doesn't want to know about problems; I'm better off covering up the problems or pretending I don't see them than dealing with them. They always shoot the messenger.

- The cost of living is going up faster than my pay.
- I am expected to be flexible in my work but the company is not flexible to my needs.
- The more you give, the more they want, and when it comes time for bonuses or raises, they find a way to justify not giving us fair payment.
- My experience isn't valued; they pay more for some kid out of college than for my years of experience and dedication to the company.
- I'm tired of other people getting credit for my work. Why should I come up with new ideas if I'm never recognized?
- If I do something right, I don't hear about it, but let me make one little mistake, and bam, the whole world knows.

Currently, most companies use money as the source of employee motivation. As Stephen R. Covey puts it, money will motivate *part* of the person but not the *whole* person. We need to stimulate the whole person: the body, the heart, the mind, and the spirit. It is about treating people well, and you don't have to throw a lot of money around to do that.

Employees look for more than monetary compensation and benefit. They want to work where they are recognized and rewarded for performance, where there is good communication, and where they feel that they are part of the success of the company. All of us have unique needs, desires, and challenges, such as career development, alignment of our values with the company's, work/life balance, the desire to make a significant contribution, and to be recognized appropriately.

In an article by Andrea Coombes titled "Show Me You Care,"[4] published by *MarketWatch*, she noted that Towers Perrin, a consulting firm, surveyed almost 90,000 workers in 19 countries, and found that the top 10 drivers of employee engagement include both the behavior and actions of senior management and the individuals' own actions and abilities. She summarized the top 10 drivers of employee engagement as follows:

1. Senior management is sincerely interested in employee well-being.
2. Organization has improved the employee's skills and capabilities over the past year.
3. Organization has a reputation for social responsibility.
4. Employee has input into decision-making in his or her department.
5. Organization quickly resolves customer concerns.
6. Management sets high personal standards.

7. Organization has excellent career advancement opportunities.
8. Employee enjoys challenging work assignments that broaden skills.
9. Employee has a good relationship with supervisor.
10. Organization encourages innovative thinking.

The article states that Julie Gebauer, a managing director with Towers Perrin, believes that many employees "are looking for a greater demonstration of senior management's interest in their day-to-day work. What employees are looking for is open communication, communication that reflects the fact that senior management really understands how the work gets done, and recognizes and appreciates that."

Further, "there are many ways that senior management can show their interest in their employees, including the organization's willingness to help employees balance work and activities outside of work, to sponsor competitive benefit programs, to focus on career development and training. Those are things that will translate to employees as senior management being interested in my well-being."

While other often-cited studies found that workers' immediate supervisors are most important to employees' sense of well-being, this study found otherwise. "It's not to say the manager isn't important, but imagine the best manager in the world working in an organization that doesn't have a good performance-management system, and doesn't have good advancement opportunities," Gebauer said.

The fact is that most people are not thriving in the organizations for which they work. They have neither excitement nor fulfillment. They have little clarity about the company's priorities. They suffer from feeling a loss of passion; feeling disempowered in their jobs with no emotional connection to their organization; coping with low-trust environments, rules, and bureaucracies; and feeling bogged down and distracted, all of which result in boredom, escapism, fear, and anger.

I.3 DIFFERENT MEDICINE FOR DIFFERENT PEOPLE

When people are ill, the medicine is not always the same for each. For example, a particular antibiotic may work for one person, while someone else may need another type. The same is true for corporate ills. The medicine that works for one organization might not work for another.

When companies decide to deploy some quality or process improvement initiatives such as Total Quality Management, Lean Manufacturing, or Six Sigma, they usually hire expert consultants to assist them with the deployment. For example, if the initiative is Lean Manufacturing (a quality program developed by Toyota that helps a company to be more efficient, or, produce more with less), the first thing consultants may do is to target a poorly performing process. Most likely, the selected process will be in production, and the consultant will apply the same set of Lean tools as Toyota applied. However, each company operates, functions, and responds differently. Each organization has a different culture and different knowledge, and what works for Toyota may not work for another company. To continue with our health care analogy: Doctors recommend what they know — to treat cancer, a surgeon will recommend surgery while an oncologist may recommend chemotherapy. A team of doctors focused on the patient's overall health may recommend something completely different when they are looking out for the whole patient instead of tackling the diseased organ.

Throughout this book, we compare the major functions of a corporation to the major functions of the human body. For the body to be healthy, every function or organ of the body needs to be healthy and working well. For corporate health, every department of the company needs to be healthy and functioning well and in balance with the others.

I.4 CORPORATE SIGMA: THE CURE

Today, with the popularity and the success of Six Sigma tools and methods, the word *Sigma* (or *Six Sigma*) has become a symbol of excellence. We introduce the new concept of Corporate Sigma as the symbol of corporate excellence. Corporate Sigma is a management program that provides the tools necessary to transform an organization into a great or visionary company. Like Six Sigma, Corporate Sigma is a quality metric that assesses the quality level, or the health and wellness, of the entire organization. We call this metric *Corporate Sigma Index* (CSI). The higher the CSI, the healthier the company is. This metric is the result of a rolled-up Six Sigma level from different organizational functions. It will be discussed in detail in Chapter 11. Similar to Corporate Sigma, Leadership Sigma is a symbol of leadership excellence, IT Sigma is a symbol of IT excellence, and Human Resources Sigma is a symbol of human resources excellence.

I.5 HOW TO USE THIS BOOK

In this book, we provide you with a distinctive set of tools that will transform your organization into a customer-driven, profitable, and continuous learning organization. It addresses the steps necessary for leaders to evolve their companies into visionary organizations. It defines the roles they should play and the principles and values that will guide them; shows you how to create a sense of purpose, possibility, and commitment; and describes how to sustain success. Also included are the tools necessary to link the entire organization together and to assess the effectiveness or the wellness of the whole organization.

The first few chapters of this book describe the role of leadership. It covers the core competencies for successful leadership needed in the 21st century and outlines the steps necessary to define corporate mission, vision, and values; to develop strategic business objectives; and to explain the importance of personal improvement. The second half of this book introduces the tools required for the improvement of the corporation. Tools discussed include Lean Manufacturing, Six Sigma, systems thinking, innovation, Design for Six Sigma (DFSS), and, finally, Corporate Sigma.

You can read each chapter individually to meet specific and immediate needs. However, we believe that the true power of Corporate Sigma comes when it is taken in its entirety as a holistic approach to ensuring a healthy, productive corporation.

NOTES

1. Jerry Krueger and Emily Killham, "At Work, Feeling Good Matters," *Gallup Management Journal*, December 8, 2005, http://gmj.gallup.com/content/20311/Work-Feeling-Good-Matters.aspx (accessed July 6, 2009).
2. Lynn Franco, "U.S. Job Satisfaction Declines," *Conference Board Reports*, February 23, 2007, http://www.conference-board.org/utilities/pressDetail.cfm?press_ID=3075 (accessed July 6, 2009).

3. Denise Kersten, "Get a Grip on Job Stress," *USA Today*, November 12, 2002, http://www.usatoday.com/money/jobcenter/workplace/stressmanagement/2002–11-12-job-stress_x.htm

4. Andrea Coombes, "Show Me You Care", *MarketWatch*, October 21, 2007, http://www.marketwatch.com/news/story/few-workers-engaged-work-most/story.aspx?guid=%7BF43DB94E-797D-4D26–9593–0B0C65948F76%7D (accessed April 15, 2009).

1

Leadership Sigma: The Brain

No institution can possibly survive if it needs geniuses or supermen to manage it. It must be organized in such a way as to be able to get along under a leadership composed of average human beings.

Peter Drucker
Author, Concept of the Corporation

The nervous system is the human body's decision and communication center. The central nervous system is made of the brain and the spinal cord, while the peripheral nervous system is comprised of nerves. Together, they control every part of a person's daily life, from breathing to blinking to walking. Sensory nerves gather information from the environment and send that information to the spinal cord, which speeds the message to the brain. The brain makes sense of that message and fires off a response. The motor neurons then deliver the instructions from the brain to the rest of the body.

Beyond managing information and delivering orders, the human brain is thought to be the source of the conscious, cognitive mind. The mind is a collection of processes related to perception, interpretation, imagination, and memories, each of which a person may or may not be aware. This is where the ability to dream, believe, and lead resides.

From a philosophical point of view, the most important function of the brain is to serve as the physical structure underlying the mind. From a purely biological point of view, the most important function of the brain is to generate behaviors that promote a person's welfare and the survival of the species.

Brains control behavior either by activating muscles or by causing secretion of chemicals such as hormones in response to information. If there is a problem processing the information or executing the instructions, that information is relayed and responded to. For example, if a person sees a cup and lifts it to drink from it, and the cup is hot, the signal of pain is transmitted to the brain, information is processed, and the person places the cup down. The brain/mind determines what a person should do next; in this example, the choices are to wait until it cools, add ice, or try again and possibly receive more pain.

The leadership of a corporation should function like the human brain; that is, it should receive information from different extremities of the corporation, process that information, and deliver clear instructions about what actions to take. If there is a problem with the delivery or execution of the instructions, that feedback is received and alternatives weighed. Just as the brain must simultaneously manage multiple functional subsystems like circulation, movement, and digestion, corporate leadership must manage multiple complex tasks. The human body can do this because many functions are involuntary — the pathways are set up, the processes defined, and the body executes the task. The mind gets involved only when it receives information that something is not running right. This allows the brain to focus on tasks that require conscious thought. Corporate leadership should operate in the same way. Some routine tasks need to be defined and allowed to operate and self-correct; management should interfere only if there is a problem. That allows the leadership mind to focus on the complex items of the business that require attention.

With the shift from the industrial age to the information age and the knowledge worker, the old command-and-control or carrot-and-stick model is obsolete. As the many corporate scandals — Enron, WorldCom, and so forth — demonstrate, great leadership is needed more than ever. The characteristics of what we call a great leader have remained constant throughout history. Leaders should move us, ignite our passion, inspire the best in us, and most important, lead by serving not only the company but also the employees. Leaders have to define a clear vision, motivate the workforce, and provide employees with the opportunity to develop and utilize their talents and strengths, listen to their concerns, and let them identify their own interests and abilities. However, the most important characteristic that a 21st century leader should possess is trust.

> Trust is one of the most powerful forms of motivation and inspiration. People want to be trusted. They respond to trust. They thrive on trust. Whatever our situation, we need to become good at establishing, extending, and restoring trust.

> **Stephen R. Covey**
> *Author*, The Speed of Trust

1.1 LEADERSHIP AND MANAGEMENT

Are management and leadership the same? No, they are not at all the same. Management is a functional part of an organization. Leadership is a trait that can be found in individuals regardless of occupation. Leadership is the ability to influence and motivate human behavior in order to accomplish a mission or goal. Management can exist in an organization with or without leadership. Management's role is to take charge or care of an organization using specific skills and processes, as well as knowledge of key business practices (usually in line with specific business objectives). Leaders show the way. A leader can manage, and often should. A manager can lead, but often does not.

You do not become a leader when you are promoted into a management position. *You become a leader when people start to follow and trust you.*

1.2 PURPOSE OF LEADERSHIP

A company is a system comprised of many departments or subsystems. Subsystems need to work together to make the whole system successful. Leadership provides the focus, direction, and inspiration to make this happen. Leadership is the brain of the organization.

Many leaders believe that their job is to be able to predict the future and lead their organization there. However, we cannot predict the future. Most attempts to predict the future based on past performance only confuse the situation, because conditions that caused past performance regularly change. Today's organizational leaders need to realize that we live in a vastly different world. Business has gone global, and with the economic and industrial boom in China, Korea, Japan, Mexico, and elsewhere, we all must operate and lead differently than we have in the past.

As time passes, the world becomes more complex and less certain. Organizations will thrive only by constantly reassessing and rethinking their business strategies, industry trends, management practices, processes, information technology, organizational learning, and human capital. To face the future, they need to be prepared to change many aspects of their business — except for their core beliefs.

> Don't tell people how to do things, tell them what to do and let them surprise you with their results.
>
> **George S. Patton**
> *U.S. Army General*

Focusing solely on uniformity, sameness, rigid roles, pleasing authority, and avoiding punishment is no longer as successful as leveraging personal potential, personal growth, personal satisfaction, and process orientation.

Different people have described the purpose of leadership in many different ways. Leaders must be agents of change. They must build confidence by clearly communicating a well-defined and clear, shared vision and its justification. They have to show confidence in the future state. Certainly, for every failing that has ever been blamed on leadership, the opposite has been implied; for example, "They didn't *know!*" = "Leaders should know."

The always applicable, if somewhat uninspiring, definition of leadership is usually some variation of "focusing and inspiring a group to enable them to accomplish a higher-level goal."

1.3 IMPORTANCE OF LEADERSHIP

Leadership is important and necessary in many circumstances. Just as leadership is important to guide children toward becoming flourishing adults, leadership is critical during times of national crisis, for a business or organization to succeed, and for a nonprofit to fulfill its mission.

Failure of leadership can lead to a continuum of results, from overt crises and corporate collapses to more insidious problems. The obvious ones, such as financial failures, are recognizable through external measures. They may result from bad decisions (as in the banking industry) or from poor ethics at the highest levels (such as the Enron scandal). Leadership failure at any level can also manifest itself quietly and slowly. This results in problems such as loss of organizational efficiency and effectiveness, higher turnover, lost work, continual changes of direction, and low workforce morale. Failure in leadership can result in an organization's speedy demise or death.

Conversely, leadership can also act as a *force multiplier*, where the leaders of the organization provide a positive influence on the behavior and attitudes of the work group around them. Over time, the individuals who were part of the work group begin to take on the traits of the leader, and the impact of the sum of these positive multipliers can create extraordinary growth in the organization. This is the quantum leap, or breakthrough point, that moves the organization to the next level.

1.4 CORE COMPETENCIES FOR SUCCESSFUL LEADERSHIP

In the past century, much of leadership thought seemed to focus on leadership style — for example, the carrot and stick. This shortchanges the subject. The leadership style that best motivates a person addresses neither the broader topic of the fundamental competencies that a leader must have nor the basic tasks the leader must perform in order to bring about organizational change.

In effect, a leader's role is to play "doctor" by assessing the current state of the organization, diagnosing both the bad and good, prescribing corrective actions, getting the "patient" to use the prescription, and then evaluating the results.

Figure 1.1 summarizes the core competency, the leadership tasks, and the organizational quality a successful leader should possess.

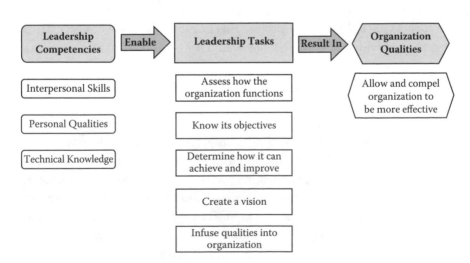

FIGURE 1.1
Core competencies for successful leadership.

1.5 LEADERSHIP CORE COMPETENCIES

Interpersonal skills, personal qualities, and technical knowledge are the competencies a leader must possess in order to lead a particular group to success at a particular time. This assumes that the leader already has a vision for what the group should become. The aptitudes may be called something else, but these are the primary competencies the leader uses to inspire the group to adopt that vision and to create the organizational qualities needed to achieve it. Unlike leadership styles, leadership competencies *are* transferrable across time and organizations.

1.5.1 Strong Interpersonal Skills

Strong interpersonal skills — including the ability to assess others' behavior, organize ideas, communicate effectively, and motivate — are essential to successful leadership. Successful leaders are 360-degree leaders. Communication and motivation happen all around leaders, with peers, subordinates, and superiors. Therefore, leaders need to be aware of how they come across to others and be able to modify this to suit the behavior and attitude of those with whom they are interacting. Leaders must be able to relate to employees as unique individuals.

Even more important is the ability to motivate, inspire, and gain the trust and commitment of people around the leader. Getting people to trust a leader is vital to long-term success. This goes beyond mere honesty. Trust begets good will, and good will between a leader and employee acts as an entry on a relationship balance sheet. How much an employee is willing to do, the "above and beyond" effort that an employee performs, is based largely on how much goodwill the leader has accumulated.

If the leader is trusted, good will accumulates freely as "return on trust" is demonstrated. A leader who asks employees to make an extra effort without having established trust will find employee morale dropping and turnover increasing. People must believe that a leader will do what he or she has promised, to the extent promised, and that the leader will always act in the best interests of the employee. Trust must be earned, but openness, honesty, and transparency in dealings with others can accelerate it.

This is why communication skills and the ability to inspire are vital to establishing trust. It is not enough to be trusting. A leader must also *convey* trust and *inspire* others to trust him or her.

Another vital component of a leader's interpersonal skills is the ability to understand interpersonal and team dynamics. This includes recognizing employees' stressed and unstressed behaviors, motivations, and needs as well as team dynamics, which define how a team reacts and performs. Factors such as company culture, personalities, team roles, existing resources, policies, procedures, and process tools affect team dynamics.

Leaders must make sure that continuous improvement is a part of everyone's daily job. Leaders should help employees find ways to do their jobs better. They should let teams do their jobs without interfering, while keeping the teams informed about things they need to know. Leaders have to know when and how to provide feedback.

Though not often mentioned, being nice, or at least *pleasant*, really helps. We're all human beings, on this earth for a limited time, and we're trying to work together in a common work environment. You might as well be pleasant about it. This doesn't mean leaders can't be tough and assertive when the time calls for it, or that you shouldn't make the difficult decisions, or that you have to be everyone's — or anyone's — friend. The latter can be counterproductive. However, many dismal leaders believe they must be "above" and "beyond" their subordinates, of a better class, and emotionally and personally distant. Bonding a team requires undertaking and completing a difficult task together. It involves getting to know each other at some deeper-than-merely-superficial level. If you are difficult to relate to or are unpleasant to those around you, you cannot be an integral part of a team (and yes, a leader must be a part of a team, *as* a leader). It's okay to be human, and to let others know that you are.

These interpersonal skills are useful in understanding how an organization functions (that is, how the people do what they do, how they work as teams and individuals) and how an organization may be able to improve itself. It is important for effective communication of the leader's vision of what the organization should become and for getting an organization to adopt and make use of those organizational qualities that are necessary to achieve it.

Overall, to be a great leader, others must trust you, have faith in you, and believe in you.

1.5.2 Personal Qualities

The right personal qualities help build confidence and make everything a leader attempts more effective. There are so many qualities that it would take more space than available here to go through them all. In this section, we'll discuss some of the most important.

A strong and balanced work ethic and good personal efficiency skills are an excellent foundation on which leaders can build. The need for these has not changed over time, but the details constantly change as technology changes. Several personal efficiency programs are available and can help you become and remain organized, so that you can accomplish more in less time. They teach how to develop a routine, use planning process and follow-through, and set priorities. In general, they can help you become a good time manager. Such programs are well worth investing in.

In today's global business environment, intercultural skills are invaluable. Being able to communicate, relate to, and understand people from around the world mandates an understanding of other people's cultures. Some cultures — for example, the Korean culture — frown on questioning superiors. Therefore, if a leader does not explain something completely to an employee from this type of culture, the employee might not ask for clarification. It is therefore important for the leader to get feedback to make certain that what was said was understood.

Habitually leveraging technology is indispensible. This means making the best (not most!) use of collaborative software such as e-mail, calendaring, instant and text messaging, and wikis. A leader must be comfortable with this technology as well as proficient at word processing and creating presentations and spreadsheets. Time and accuracy are lost by doing these poorly, and their appearance distracts from their message. Even more time and energy are spent handing these off to someone else — for example, an administrative assistant — to get these done, which inevitably results in misinterpretation and reworking. Leaders benefit from learning how to become fast at putting their thoughts into documents.

Excellent communication skills are mandatory. Communication requires not only expression but also a talent for really listening. As Norm Augustine, former CEO of Lockheed Martin, once said, "When was the last time you heard someone criticized for listening too much?" Leaders should make their expectations clear, while listening to others' concerns — for example, to employees' ideas about things that affect their work — with the respect and dignity they deserve.

When committing thoughts to documents, a leader must be clear and concise. Too many have fallen into the trap of being sesquipedalian (using multisyllabic words) to project superiority. Clarity and concision are hard to come by. Being good at both allows people to focus on your ideas and your message, and not be distracted by your form.

A leader must stimulate confidence in others. There are many ways to do this, and likely the best is to establish a history of success. Take on responsibility and deliver results. Personal behavior engenders trust as well. Being consistent, calm, sincere, and assertive is next best. Be gently persistent. How you treat people affects how they trust you. Make an effort to understand another's point of view, and keep favoritism out of the picture.

Business and process modeling techniques — as well as analytical tools such as affinity diagrams, control charts, Ishikawa (cause and effect) diagrams, process maps, swim-lane (organization structure) charts, to name a few — help a leader make sense of what is observed. Knowing when and how to use these is vital.

It is especially important that leaders know when and how to impose something on an organization without asking for input — that is, when to be autocratic versus when to elicit — and how to listen to input from others.

Leaders who have a desire for self-improvement and who can visualize themselves succeeding will acquire and refine such personal qualities. Having an inquisitive nature and being a quick learner (yes, this can be learned) propel this desire. Continuing education and professional networking provide mental stimulation and add fresh ideas and perspectives for a leader.

Such personal qualities and skills are needed when a leader needs to either find out or set an organization's objectives, select ways improve the organization, create and communicate the vision of what an organization is to become, and monitor the results of change.

1.5.3 Technical Knowledge

Technical knowledge includes those skills related to the organization's products, services, or processes used to create them. Every leader, even those who are not in direct supervisory positions, should have this knowledge because

- Leaders must understand what they are told by others, in order to understand completely the issues raised and to comprehend the usefulness and practicality of the corrective actions being proposed.
- Leaders must recognize when subordinates are misspeaking, whether nonsense, lies, deception, or exaggeration. There are few things quite so damaging as taking at face value a technical statement made in jest.
- Leaders must be respected by subordinates; having technical knowledge is highly valued and respected by many technical workers.

A particularly difficult situation occurs when a leader is in charge of a group tasked with developing and applying new technology. In such cases, it is difficult for the leader to understand the technology, since, by definition, no one really knows it yet. On the other hand, team members face great technical challenges that the leader cannot begin to appreciate, give advice on, or help with. In such cases, the leader must rely on personal skills — an inquisitive nature and the ability to learn quickly — to be able to lead, and must also encourage the team, cheer them through their doubts, recognize and reinforce achievements, help them to find ways to work better, and take down barriers.

Lacking technical knowledge can lead to a lack of respect from the team that may not be obvious to the leader. In a recent engagement, we worked with a team of competent individuals under a technically incompetent manager. The team goal was to support the internal use of a complex analytical software application. The manager insisted (and likely truly believed) that he knew how the application worked, but it was clear every time that he discussed the application with the team members that he had only a vague idea. Worse, he had no notion of how long a given team member's assignment should take. To complicate matters, he never kept a history of assignments, estimates, and actual results from which to learn. He would regularly over- or underestimate by at least an order of magnitude. The team members would work near miracles that were not appreciated or were sometimes given so much time for an assignment that it left them wondering what they didn't know about it.

In practice, they managed the manager by bucketing all the allotted time together, and misstated progress on individual tasks, in order to optimize the achievement of most. The team members recognized the manager's lack of knowledge and openly joked about it when he was not present. He had little credibility with the team, which became demoralized because they felt underappreciated. They became a dysfunctional team without an effective leader. Without competent technical knowledge, the manager failed to earn the team's respect and could not have improved the team dynamics even if he had tried.

> The greatest leaders are those that serve others. A good leader exists for the people, not the other way around.
>
> **Rick Warren**
> *Author*, The Purpose Driven Life

What is the right leadership for the twenty-first century? The answer is, the same qualities that were needed in the past. The leadership competencies that have applied over the years still apply, as do core beliefs such as give more than you get, look after people, and get them to believe in and trust you.

1.6 LEADERSHIP TASKS

Good leaders embody core competencies in themselves and are able to instill the organization with the qualities that not only allow but actually *compel* it to be more effective.

1.6.1 Assess How the Organization Functions

What do the people in the organization do? What is their technical knowledge? What best practices have they adopted? What benchmarks measures are in place? What are the organization's strengths and weaknesses? How do the people in the organization do their tasks? How do they work as individuals and as teams? The leader must inspect the organization with an open mind.

1.6.2 Know the Organization's Objectives

In most cases, the organization's objectives are set by top management, who determine what is needed to survive in the market in which the company competes. What are its opportunities in the marketplace? Are the objectives compatible with corporate strategy and values? Are they appropriate given internal and external comparisons of objectives?

1.6.3 Determine How the Organization Can Achieve Its Objectives and Improve

This objective results from the previous two points, based on external benchmarks and an evaluation of the organization's abilities and weaknesses.

1.6.4 Have a Vision for What the Organization Should Become

This is perhaps the most difficult part of leadership — knowing the direction in which to lead. The leader must have a good grasp of trends in the market, in technology, and in the organization's culture and capabilities.

This requires clear and logical thought as well as creativity and innovation. Equally important, vision is vastly improved through collaboration with other key members of the organization.

The net result of the above is a set of qualities that the organization must possess. There are many criteria. Among them are corporate values and ethics, financial performance criteria, morale, policies, processes, procedures, physical environment, market placement and perception, internal performance feedback and improvement programs, and so on. The importance of each will vary from time to time and from organization to organization. The leader cannot come pre-equipped with a solution, a preconceived notion, or a bottled elixir. That was for another organization, at a different time, and might not apply at all here and now. It is important to remember that these solutions must be tailored to the moment and for the future insofar as it can be seen. This is not easy.

1.6.5 Infuse Leadership Qualities into the Organization

The good leader is contagious; his or her qualities rub off onto those around them. Over time, the leader's qualities are understood by the individuals and teams in such a way that they — and thus the entire organization — adopt and use them. Organizational inertia, the tendency to continue doing what has been done, has to be overcome. This requires communicating with all levels in the organization, as well as the ability to inspire, persevere, explain, convince, and incentivize. Leadership style must be picked with care. Getting people to understand and agree is vital, but getting them to *perform* is even more difficult. This is where a leader must act as a champion, monitor the organization, encourage, reinforce, reward, promote, and control. Expect, but also *inspect*.

1.7 IMPROVING LEADERSHIP

I not only use all the brains that I have, but all that I can borrow.

Woodrow Wilson
Twenty-eighth president of the U.S.

There can be no improvement without measurement, feedback, and learning. Direct measurement of leadership is difficult. Traditionally, it is done by measuring the tangible, quantifiable results, such as balanced scorecards, earnings, growth, or various returns such as return on investment. Nonfinancial measures, such as customer and employee satisfaction, completion of specific improvement plans, or achievement of individual performance improvement or projects are also used. Each of these is merely an indirect consequence of leadership.

Direct measurement of leadership effectiveness is often implemented through qualitative surveys, which generally survey, on a subjective scale, such things as vision, customer focus, quality commitment, integrity, accountability, communication, team building, initiative, and open-mindedness. They are often administered as 360-degree feedback, meaning that subordinates, peers, and superiors are asked to complete them, as is the leader who is being measured or evaluated. Regardless of method, it is important to keep two things in mind. The first is that there is agreement that whatever is measured is, in fact, important to the organization. Thus, the measures are very organization and time specific.

The second is that there must be feedback. Jeffrey A. Sonnenfeld, founder and president of the Chief Executive Leadership Institute, asserted in the *Harvard Business Review* that a "lack of feedback is self-destructive."[1] This implies that feedback at the highest levels of leadership is required to help modify behavior and improve performance, although it is hard to measure such skills. People and organizations cannot learn without proper feedback.

Systems thinking can be used positively to effect leadership improvement. This type of thinking is a paradigm shift from the usual problem-solving techniques to a unique approach where the problem is considered as part of an overall system. In this view, the leader is one component of an organizational system and, therefore, should not be considered in isolation; rather, the organization should be looked at holistically. The danger in looking at improvements to only one component in a system is that changes to that one component might lead to detrimental effects in other areas, or, at the very least, to a silo effect (lack of communication). Viewing the linkages and interactions between the leader and other components of the whole organization is critical.

1.8 DEVELOPING LEADERSHIP

Good leaders usually come from companies that have effective leadership development programs in place, although having these programs in place does not guarantee good leaders. The majority of companies that have outstanding leaders have also incorporated Lean Six Sigma into their leadership development process. The inverse is also true: the majority of leadership development processes that incorporate Lean Six Sigma have outstanding leaders.

Lean Six Sigma is an organizational competency companies use to establish continuous quantified improvement. It is not an elixir. It is a proven process with clearly defined steps that qualified individuals and teams can apply to achieve tangible improvement. The success of Lean Six Sigma depends heavily on the topmost leaders embracing it, believing in it, championing it, and properly applying it.

In some situations, leaders have given lip service to Lean Six Sigma, adopting it because it (whatever "it" is) was successful for a competing company. They, themselves, never really understand it. Despite memos and edicts to the contrary, they are not able to convince the organization to adopt it, because their employees sense the leader's insincerity and see their lack of knowledge. In this situation, Lean Six Sigma, like any other valuable process, will fail, not because it doesn't work, but because a leader lacks the knowledge and commitment to implement it. Enlightened and informed leadership is vital to Lean Six Sigma's success.

1.9 LEADERSHIP AND SYSTEMS THINKING

Today, with a world hungry for change and with multifaceted, global organizations, leaders have many challenges. How should leaders communicate corporate strategy? How do they align the whole organization and minimize wasted activities so that all employees are working efficiently toward a shared vision? How do they measure the organization's effectiveness? How do they promote a culture of agility to respond to the rapidly changing business climate they face? Most business leaders wrestle with these questions each day. To succeed they need to think about the whole organization as a system. They need to understand that an organization is more than its people; it also includes values, structure, processes, policies, regulations, and supervision, to name a few.

An entire corporate system can succeed only when leaders collaborate in and across a number of functional departments or subsystems. The whole system can fail if leadership at a high level fails, particularly when several senior managers are involved (referred to as a systemic failure of leadership). In cases of systemic failure, individual leaders who operate at a lower subsystem level should be free of blame. The leadership of subsystems may individually be successful but that may not be sufficient to cause the whole system's success. Whole-system success requires goal setting, development, incentives, communication, reviews, rewards, accountability, and so on.

Using systems thinking, a leader evaluates not only the tactical consequences but the strategic consequences as well. Consider this example: a farmer has just found a field of tomatoes infested with beetles. The farmer decides to spray a pesticide on the field to eliminate the beetles. The beetles die and the farmer's crops are saved, or so he thinks. However, the farmer has failed to realize that the pesticide he was using not only got rid of the beetles but the honeybees as well. Without the honeybees pollinating the crops, some of his other crops fail. In this example, the farmer — a leader in a subsystem — provided corrective action to resolve a tactical problem but failed to see how the action affected the system strategically. Leaders must be able to evaluate the cause and effect of a solution in not only a tactical sense but a strategic sense as well.

> The use of lower-level models is problematic when applied to higher-level systems.
>
> **Mary Jo Hatch**
> *Author*

In Corporate Sigma, the leadership needs to be able to think in terms of the system. This means that before leaders consider making any type of change to a department or subsystem, they need to evaluate how it will affect tertiary elements of the organization. In his essay, "Systems Thinking and Leadership," Colonel George Reed of the U.S. Army said it best: "If not well considered, today's solutions become tomorrow's problems."

NOTES

1. Jeffrey A. Sonnenfeld, "What Makes Great Boards Great," *Harvard Business Review* (September 2002).

2

Corporate Beliefs: The Soul

There is nothing more pathetic than a man with eyesight but no vision.

Helen Keller
Author and activist

In many religions, the soul is the eternal part of a person. It is usually thought to consist of one's inner awareness and personality, and can be synonymous with the spirit, mind, or self. The dictionary defines soul as "An entity which is regarded as being an immortal or spiritual part of the person and, though having no physical or material reality, is credited with the functions of thinking and willing, hence determining all behavior."[1] This capacity of the soul to think and determine behavior allows the creation of vision. Mary Wollstonecraft Shelley believed that "Nothing contributes so much to tranquilizing the mind as a steady purpose — a point on which the soul may fix its intellectual eye."[2] She was describing the innate need of the soul to have a vision — a point to focus on and guide it. Just as human beings have this need, the corporation, which also has a soul, needs a vision to guide it.

Corporations that have embraced this ideal have noticeable characteristics. They show passion, commitment, and the ability to achieve extraordinary success. They are soulful, and it shows in the ways they conduct their business, energize their employees, and exist within their communities. On the other hand, corporations without soul usually appear disorganized, distracted, and unproductive.

Many studies have shown that companies that adhere to a well-defined core ideology and that have a clear organizational mission, vision, and core values become very successful. Jim Collins and Jerry Porras provide a well-documented example of such study in their book, *Built to Last*.[3] The study shows the existence of high ideals in visionary companies not only when they were successful but also when they were struggling just to survive.

In recent years, many companies have become interested in writing mission and vision statements, which they sometimes mount on the walls when you enter the company. The problem is that these statements rarely have anything to do with what the company is trying to achieve. They do it because some quality program requires it. They do it to answer to an auditor. They do it to look good in the eyes of potential customers. They do it because it looks sexy. If you ask employees at these companies if they have a mission and vision statement, they will quickly answer yes — but when you ask if they can tell you what it is, they usually do not have a quick response. Most of the time, they don't remember it and they have to look for it. Some companies have it printed on a small card or on the back of business cards, so employees can recite it to an auditor.

To be truly effective, an organizational vision statement must (the theory states) be assimilated into the organization's culture. Organizational leaders have the responsibility of communicating the vision regularly. As Peter M. Senge simply puts it, "mission and vision statements are not just a thing that companies should have."[4] They are what the company is all about. Everybody in the company should know it. Everybody should constantly talk about it. Everyone should make it his or her daily business.

This chapter describes the corporate "soul," and it will help you to clearly define it and utilize it throughout your organization to significantly improve your company's effectiveness and increase the bottom-line results.

2.1 CORPORATE CULTURE

Whenever individuals work together with a common purpose, work strategies and thinking processes develop and an organizational culture is created. Corporations have belief structures in which they operate, and we call this belief structure "the corporate culture." Corporate leadership greatly influences corporate culture. Everyone who has ever worked for an organization played some role in shaping its culture. Organizational cultures evolve over time and for many complex reasons.

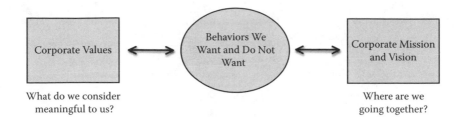

FIGURE 2.1
Corporate culture.

Corporate culture (see Figure 2.1) is the personality of the organization — "the way things work around here" — and is based on people's perceptions and assumptions about how things are accomplished within that particular organization. Culture is to organizations as personality is to people. When we speak of corporate culture, we are referring to the habits, attitudes, shared beliefs, behaviors, and expectations. It guides how employees think, act, and feel, and it drives action in the organization. It is the "interior" domain that unifies the organization. The corporate culture is the organization's shared mental model that drives behaviors and performance levels.

The corporate culture is not the ideals or the corporate mission or the vision. It is a reflection of daily work, communications, beliefs, and behaviors that result in a common corporate mission, values, and vision.

Another way to view corporate culture is as a system with inputs from the environment and outputs such as behaviors, technologies, and products. The system reflects the way work is done, how authority is exercised and distributed, and to what degree it is formalized, standardized, and controlled through systems, with emphasis given to policies, procedures, and performance and results requirements.

Initially, leaders and the common purpose for which the company was created shape corporate culture. It then evolves within the constraints of the environment, technology, values of the leadership, and performance expectations. People's experiences, leadership style, company structure, geographic location, decision-making methods, and the size of the company all affect the initial culture.

Corporate culture is directly linked to the brand of the corporation, as defined by its corporate mission, values, and vision (see Figure 2.2). In the next sections of this chapter, we describe how to define the corporate mission, values, and vision, and how we create them.

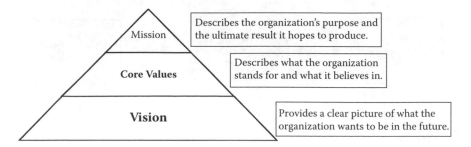

FIGURE 2.2
Corporate mission, core values, and vision.

2.2 ORGANIZATIONAL MISSION

The organizational mission consists of an organization's identity and indicates its reason for existing: why, to what extent, and for whom does it exist? What is the primary function? Which basic need does it fulfill, and who are its most important stakeholders? What is its ultimate objective? This, the organization's "genetic code," is meant to help employees build a common understanding of the main objective, increase their devotion, and provide an explanation for why their organization is different from the others. It describes the primary purpose of their existence, defining for the employees "who we serve, what we provide, and how we will provide it." An effectively formulated and forcefully articulated mission creates unanimity in the behavior of employees, strengthens their single-mindedness, and improves the atmosphere of mutual communication within the organization.

When developing your mission statement, here are some questions to use as a guide:

- Who are we?
- What do we stand for?
- What do we do?
- Where are we now?
- For what purpose and why does our organization exist?
- What is our identity?
- What is our primary function?
- What is our ultimate primary goal?
- For whom do we exist?
- Which factors make us unique?
- Who are our most important stakeholders?

- Why do we do what we do?
- Which fundamental need do we fill?
- What is decisive for our success?
- How do we know when we are successful?

Research shows that companies with a purpose beyond just making a profit succeed.[5] Many companies have "to maximize return on investment to shareholders" as their mission statement. Of course, making money is important but it should not be at the expense of an ideal organizational purpose. Jim Collins and Jerry Porras (2004) stated in *Built to Last* that visionary companies pursue broader, more meaningful missions, like helping the community and employees, not just making profits. Improving the bottom line should not dictate everyday decisions. They elaborated that profitability — like oxygen, food, and water — is an important and necessary condition for the company to survive. It is not the point of life, but without it, there is no life.

A mission statement should outline the function the company serves, for whom the company performs this function, and what process the company follows to fulfill this function. An effective mission statement is best developed with input from all levels of an organization. It should be specific, crisp, clear, engaging, and to the point — one to two sentences long in order for it to be easily understood by all levels of the company. Humor, sarcasm, and cynicism are not good components of an effective mission statement. Simplicity, honesty, and frankness are. It should not describe how good the service or product you provide is. It should truly reflect your business and not someone else's. It is who you are, not what you wish to be. For a list of familiar companies' mission statements, see Table 2.1.

When defining the company's mission, the "five whys" method is an effective way to get to the heart of it. You start with a statement such as "We make these products" or "We deliver these services," and then ask, "Why is that important?" or "Why do we do that?" To each answer, ask "why" again. Generally, after doing this five times (five whys), you will find that you are getting down to the primary purpose of your organization. If not, continue the process.

2.3 ORGANIZATIONAL CORE VALUES

People make decisions on a daily basis. These decisions reflect their beliefs and their values. Similarly, organizations make decisions and their decisions reflect the organization's beliefs and values. Core values are the

TABLE 2.1

Sample Mission Statements

Company	Mission Statement
Lexus U.S.	To attract and retain customers with the highest value products and services and the most satisfying ownership experience in America.
Motorola	The company exists to honorably serve the community by providing products and services of superior quality at a fair price.
Merck	We are in the business of preserving and improving human life. All of our actions must be measured by our success in achieving this goal.
3M	To solve unsolved problems innovatively.
General Electric	Improving the quality of life through technology and innovation.
Nike	To experience the emotion of competition, winning, and crushing competitors.
Walt Disney	To make people happy.
Becton Dickinson	To help all people lead healthy lives.
Marriott	To make people away from home feel they are among friends and really wanted.
Mary Kay	To give unlimited opportunity to women.
Walmart	To give ordinary folk the chance to buy the same things as rich people.
Sony	To experience the sheer joy of advancing and applying technology for the benefit of the public.
Bausch & Lomb	Dedicated to perfecting vision and enhancing life.
Starbucks	To be premier purveyor of the finest coffee in the world while maintaining our uncompromising principles while we grow.
American Family Insurance Group	To provide financial protection to an expanding customer base with a commitment to best value.
Aquila, Inc.	To exceed expectations in providing safe and reliable electric and natural gas services.
Chiron Corporation	Protecting people through innovative science by working to cure cancer, providing safe blood, and preventing infectious diseases.

set of beliefs that influence the way people and groups behave; they are the "soul" of the organization. They create a foundation of attitudes and practices that support long-term success and provide reference points for shaping and building the business. Collins and Porras stated that organizational core values are the organization's essential and enduring tenets, a small set of timeless guiding principles with intrinsic value.[6] The key is not *what* core values an organization has, but that it *has* core values. A company should remain true to these core values and should not change its core values in response to market fluctuations. Rather, it should change markets, if necessary, in order to remain true to its core values.

Organizational values are deeply embedded principles that guide all organizational decisions. They are a set of beliefs that specify common expectations and ideal behavior in a company. They determine how people must act in order to realize the organizational mission and vision. They guide the principles that support people's behavior at work. These values express the way employees treat each other and how they see customers, shareholders, suppliers, and the community. If the principles and values of the employees are aligned with those of the organization, then their efforts and contribution will be optimal. Therefore, core values are strongly related to the personal ambitions of the employees. Since organizational core values are the central and enduring tenets of the organization, they form the "glue" that holds an organization together as it grows, decentralizes, diversifies, and expands. Core values remain fixed while business strategies and practices endlessly adapt to a changing world.

When the values of the employees in the organization are similar to those of the company they work for, their values are aligned. When the values of the employees are different from those of the company they work for, there is values misalignment. A study conducted in 2007 by C02 Partners, a leadership development firm, shows that one in three U.S. workers say their employer's core values are not consistent with their own.[7] Forty-four percent said their values were consistent, 11% said they were uncertain about their own core values but never felt uncomfortable working for their employer, and 10% said they didn't feel their core values had much connection to the work they do.

Other studies show that corporations that seek to align the values of the organization with the values of employees are more successful, more enjoyable to work for, more focused on the needs of their employees and their customers, and usually attract and retain talented people. On the other hand, corporations that don't have great alignment tend to be more inward looking, bureaucratic, and stressful to work for, and have difficulty attracting and retaining talented people.

To create values alignment, executives need to understand their employees' values as well as how their employees perceive the organization's values. This initial step will outline what values the employees consider important to run the business and identify any values gaps that need completing in order to create alignment. This information will allow organizations to choose core values that are meaningful to all employees. This alignment is very significant not only because happy employees create happy customers but also because the core values that an organization chooses provide employees with guidance in making daily decisions. A robust set of organizational core values allows managers to trust their employees to make the right decisions that reflect the values of the organization. (See Figure 2.3.)

In order for the organization to harvest the benefits of a robust set of core values, these values must be lived by the senior management in the organization. When only lower-level employees are held to these values, cynicism is inevitable. We have often heard employees say that company values do not apply to management, they just apply to them. The organizational core values must become part of the organizational fabric of a company at all levels. To be fully realized, they have to be integrated into every aspect of the organization's culture, mainly in the organization's relations with employees, customers, and the community as a whole.

Core values are effective when integrated into all levels and functions of the organization and communicated to ensure that all employees understand and believe in them. They should be practiced daily and aligned to the corporate systems including rewards, information sharing, measures, meetings, teams, and so on. Management must correct those who violate the core values and recognize those who practice them. This is the only way that the core values become habits and self-sustaining. See Table 2.2 for a list of familiar companies' core values.

	Employees	Customers	Stakeholders	Owners
Be ethical	X	X	X	X
Treat others with dignity	X	X	X	X
Be honest	X	X	X	X
Respect the individual	X	X	X	X
Be profitable	X	X	X	X

FIGURE 2.3
Integration of Core Values.

TABLE 2.2

Examples of Core Values

Company	Core Values
Motorola	Continuous self-renewal Treat each employee, as an individual, with dignity Honesty, integrity, and ethics in all aspects of business
Merck	Honesty and integrity Corporate social responsibility Science-based innovation, not imitation Unequivocal excellence in all aspects of the company
3M	Absolute integrity Respect for individual initiative and personal growth Tolerance for honest mistakes Product quality and reliability
Hewlett-Packard (1950s)	Respect for the individual Affordable quality and reliability Collaborative creativity Community contribution and responsibility Profitable growth
General Electric	Interdependent balance between responsibility to customers, employees, society, and shareholders Individual responsibility and opportunity Honesty and Integrity
American Express	Customer commitment Quality Integrity Teamwork Respect for people Personal accountability
Armstrong World Industries, Inc.	Respect Integrity Diversity Service
Becton, Dickinson and Company	Treat each other with respect Do what is right Always seek to improve Accept personal responsibility
Chiron Corporation	Transparency Alignment Execution Accountability

When defining organizational core values, leaders should consider the following questions:

- What do we stand for?
- What is essential in our attitude?
- What do we believe in?
- Which values are precious to us?
- How do we treat each other?
- How do we work together?
- How do we think of ourselves?
- What are the desired characteristics of our cultural and leadership style?

2.4 ORGANIZATIONAL VISION

If you search the Internet for the definition of "vision," a common theme emerges: "Vision is an image of the future we seek to create." Visions are deceptively simple to define, yet difficult to achieve. An organizational vision is a statement about what your organization wants to become. It contains the most ambitious dream of the organization; it is an image of its desired future, its long-term dreams and intentions, what it wants to achieve, where it goes from here, how it sees a desirable and achievable shared future, and so on. It should echo with all members of the organization and help them feel proud, excited, and part of something much bigger than themselves. An organizational vision is much more then the words on paper — it is the feeling, the *mental image*, that those words produce when participants believe them to be true.

A corporate vision statement is a short, concise, and inspiring description of what the organization intends to become and achieve at some point in the future; it is often stated in competitive terms. It is the image that a business must have of its goals before it sets out to reach them. It describes aspirations without specifying the means required to achieve them. It provides a shared vision of a desired and feasible future, as well as the route needed to reach it. It indicates what the organization wants to achieve, what is essential for its success, and which critical success factors make it unique. It shows where and how the organization wants to distinguish itself from others.

This implies that the organizational vision provides insight into *core competencies*: the fields in which the organization excels, the reasons why customers use its products and services, and the principles of the employees. Standards, values, and principles are also part of the organizational vision. The vision, in contrast to the mission, includes a timeline. An effectively formulated vision guides personal ambitions and creativity, establishes a climate that is fertile for change, strengthens the organization's belief in the future, and therefore releases energy in people.

An organizational vision statement must be assimilated into the organization's culture in order for it to be truly effective. Leaders in many organizations are responsible for bringing the vision to life. They achieve this by communicating the vision regularly, by creating narratives that illustrate the vision, and by acting as a role model who embodies the vision. Leaders create short-term objectives compatible with the vision and encourage others to craft their own personal vision compatible with the organization's overall vision.

Features of an effective vision statement are

- Clarity and lack of ambiguity
- A vivid and clear picture
- A picture of a bright future (hope)
- Memorable and engaging expression
- Realistic and achievable aspirations
- Alignment with the organization's values and culture

There is no magic formula for developing an effective organizational vision, but Collins and Porras suggest that there are three conditions necessary for an aim to take root in an organization.[8] First, it must reflect the inner personal needs, values, and motivations of members of the organization. Second, there must be an authentic personal commitment. Third, communication and reinforcement are vitally important.

When you begin the process of strategic planning, visualization comes first. When visualizing the change, ask yourself "What is our preferred future?" and be sure to

- Draw on the beliefs, mission, and environment of the organization.
- Describe what you want to see in the future.
- Be specific to each organization.
- Be positive and inspiring.
- Do not assume that the system will have the same framework as it does today.
- Be open to dramatic modifications to current organization, methodology, teaching techniques, and facilities.

TABLE 2.3

Samples of Organizational Vision Statements

Company	Vision Statement
Ford Motor Company	To become the world's leading consumer company for automotive products and services.
PepsiCo.	We want to sell a variety of products on a daily basis to every living person on the earth.
Microsoft	A computer on every desk and in every home.
General Motors Corp	To be the world leader in transportation products and services.
One Laptop per Child	One laptop per child.
Alcoa	To be the best company in the world.
Anheuser-Busch Companies, Inc.	Through all our products, services, and relationships, we will add to life's enjoyment.
Applied Materials, Inc.	We apply nonmanufacturing technology to improve the way people live.
Aquila, Inc.	To provide energy for better living.
Becton, Dickinson and Company	To eliminate unnecessary suffering and death from diseases, and in doing so, become one of the best performing companies in the world.
Chiron Corporation	To create value by transforming the practice of medicine through biotechnology.

Without vision, we get stuck in the middle of the process of change. The vision motivates and challenges its members as it builds self-esteem. It is not a business plan; it is a holistic view of the organization. It must help people realize their potential.

Tichy and Mary Anne Devanna
Authors, The Transformational Leader

2.5 SHARED VISION — THE SECRET

In Section 2.4, we described organizational vision and the key characteristics of an effective vision. Shared vision allows ordinary people to do extraordinary things. It generates new levels of inspiration and energy to change the current situation and create a new future. Proverbs 29:18 states that "Where there is no vision, the people perish."

It is important to realize that organizations do not have visions, people do. Shared visions emerge from personal visions, and personal visions come from an individual's deep caring. Therefore, it can be said that shared visions arise from a common caring. A shared vision clarifies what is important and empowers people to take initiative. It nurtures analytical thinking, encourages focus and creativity, and highlights the need for change.

> Shared vision will not direct the precise manner in which we cut through the forest, but simply serve as the mechanism for ensuring that we're in the right forest in the first place.

> **Stephen R. Covey**
> *Author*, Principle-Centered Leadership

> For a shared vision to be effective, it needs to be accepted by all members of the organization. A vision shared by the members of an organization helps them to set goals that advance the organization and is an important for motivation and empowerment. Therefore, leaders need to allow and enable all members of the organization to have their own visions. They should allow people at every level of the organization, in every role, to speak openly and to really be heard about what really matters to them. It is in this openness that the sense of shared vision grows.
> The content of a truly shared vision cannot be dictated, it can only emerge from a coherent process of reflection and conversation.

> **Peter Senge**
> *Author*, The Fifth Discipline

The power of shared vision is evident throughout history. A perfect example is Mahatma Gandhi's vision of achieving freedom through the path of nonviolence. He followed the principle of Satyagraha, which is based on truth, government by consensus, persuasion through decision and reason, education of the community, decisive actions, and mass civil disobedience. He believed in living a simple life and proved to the world that freedom could be achieved through nonviolence. He had a specific image of postcolonial India and he talked of that image at every opportunity and to everyone who would listen. He achieved the impossible; ultimately, 200 million people shared his vision and followed in his path toward that vision, defeating the British without resorting to violence.

A recent example of shared vision is that of President Barack Obama, the first African American president of the United States. Obama announced his intention to run in February 2007; that he would win was viewed as a long shot. Young and relatively inexperienced and facing what many thought were insurmountable barriers due his skin color and Muslim name, he remained consistent in his vision to "Bring about real change, change that we can believe in." At rallies throughout his campaign, the chant of "Yes, we can" caught fire as his vision became a shared vision. Barack Obama was nominated at the 2008 Democratic National Convention with Delaware senator Joe Biden as his running mate. As the presidential race became more heated, the values on which Obama's vision were based remained consistent: "challenge ideas, not the personal integrity of opponents," "focus on hope, not fear," and "believe in the basic goodness of the American people." Despite attempts to link Obama with an unpopular religion, terrorists, and to question his citizenship, he won a significant victory: 53% of the popular vote and 364 electoral votes, rivaling John McCain's 46% of the popular vote and 173 electoral votes.

Barack Obama's vision to "Bring about real change, change that we can believe in" — his passion for change — is the pillar of his success. Most Americans shared his vision. Although he was one of the least likely candidates, the shared vision he inspired gave Americans hope that together they could beat the odds.

In his acceptance speech, he recognized that people voted not for him but for his vision, which they shared: "And I know you didn't do it for me." There is nothing in human affairs as powerful as a shared vision. It will move mountains. Leaders who understand the power of shared vision hold the secret in their hands. It is the key to business success.

NOTES

1. *Webster's New World College Dictionary* (Cleveland: Wiley, 2004), s.v. "soul."
2. Mary Wollstonecraft Shelley, http://www.quotationspage.com/quote/1936.html (retrieved July 7, 2009).
3. Jim Collins and Jerry I. Porras, *Built to Last: Successful Habits of Visionary Companies* (New York: Collins Business, 2004).

4. Peter M. Senge, *The Fifth Discipline: The Art and Practice of The Learning Organization* (New York: Broadway Business, 2006).
5. Collins and Porras conducted an excellent example of such research at Stanford's Graduate School of Business; Collins and Porras, *Built to Last*.
6. Collins and Porras, *Built to Last*.
7. Human Resource Planning Society, *Human Resources Strategic Agenda Update*, no. 33, http://www.hrps.org/hrps_sau_33_b.pdf (retrieved July 7, 2009).
8. Collins and Porras, *Built to Last*.

3

The Road to Corporate Wellness

Vision without action is a dream. Action without vision is simply passing the time. Action with Vision is making a positive difference.

Joel Barker
Author and futurist

In Chapter 2, we outlined the importance of a well-defined vision in an organization. The leader's role is to implement a comprehensive management system in order to steer the entire business toward this vision. This system should align strategic business goals with management goals, operational performance plans, and employee development plans. This requires that management and employees work together to report and provide feedback to one another to help achieve these goals, and that everyone in the company be involved in working toward achieving the same objectives. Many organizations devote extensive resources to developing a corporate strategy. This strategy will fail to realize its benefits unless it is well defined, well communicated, and translated into actionable initiatives.

Sufficient performance measures to guide organizations in today's rapidly changing and complex economy are necessary. The Corporate Balanced Scorecard provides a powerful framework for translating strategy into action and then results, as well as a means to measure the critical parameters of corporate success. The scorecard presents the mechanism for aligning the various activities, processes, and groups throughout the organization with strategic goals and measures that are based on the corporate mission, values, and vision. It also links individual performance to corporate strategy and provides a constructive mechanism for holding people accountable for results.

Creating a strategy-focused organization is a major culture change for many organizations. Success in achieving this change requires

- Reliable executive support and involvement
- Education, communication, and visibility of the strategy and measurements of its effectiveness throughout the organization
- Tools that enable users at all levels to understand the key drivers of the measures
- Cascading the strategy to operations so that alignment between strategy and implementation occurs at all levels of the organization

3.1 CORPORATE BALANCED SCORECARD

The Corporate Balanced Scorecard (CBSC) concept was developed by Robert S. Kaplan and David P. Norton in the early 1990s in a series of journal articles.[1] They initially focused on organizational performance, specifically the financial measures.

The Balanced Scorecard is a concept that helps managers at all levels monitor results in their key areas. It also offers a comprehensive view of the business, which helps organizations function in their long-term interests. The scorecard provides feedback on both the internal business processes and external outcomes to continuously improve strategic performance and results. According to Kaplan and Norton, "The Balanced Scorecard provides managers with the instrumentation they need to navigate to future competitive success."[2]

Although the scorecard began with financial measures, it expanded to focus on operations, marketing, and development. The Balanced Scorecard sometimes is referred to as a "strategic linkage model" or "strategy map."

The main objective of the Balanced Scorecard is to identify a set of measures that reflect future performance. These measures are aligned with an organization's vision and strategy. They include financial, customer, internal business processes, and learning and growth perspectives. The financial perspective includes traditional financial measures such as revenue growth, return on investment or return on assets, market share, and earnings per share. The customer perspective measures the importance of such things as timeliness, quality, performance, cost, and service, which contribute to customer satisfaction. The internal business process perspective measures the critical internal activities and processes that the

TABLE 3.1

Balanced Scorecard Perspectives

Perspective	Key Question
Financial	To succeed financially, how should we appear to our stakeholders?
Customer	To achieve our vision, how should we appear to our customers?
Process	To satisfy our customers and shareholders, at what business processes must we excel?
Learning and Growth	To achieve our vision, how will we sustain our ability to change and improve?

organization employs to meet its customers' expectations. The learning and growth perspective measures the organization's capability to change and innovate for the future. Examples of such measures may include time to market for new product development, human capital training and development, and process improvement.

Kaplan and Norton's Balanced Scorecard describes strategy and performance management from four perspectives — financial, customer, process, and learning and growth (see Table 3.1).

Figure 3.1 shows the linkage between the corporate mission, values, and vision and the four quadrants of the Balanced Scorecard.

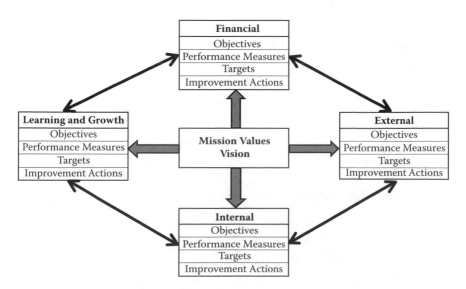

FIGURE 3.1
Balanced Scorecard's four quadrants.

According to Kaplan and Norton,[3] the Balanced Scorecard benefits an organization by

- Focusing the whole organization on the few vital inputs needed to create breakthrough organizational performance
- Helping integrate various corporate initiatives, such as quality, human resources, operations, and customer service into the organization
- Cascading strategic business goals and measures to the rest of the company, including department managers, operators, and other employees, so that they can observe what is required at their level to roll into overall performance

The role of a Balanced Scorecard is to identify the key metrics across all levels of an organization with the main purpose of aligning organizational business goals and objectives with the activities at the operating levels. The basic requirements of the Balanced Scorecard include

- Measurement of objectives for each of the four perspectives
- Definition of a quantitative metric or "score"
- Target value
- Target date
- Recurring measurement cycle

3.2 THE FOUR PERSPECTIVES

Implementing Balanced Scorecards typically includes four steps: (1) translating the vision into operational goals; (2) communicating the vision and linking it to individual performance; (3) business planning; and (4) feedback, learning, and strategy adjustment, when necessary.

3.2.1 Financial Perspective

The financial perspective examines the financial soundness of the corporation. How do shareholders see the company? What does it mean for our shareholders? Its purpose is to assess whether the company's implementation of its strategy is contributing to the bottom-line improvement of the company. It represents the long-term financial strategic objectives of the organization.

Kaplan and Norton described three possible stages in the financial perspective: rapid growth, sustain, and harvest.[4] Financial objectives and measures for the growth stage branch from the development and growth of the organization, which lead to increased sales volumes, acquisition of new customers, and growth in revenue. The sustain stage is characterized by measures that evaluate the effectiveness of the organization to manage its operations and costs by calculating the return on investment and the return on capital employed. Finally, the harvest stage is based on cash flow analysis using measures such as benefits periods and revenue volume.

Depending on the industry, some of the most common financial measures that are incorporated in the financial perspective include revenue growth, cost, profit margins, cash flow, shareholders value, return on investment, investment level, and operational costs and percentage of sales.

3.2.2 External Perspective

Most companies realize that in order to be successful, they need to focus mainly on the customer.

The customer perspective defines the value proposition that the organization applies in order to satisfy their customers and therefore generate more sales. If the customers are not satisfied, they will eventually find other suppliers that will meet their needs. Poor performance from this perspective is therefore a leading indicator of future decline, even though the current financial picture may look healthy. Customers will tell twice as many people about bad experiences than about good ones. A dissatisfied customer will tell eight or nine people about the bad experience (some numbers are as high as nineteen). However, about 70% of upset customers will continue to be customers if their complaints are resolved satisfactorily.

It is important to define key customers, what services or products they expect from the company, and to understand how the company will meet their needs. It is also important to define how the company will measure customer satisfaction and dissatisfaction. The measures that are chosen for the external perspective should measure both the value that is delivered to the customer (time, quality, performance, service, and cost) and the outcomes that result from this value proposition (such as customer satisfaction, market share). Common measures of the external perspective are

- Market share
- Market growth

- Percentage of customers who terminate their relationship with the organization due to dissatisfaction
- Degree of customer satisfaction
- Time needed to answer a complaint
- Time needed to solve a complaint
- Degree of customer loyalty
- Sales loss as a result of dissatisfied customers
- Percentage of orders delivered late
- Number of customer complaints
- Percentage of customer returns

3.2.3 Internal Perspective

This perspective concentrates on primary business processes in order to create value for customers; that is, it focuses on all of the activities and key processes required for the company to excel and continuously satisfy customers and on the processes that add value to the customers.

Metrics based on this perspective allow managers to know how well their business is running and whether its products and services conform to customer requirements. Usually cost, quality, throughput, productivity, and time are some of the measures used in this perspective. To select adequate measures that have the greatest impact on the clients, Kaplan and Norton propose using certain clusters that group similar value-creating processes in an organization. The clusters for the internal process perspective are operations management, customer management, innovation and new products and services, and regulatory factors.

Some of the most common measures used are down time, failure rate, response time to a service request, lead time for product development, time needed to launch a new product on the market (time-to-market), degree of satisfaction of employees, percentage of personnel turnover, percentage of rejects, percentage of scrap, percentage of safety incidents, percentage of processes that are meeting Six Sigma level, and percentage of delayed orders.

3.2.4 Learning and Growth Perspective

The learning and growth perspective supports the other three perspectives. It focuses on an organization's actual resources, mainly the internal skills, attitudes, and capabilities of the employees and the organizational learning ability required to support the value-creating internal processes. This includes employee training and corporate cultural attitudes related to both individual and corporate self-improvement (Chapter 4 addresses self-improvement methods). In an environment that is hungry for change, it is becoming necessary for employees to be in a continuous learning mode. Metrics can be put into place to guide managers to focus training and learning where they can help the most. By enabling employees with knowledge, innovation, and an advanced skill set, they can build and enhance innovative business processes that in turn help retain and acquire new customers, and ultimately achieve the organization's financial objectives.

The learning and growth perspective is mostly concerned with the human capital, the systems, and the climate of the organization. This is the infrastructure needed in order to achieve the organizational objectives enumerated in the other three perspectives.

Some of the most common measures include the following:

- Availability of strategic information
- Experience level of employees regarding information exchange
- Percentage of communication failures
- Percentage of available competences
- Number of required training courses
- Percentage of qualified employees
- Percentage of employees who are trained in essential skills
- Percentage of employees who need crucial skills
- Cost to train employees
- Cost to train executives and managers
- Training costs as percentage of sales
- Number of solved problems
- Number of suggestions per employee
- Number of suggestions implemented
- Percentage of employees with a competence profile
- Degree of existence of innovative technology
- Percentage of available strategic skills
- Average time that employee stays in the same position

3.3 CORPORATE CRITICAL SUCCESS FACTORS

Corporate critical success factors are derived from the mission statement. They are the things at which the organization must be very good in order to survive, and therefore must be of dominant importance to the organization's success. These key strategic factors determine the competitive advantage of an organization. They are characteristics by which the organization wants to differentiate itself from other companies in order to be unique in the market and are related to its core competencies and the four perspectives. The critical success factors form the connection between the corporate mission, core values, and vision and the remaining Corporate Balance Scorecard components. Some questions that help identify the corporate critical success factors include the following:

- What is our competitive advantage?
- How do we generate profit?
- Which skills and capabilities make us distinctive?
- How do shareholders see us?
- How do our customers see us?
- How do our key business processes perform?
- How can we remain successful in the future?

3.3.1 Corporate Objectives

Corporate objectives are the desired and measurable outputs that must be achieved. They are the indicators of how a business is performing relative to its strategic objectives. They describe the projected short-term results that should be achieved in order to realize the long-term corporate shared vision. These objectives are critical and must be measurable, strategically relevant, and consistent. They come directly from the critical success factors and form rational milestones. Specifying corporate objectives will occur at a later phase through corporate performance measures and targets. The objectives form part of a cause-and-effect chain, resulting in the final corporate objective.

Corporate objectives must be linked to each stakeholder.

- *Employees:* Which objectives do we want to achieve in order to improve the quality of the work?
- *Customers:* Which objectives do we aim for to satisfy our customers?
- *Shareholders:* What do our shareholders expect of us? Which objective do we aim for to satisfy our shareholders on a continuous basis?
- *Suppliers:* Which objectives do we aim for in order to increase our added value?
- *Community:* Which objectives do we aim for in order to serve our community effectively and be a good corporate citizen?

3.3.2 Corporate Performance Measures

Corporate performance measures are indicators that are related to the critical success factors and the strategic objectives, and are used to assess the performance of specific key processes. They are the standards by which the progress of the strategic objectives is measured. They are necessary when putting strategic plans into action, and they provide management with the appropriate directions to make sound decisions regarding changes in key processes. Therefore, performance measures make the corporate vision and objectives measurable.

3.3.3 Corporate Targets

Corporate targets are the quantitative objective of a performance measure. It is a value that an organization seeks to achieve, the understanding of which can be measured using performance measures. In other words, targets specify values to be attained.

3.3.4 Corporate Improvement Actions

Corporate improvement actions are strategies carried out to realize the corporate shared vision. The following questions drive improvement actions in companies: How can we control the performance of key business processes? How can we improve the profit margin? How can we improve employee engagement and productivity? Corporate improvement actions must be selected in a way that results in the greatest contribution to the corporate shared vision.

3.3.5 Strategic Alignment by Cascading the Balanced Scorecard

Cascading the Balanced Scorecard is a method designed to bridge the considerable learning gap that exists in most organizations. It is the process by which Balanced Scorecards are developed at every level of the organization. Communicating and linking the CBSC is critical to its successful implementation.

To convert the strategic vision of an organization into action, it is necessary to link the Corporate Balanced Scorecard (CBSC) to the Balanced Scorecard of departments (subsystem level) and teams (components level), as well as the individual performance plans of managers and employees (process level) at lower levels of the organization. Each business unit or department sets up its own specific scorecards. Each team develops a team scorecard based on the scorecard of its business unit. Then, with the help of the team leader, each team member translates the team scorecard into his or her own individual performance plan, which concentrates on the individual's job and the person's unique contribution to the team goals.

The organizational mission, formulated in the CBSC, applies to all organizational levels. The organizational vision and linked critical success factors, objectives, targets, and improvement actions are adjusted and fine-tuned to meet the needs of the related business units and teams. The corporate objectives in the CBSC form the initial point for linking the CBSC to the scorecards at lower organizational levels.

Figure 3.2 illustrates how the corporate scorecards cascade throughout the organization. For each objective, a determination is made as to whether the respective business unit significantly influences a given objective and if improvement actions can be formulated to directly influence the accomplishment of this objective. If the answer is "yes," the objective is incorporated into the scorecard of the respective business unit. To help prioritize improvement projects, you can use the worksheet (Table 3.2) to summarize the scorecards including requirements, objectives, measures, targets, and the necessary improvement actions.

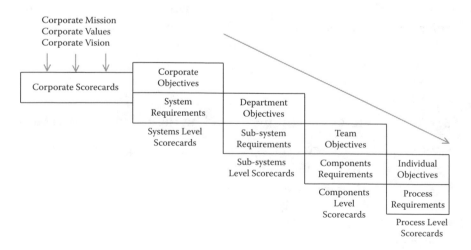

FIGURE 3.2
Cascading the Balanced Scorecard.

TABLE 3.2

Corporate Balanced Scorecard Worksheet

Mission, Values, Vision					
Perspective					
Corporate Scorecards	Systems Requirements	Objectives	Measures	Targets	Improvement Actions
Department-Level Scorecard	Subsystems Requirements	Objectives	Measures	Targets	Improvement Actions
Team-Level Scorecard	Components Requirements	Objectives	Measures	Targets	Improvement Actions
Personal-Level Scorecard	Process Requirements	Objectives	Measures	Targets	Improvement Actions

3.4 STRATEGY MAP

Mapping a strategy is an important way to evaluate and make visually explicit an organization's perspectives, objectives, and measures, and the causal linkages between them by organizing objectives in each defined perspective, and depicting the strategic relationships among them. It serves as a way to evaluate objectives to make sure that they are consistent and comprehensive in delivering the strategy.

The strategy map is a visual way to communicate to different parts of the organization how they fit into the overall strategy. Because it can be created at different levels of an organization, it facilitates cascading a Balanced Scorecard through an organization. Each level's map then can be viewed for alignment with the overall strategy map.

3.5 CASE STUDY: ACME CIRCUITS

Acme Circuits is a fictitious manufacture of high-technology, low-volume, bare printed circuit boards. Acme Circuits designs and manufactures double-sided and multilayer circuit boards at their sole facility in Cleveland, Ohio. Current annual sales volume is 8 million (8M) US dollars per year. Acme Circuits customers are typically research and development companies working on low-volume, initial product launches. Because the products they supply are being used for qualification and design testing, their customers are very demanding about the quality and the timely delivery of the product. As the quick-turn market expands to overseas competition, there is greater pressure on Acme Circuits to deliver on time and with zero defects. If Acme Circuits can meet these rigid demands, they will gain market share from their overseas and local competition and achieve their goal to meet or exceed financial expectations.

Acme Circuits has decided to deploy the Corporate Balanced Scorecard methodology as the tool to meet these demands and grow their company.

3.5.1 Acme Circuits' Corporate Balanced Scorecard

Acme Circuits critical success factors (enumerated in Table 3.3) are broken down into the four perspectives — financial, internal, external, and learning and growth. Table 3.4 shows Acme Circuits' Corporate Balanced

TABLE 3.3

Acme Circuits' Critical Success Factors

Acme Circuits' Critical Success Factors	
Financial	**External**
Grow profitability	Key supplier in quick-turn prototype PCB market
Meet or exceed financial expectations	High quality, zero defects
	Deliver on time
Internal	**Learning and Growth**
Stable control of internal processes	Stay current with market trends
Minimize equipment downtime	Continuous development of workforce
Increase sales	Open communication
Eliminate remakes	Motivate workforce

Scorecard. For each of the four perspectives, the critical success factors and corporate objectives, corporate performance, corporate targets, and corporate improvement actions are listed. Completing the CBSC worksheet is important because it shows exactly how each success factor will be achieved and what the metric is to measure success. The last column, corporate improvement actions, lists all the tactical projects that need to be executed to meet the strategic objectives, also called the corporate critical success factors.

3.5.2 Acme Circuits' Strategic Map

You can see the position of Acme Circuits objectives, within the four perspectives and their mutual relationships in Figure 3.3. In this cause-and-effect chain, Acme Circuits' objectives are interrelated and affect one another. In this figure, all first-level organizational strategic objectives are formulated and illustrated; they all lead to a final objective — namely, to meet or exceed financial expectations. The cause-and-effect chain is a handy tool for communicating the CBSC to lower organizational levels.

It is important to note that each measure for each perspective in a Balanced Scorecard is chosen based on the corporate vision and strategy. For each measure, there is a defined goal, a target, and specific initiatives to translate the goal into action. Cause-and-effect relationships among the measures clearly define how the different variables contribute to achieving strategic goals. This becomes a communication mechanism that demonstrates the significance of the strategy and how different perspectives and departments contribute to achieving the strategy. Later, we

TABLE 3.4

Acme Circuits' Corporate Balanced Scorecard

Corporate Critical Success Factors	Corporate Objectives	Financial		Corporate Improvement Actions
		Corporate Performance Measures	Corporate Targets	
• Grow profitability	• Higher return on each order	• Net profit	• Increase of 20% in 3 years	• Outsource unprofitable and infrequently used special finishes • Modify purchase orders to include cost-adders • Implement Lean principles to increase process speed
• Meet or exceed financial expectations	• Satisfy quarterly strategic objectives	• Overhead as % of profit • COQ as % of profit	• Reduce by 3% in 2 years • Reduce by 5% in 2 years	• Implement Six Sigma principles to eliminate defects • Deploy Corporate Sigma program organization-wide • Eliminate waste in processes using Lean methods • Find lower cost supplies (paper products, cleaning products, office supplies, etc.) • Use Six Sigma tools to identify and reduce variation in poor performing processes • Invest more in preventive measures to reduce external failure costs (FMEA)

External

Corporate Critical Success Factors	Corporate Objectives	Corporate Performance Measures	Corporate Targets	Corporate Improvement Actions
• Key supplier in quick-turn-prototype PCB market	• Increase market share	• Market share percentage	• 10% increase in 3 years	• Expand activities in foreign markets • Launch marketing campaign targeting quick turn • Trade magazine ads
• High quality, zero defects	• Reduce remakes and reworks	• DPMO measurement • Sigma measurement	• 5 Sigma level in 5 years	• Offer discounts for responding to ads
• Deliver on-time	• Improve on-time delivery metric	• OTD %	• Increase OTD to 98% in 3 years	• Implement Corporate Sigma program • Train Green and Black Belts • Use DMAIC to continuously improve • Use Lean to eliminate waste in the process • Provide training for all operators in Lean Six Sigma

Internal

Corporate Critical Success Factors	Corporate Objectives	Corporate Performance Measures	Corporate Targets	Corporate Improvement Actions
• Stable control of internal processes	• Processes are available 24•7•365	• C_p measurement	• Bring C_p to 1.33 for all key processes within 2 years	• Reduce supplier base • Identify all key processes • Gather and plot average C_p data for all key processes
• Minimize equipment downtime	• Processes are available 24•7•365	• Downtime metric	• Reduce downtime by 20% in 2 years	• Use C_p data to monitor and control processes

(continued)

TABLE 3.4 (CONTINUED)

Acme Circuits' Corporate Balanced Scorecard

		Internal		
Corporate Critical Success Factors	Corporate Objectives	Corporate Performance Measures	Corporate Targets	Corporate Improvement Actions
• Increase sales	• Increase gross sales dollars	• Annual gross sales	• Increase annual gross sales from 12M to 20M within 4 years (2M per year)	• Collect PM data • Use PM data to upgrade unreliable equipment • Create plan to assure maintenance staff is available when needed
• Eliminate remakes	• Reduce remakes and reworks	• Remake as percent of profit metric	• Reduce metric from 12% to 5% in 3 years	• Add to outside sales force • Aggressively pursue substrate and aerospace markets • Provide early-pay discounts • Implement Lean office practices to Sales Department • Implement Lean and Six Sigma methods throughout organization • Identify and conduct LSS projects to reduce remakes • Use remake metric as key results expected (KRE) for product managers • Provide incentives to departments for meeting remake reduction goals

Learning and Growth

Corporate Critical Success Factors	Corporate Objectives	Corporate Performance Measures	Corporate Targets	Corporate Improvement Actions
• Stay current with market trends	• Increase knowledge of workforce • Use knowledge to make process improvements • Use knowledge to increase process capabilities	• Number of revisions to processes due to Innovation	• At least 30 process innovations per year	• Production teams receive specialized training • LPC•600 training for all of production • Hold monthly process innovation meeting • Record actions and results from process innovation meeting
• Continuous development of workforce	• Improve competencies of workforce to drive quality	• Improved first-time quality (FTQ) measurement	• Improve FTQ by 20% in 3 years	• Provide Corporate Sigma and LSS training to all of workforce • Add FTQ as KRE for appropriate managers and personnel
• Open communication	• Reduce or eliminate communications issues that have resulted in remakes	• Reduction in the number of remakes and rework that were allocated to poor communications or wrong information provided	• Reduce "poor communication" defect rate by 50% in 2 years	• All managers and leaders will receive team coaching and leadership training in Corporate Sigma ideology

(continued)

TABLE 3.4 (CONTINUED)

Acme Circuits' Corporate Balanced Scorecard

		Learning and Growth		
Corporate Critical Success Factors	Corporate Objectives	Corporate Performance Measures	Corporate Targets	Corporate Improvement Actions
• Motivate workforce	• Culture shift	• Increased Employee Satisfaction Index (ESI)	• Increase ESI metric by 75% in 2 years	• Foster interdepartmental communications • Add vision boards for key process results in each department • Add poor communication metric to manager KREs • Deploy Corporate Sigma program • Create Personal Balanced Scorecards (PBSC) that align directly to the Corporate Balanced Scorecard (CBSC) • Hold employee satisfaction meeting with third party once a quarter at off-site location for the next 8 quarters • Institute employee feedback system

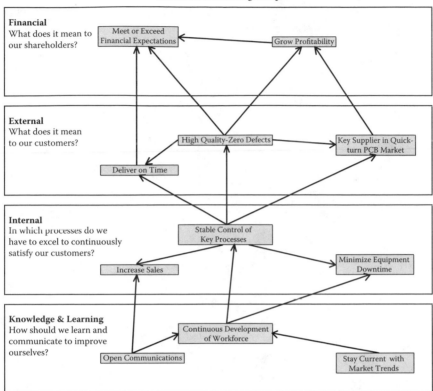

ACME Circuits Strategic Map

FIGURE 3.3
Acme Circuits strategic map.

translate these measures into corporate requirements, which we call systems requirements.

NOTES

1. Robert S. Kaplan and David P. Norton, "The Balanced Scorecards — Measures That Drive Performance," *Harvard Business Review*. This article sparked interest in the method, which led to the authors' bestselling book, *The Balanced Scorecards: Translating Strategy into Action* (Cambridge, MA: Harvard Business School Press, 1996).
2. Kaplan and Norton, *The Balanced Scorecards*, 2.
3. Kaplan and Norton. *The Balanced Scorecards*.
4. Stella Mooraj, Daniel Oyon, and Didier Hostettler, "Balanced Scorecards: A Necessary Good or an Unnecessary Evil?" *Strategy Implementation: Readings*, ed. P. J. Smit, M. A. Van der Merwe, and P. N. Palmer (Lansdowne, South Africa: Juta Academic, 2000), 140.

4

Human Capital: The Heart

> Your work is to discover your work and then with all your heart to give yourself to it. Irrigators guide water; arrow makers straighten arrows; carpenters bend wood; wise people shape themselves.
>
> **Buddha**

If you ask any executive "What is the most valuable asset in your company?" he or she will quickly respond, "People are our most valuable asset," "Our employees come first," "We're only as strong as our people." Yet a growing number of American companies are learning that they have long overlooked and mismanaged one of their most critical assets: human capital. When we look at what is happening in corporate America, there is a real disconnect between the typical executive response and the reality of how people are valued in the workplace on a daily basis. Executives seem to be in denial about the failure of company programs and rhetoric to realize the full potential of their people.

Several business leaders and studies examine the fact that employee satisfaction and engagement are critical to the success of the corporation. We believe that if employees are the heart of the corporation, they need to be fully connected to the arteries and veins of the company. Only in that way can both succeed. By integrating employee personal scorecards with corporate scorecards, that connection is made and companies are better able to maximize and engage the hearts of their employees.

> Human capital issues are at the top of the agenda for today's CEO. Enlightened executives have realized that human capital represents a real sustainable competitive advantage. Yet, organizations continue to treat human capital as a non-strategic asset. In fact, many continue to witness

employee goals misaligned to the business strategy, training initiatives yielding only incremental improvements and skill gaps prohibiting the successful execution of strategy. Today, with knowledge workers accounting for over 50% of the workforce, the challenge for most organizations is how to ensure their employees have the right capabilities and are motivated to execute their strategy.

Palladium Group, 2007

As Mary Kay Ash, the famous entrepreneur and founder of Mary Kay cosmetics, who based her business on a belief in people, said, "People are definitely a company's greatest asset. It does not make any difference whether the product is cars or cosmetics. A company is only as good as the people it keeps."[1]

Organizations typically spend a significant amount of resources generating new business and cutting costs but doing very little to satisfy and motivate employees despite undeniable evidence from many studies demonstrating the strong relationship between employee satisfaction and corporate financial performance. For example, in the book *The Enthusiastic Employee: How Companies Profit by Giving Workers What They Want*, Sirota and colleagues conclude from the results of thirty years of research that enthusiastic and satisfied employees always outperform the unhappy and dissatisfied employees.[2] Without engaged people to run the equipment and execute the business processes, there would be no product or service to deliver; in fact, there would be no company at all without the people, the employees, to make it work.

> There is one key to profitability and stability during either a boom or bust economy: employee morale.

Herb Kelleher
Cofounder, Southwest Airlines

4.1 EMPLOYEE SATISFACTION

Employee satisfaction means different things to different people. Merriam-Webster's dictionary defines satisfaction as "anything that brings gratification, pleasure, or contentment."[3] In general, people most often associate satisfaction with happiness and comfort.

In the workplace, three basic things affect an employee's overall sense of satisfaction. All of them must be met for employee satisfaction to be high. First, people need to personally value the work they perform each day. One of the authors had a manager who told him that if at the end of the day he would be willing to pay himself for the work he had accomplished during the day, then it had been a productive day. If he had too many days where he would not pay himself for the activities of the day, then it was time for a change.

Second, people need to like working with their co-workers. When conflicts arise, they need to be assured that the focus is on the issues — not on personalities. Think about a time you worked on a "hot" issue and felt very good about it when it was over. Most likely, the people on the team liked their jobs and enthusiastically threw themselves into the work. Enthusiasm is contagious. It is easy to understand why part of an employee's individual satisfaction at work is linked to the satisfaction of his or her peers.

Third, people need to have confidence in their leadership and believe that their managers are making the best choices possible. Linked to this is the reassurance they feel when co-workers also have confidence in their leadership. This shared confidence is also contagious and helps people stay focused during rough times for the company.

The organization's leadership plays a big role in developing employee satisfaction. They need to create a work environment that aligns the employees' values, goals, and actions to an inspiring organizational mission, values, and vision, create a challenging work environment, and most important, provide support for employee personal development and abilities. Leaders can do this by

- Demonstrating characteristics that contribute to employee satisfaction and morale
- Having a clear and defined organizational vision
- Relating the corporate vision to the daily work
- Having excellent communication with the organization
- Driving effective communication within the organization
- Giving recognition for a job well done and regular performance feedback
- Creating a pleasant atmosphere and workplace

All of these will lead to confidence in senior management's abilities.

4.2 PERSONAL BALANCED SCORECARDS

Companies not only need to hire the right people with the right skills and put them in the right place where they are most effective, they also need to hire people who are constantly improving themselves. By improving the employee, the company will improve.

There are many personal improvement methods out there, but one method that we found effective is the Personal Balanced Scorecard (PBSC), which was developed by Dr. Hubert Rampersad.[4] PBSC is a structured method that helps individuals define their performance measures, personal mission, critical success factors, vision, key roles, objectives, targets, and improvement actions.

Similar to the Corporate Balanced Scorecard, PBSC also has four perspectives: financial, external, internal, and knowledge and learning. Financial refers to personal financial stability. To what degree are you able to meet your financial needs? External refers to the relations with your spouse, children, friends, employer, colleagues, and others. How do they see you? Internal refers to your physical health and mental state. How can you control these in order to create value for yourself and others? Last, knowledge and learning refers to your skills and learning ability. How do you learn, and how can you remain successful in the future? Quantity of professional literature read, number of workshops and seminars attended, number of articles published, MBA diploma, study expenditures, or number of necessary skills are good examples. These four basic perspectives form the critical part of a person's personal ambition. Along with the personal critical success factors, it creates a link to such things as performance measures, objectives, targets, and improvement actions.

The Personal Balanced Scorecard serves as a guide for people who want to achieve more in their lives. This involves skills, personal habits, and behaviors. These are essential to good personal well-being and to being a successful person. Personal ambition in every individual is essential to success. Having vision, mission, and key roles allows a person to express his or her values, ideals, personal intentions, identity, and driving force. More important, it will provide people more insight about themselves.

Rampersad's Personal Balanced Scorecard model has two components: personal branding or personal ambition, which includes personal vision, personal mission, and personal key roles, and the actual Personal Balanced

Scorecards. which include personal critical success factors, personal objectives, personal performance measures and targets, and personal improvement actions.

4.3 PERSONAL VISION

If you ask 100 people what they want to do in their lives or if they have a personal vision or dream they want to achieve, 99 of them will have no answer. When we were children, most of us dreamed about our future. For a variety of reasons, as we grow up some of us lose those dreams. Often we are told our dreams are unrealistic and we become discouraged. Having a personal vision or dream is an important guide to personal success in our work as well as our personal lives. Feodor Dostoyevsky said, "The secret of man's being is not only to live but to have something to live for."[5] We humans were born to dream, so when you dream, dream big and believe that you will achieve it.

> I noticed an almost universal trait among Super Achievers, and it was what I call Sensory Goal Vision. These people knew what they wanted out of life, and they could sense it multi-dimensionally before they ever had it. They could not only see it, but also taste it, smell it, and imagine the sounds and emotions associated with it. They pre-lived it before they had it. And the sharp, sensory vision became a powerful driving force in their lives.
>
> **Stephen Devore**
> *Author*

Think about people who have become household names, such as Oprah Winfrey, Bill Gates, J. K. Rowling, Condoleezza Rice, Michael Jordan, and Jack Welch, to name a few. They all identified and leveraged their authentic dream, responded to it with love and passion, succeeded by living according to it and doing work they love, had faith in themselves, and had the courage to pursue their dream. They worked very hard to realize their dream or personal vision.

A personal vision is a picture of the future you want to create and a description of how you will go about realizing it. It includes such things as where you are going; which values and principles will guide you on your way; what you want to achieve; what you want to be; what talents, skills, and experience you need; the ideal characteristics you want to possess; your ideal job situation; and where you want to be at the end of your life. Your personal vision takes care of inner guidance and determines what actions you must take today in order to reach those goals. It functions as an ethical compass and is a concrete translation of your inner longings; keeping in mind the four perspectives, it gives direction to your efforts.

If your personal vision is "Always act and serve out of love," your personal vision statement might be "I want to realize my vision by …"

1. Inspiring others and earning their respect.
2. Always paying attention to optimize my spiritual development, my emotional balance, and my physical health.
3. Purposefully controlling my learning process, and, on this basis, being intuitive and creative.
4. Developing my moral character and personal integrity.
5. Maintaining my financial independence.

The four basic perspectives — internal, external, knowledge and learning, and financial — are clearly recognizable in this example. These perspectives must be an integral part of personal ambition for you to formulate your PBSC.

4.4 PERSONAL MISSION

Your personal mission statement encompasses your philosophy of life and your overall objectives. It indicates who you are, what you stand for, what makes you unique, what your success depends on, what your life objectives are, what you live for, what your core beliefs are, what your deepest aspirations are, what makes you happy, how you want others to see you, and what you are most proud of.

These are seemingly easy questions, but they are difficult to answer. They are central to your sense of self. "Who am I?" is an identity question. It initiates self-examination of your *personal identity* (the unique position you find yourself in) and a voyage of discovery.

Without knowing what I am and why I am here, life is impossible.

Leo Tolstoy
Author, Anna Karenina

A personal mission statement might be "To be authentic and gracious, create joy and deeper meaning in others' lives based on my uniqueness." A personal mission is aimed at *being*, and personal vision at *becoming*. Through your mission and vision, you will be able to give direction to your life.

> When you discover your mission, you will feel its demand. It will fill you with enthusiasm and a burning desire to get to work on it.
>
> **W. Clement Stone**
> *Businessman, author, philanthropist*

4.5 PERSONAL KEY ROLES

Key roles relate to the way you wish to fulfill the many essential roles in your life and thereby realize your personal mission and vision. They indicate the types of relationships you would like to have and how you connect with your friends, family, customers, and others, and who the most important people in your life are and your relationship to them, and for whom you exist. This formulation of your key roles will also result in work–life balance and a better self-image, which in turn improves your learning ability.

Key roles are concerned primarily with the external perspective in the PBSC. You should then identify elements of them as critical success factors, which you can then translate in the PBSC to personal objectives, performance measures, targets, and improvement actions. This will create work–life balance. Some examples of personal key roles:

- *Spouse:* To build a future together, in which I give and receive love, respect, and trust.
- *Mother:* To be a support to my children and be there while they strive toward a happy life.
- *Friend:* To be someone my friends can always count on and to never disappoint them.
- *Manager:* To help make the organization for which I work successful and, through this, serve the community.

Personal ambition is a set of guiding principles that embody your values and clearly state who you are, where you are going, where you want to be, and the roles are you fulfilling. The personal ambition statement is your personal brand. You must have a personal ambition statement if you expect exceptional success, since people who perform at their peak attract success. Keep the personal ambition you desire to achieve at the forefront of your mind each day. It is your personal lighthouse keeping you steadily on course. Personal ambition statements are most effective when they are grounded in

- The four perspectives — financial, external, internal, and knowledge and learning
- Unselfishness *and* authenticity
- Your dream, uniqueness, genius, skills, principles, and values (specific to each person but include ethical starting points)
- Your personal mission statement (short, clear, simple, concrete, and formulated in the present tense; it may be used as a guideline)
- Unique and recognizable as such to others
- Formulated positively, in an arresting manner, and durable (the mission is not time bound; the vision is — for example, approximately ten years)
- An ambitious and inspiring personal vision that gives direction to personal initiative and creativity, and combines personal power and energy
- A personal mission that indicates how you want to distinguish yourself in society
- Self-image, self-knowledge, self-acceptance, and self-development (it requires a positive image of yourself and others)

Not the maker of plans and promises, but rather the one who offers faithful service in small matters. This is the person who is most likely to achieve what is good and lasting.

Johann Wolfgang von Goethe
German poet, novelist, and dramatist

4.6 PERSONAL CRITICAL SUCCESS FACTORS

The personal critical success factors (CSFs) are derived from personal ambition. They are related to the four perspectives. A personal ambition without them results in an incomplete PBSC. The personal CSFs form the bridge between personal ambition (long term) and personal objectives, performance measures, targets, and improvement actions (short term). To make this link, identify your personal core competencies in your personal ambition as they relate to the four perspectives. You can then translate your personal CSFs into concrete personal objectives. They are the factors that make you unique and where you can further develop yourself and make a difference.

4.7 PERSONAL OBJECTIVES

The central question here is, which measurable short-term personal results do I want to achieve? Personal objectives describe a result that you want to achieve in order to realize your personal ambition. Your personal objectives are derived from your personal CSFs and from an analysis of your strengths and weaknesses. Each personal CSF has one or more personal objectives related to one of the four scorecard perspectives. Make a list of all your strengths and weaknesses. Weaknesses include things you do not do well and habits that restrict you, have an unfavorable influence on your life, and deliver poor results.

It is also important to focus on areas where you are accomplished in order to make your performance even better. When analyzing your strengths, ask yourself the following questions:

- What are some of the strengths that have contributed to my success up to the present?
- How might these create problems for me in the future?
- Which problems would I like to solve first?

While analyzing your shortcomings, you should think about the following questions:

- What are my biggest shortcomings?
- Has anyone ever mentioned any of these shortcomings to me?
- Can I describe a situation where any of these shortcomings would be a serious handicap?

You could also ask yourself, what is the most important challenge I face regarding my work and career? Factors that may be related to these questions are, for example, aptitude, talent, ability, intelligence, goal orientation, perseverance, self-control, health, integrity, creativity, tolerance, enthusiasm, the home and work environments, responsibility, job prestige, status, power, freedom, having more free time, and so on. Some examples of personal objectives are appreciation from customers, improved leadership skills, inner peace, and greater knowledge. Your objective could be to develop a dynamic, charismatic personality and to become a highly competent, strong, disciplined, calm, and decent individual.

4.8 PERSONAL PERFORMANCE MEASURES

Personal performance measures are standards by which to measure the progress of your personal objectives. With these, you can assess how you are functioning in relation to your personal critical success factors and objectives. Without performance measures and targets, it is difficult to coach yourself with feedback. Performance measures related to your objectives urge you to action and give you a certain direction. They measure the changes and compare you with the norm, and, therefore, in time, give you information about steering yourself. This section of the PBSC deals with the following questions: How can I measure my personal results? What makes my personal objectives measurable? Some examples of personal performance measures are body weight, number of innovative ideas, ratio earnings and expenses, and number of hours of quality time with my family.

4.9 PERSONAL TARGETS

A personal target is a quantitative objective of a personal performance measure. It is a value that is pursued and then assessed through a personal performance measure. Targets indicate values that you want to achieve, and depend on your level of ambition. Some examples of personal targets are a salary increase of 5% in the current year, a minimum salary increase of 15% in two years, and to lose a minimum of 15 lbs. before December 31.

4.10 PERSONAL IMPROVEMENT ACTIONS

Personal improvement actions are strategies used to realize your personal ambition. They help to develop your skills, improve your behavior, master yourself, and improve your performance. *How* is central here: How do I want to achieve my personal results? How can I realize my personal objectives? How can I improve my behavior?

Step by step. I can't think of any other way of accomplishing anything.

Michael Jordan
Professional basketball player

Dr. Hubert Rampersad, a world-renowned expert on human resources and the originator of Personal Balanced Scorecards, was kind enough to allow us to share his Personal Balanced Scorecards to illustrate the application of this effective tool. Taken together, Table 4.1 and Table 4.2 summarize Dr. Rampersad's Personal Balanced Scorecard. For each personal objective, he specifies metrics, targets, and the steps needed to achieve his personal goals. Table 4.2 is a good example of a PBSC.

We have seen many companies spending hundreds of thousands of dollars on employee satisfaction surveys each year. Yet, in many cases, the results show that employee satisfaction continues to decline each year.

TABLE 4.1

Hubert Rampersad's Personal Ambitions

My Personal Vision

To live life completely, honestly, and compassionately and to serve the needs of mankind to the best of my ability. I want to realize this in the following way:

Enjoy physical and mental health

Passionate and compassionate to inspire others, earn their respect, and always serve out of love

Energize innovative organizations where human spirit thrives and which model the best practices in business performance and personal integrity

Experience enjoyment in my work by being full of initiative, accepting challenges continuously, and to keep on learning

Achieve financial security

My Personal Mission

Enjoy the freedom to develop and share knowledge, especially if this can mean something in the life of others.

My Personal Key Roles

In order to achieve my vision, the following key roles have top priority:

Spouse: Rita is the most important person in my life

Father: Guide Rodney and Warren on the road to independence

Coach: Love to serve learning individuals and innovative organizations to unlock their potential

Student: Learn something new every day and always be a scholar

TABLE 4.2

Hubert Rapersad's Personal Balanced Scorecard

Personal Critical Success Factors	Personal Objectives	Internal — Personal Performance Measures	Personal Targets	Personal Improvement Actions	Progress — In Progress	Progress — Reached My Target
To live life completely, honestly, and compassionately	Be happy	Level of feeling happy	> 80% of my time	Accept new challenges continuously, update my PBSC frequently, ask for feedback, and be more patient.	X	
Enjoy physical and mental health	Emotionally strong	Number of hours of sleep	7 hours per day	Not endlessly continue activities but define a deadline and stick to it. Pay attention to the quality of sleep, not the quantity.	X	
	Be physically strong and fit	Weight	By June 1 lose at least 15 lbs.	Continue current diet, less candy, red wine instead of beer, and healthy food (fruit/vegetables).		X
		Body fat	By May 1 decrease from 47.4% to 29.1%	Initiate a training roster, at least 2 times a month, a 20 mile bicycle trip, golf once a week, 3 times a week exercises at home, and rejoin tennis club.	X	
Experience enjoyment in my work	No stress	Level of stress	Decrease by at least 75% within 6 months	Learn to do yoga effectively. Balance times of stress with times of pure relaxation and leisure.		

External

Personal Critical Success Factors	Personal Objectives	Personal Performance Measures	Personal Targets	Personal Improvement Actions	Progress	
					In Progress	Reached My Target
Serve the needs of mankind	Satisfaction	Degree of satisfaction of others with regard to my actions	Satisfaction score of at least 80% within half a year	Act more helpful without trying to gain profit from it. Provide positive recognitions and say "I'm sorry" and "thank you" more often.	X	
Be passionate and compassionate to inspire others, earn their respect, and always serve out of love	Be of greater value to others	Appreciation score on delivered added value	At least 80% within one year	Be more helpful. Inspire and encourage others to commit to their own dreams. Act as a role model. Encourage creativity and innovation in others. Be more involved in their situation.	X	
Love to serve learning individuals and innovative organizations to unlock their potential	High Personal Brand awareness	Awareness score of my Personal Brand	At least 25% of my domain is aware of my brand within 1 year	Promote my Personal Brand more actively, publish more articles, attend networking groups, and network with fellow professionals.	X	X
				Make effective use of Internet. Develop a network in North America. Identify subset of branding tools and branding channels that will reach my target audience effectively. Update my Web site contents and launch my blog.	X	
		Percent of my revenue spent on Personal Branding	20% per year	Focus more on Personal Branding instead of marketing and sales. Develop initiatives to benefit from the positive trends in Personal Branding.		

(continued)

TABLE 4.2 (CONTINUED)

Hubert Rapersad's Personal Balanced Scorecard

| Personal Critical Success Factors | External | | | Progress | |
	Personal Objectives	Personal Performance Measures	Personal Targets	Personal Improvement Actions	In Progress	Reached My Target
Energize innovative organizations where human spirit thrives and that model the best practices in business performance and personal integrity	Be appreciated by my customers	Satisfaction score of my customers	At least 90% within 1 year	Ask for feedback from customers and document this. Demonstrate effective emotional responses in a variety of situations. Encourage creativity and innovation in organizations. Develop initiatives to benefit from the positive trends in outplacement field.		
Rita is the most important person in my life	Be a good husband	Number of loving and appreciating feedback received from her	Minimum of once per day	Make loving remarks myself. Be open for her real needs. Go on vacation together three times a year. Create work/life balance based on this.		

Personal Critical Success Factors	Personal Objectives	Personal Performance Measures	Personal Targets	Personal Improvement Actions	Progress	
					In Progress	Reached My Target
Guide Rodney and Warren on the road to independence	Be a good father	Number of times they involve me in their decisions	Whenever needed	Show more patience; listen to them more and more carefully. Take an interested position, not a correcting one. Periodically inform, coach, advise and facilitate. Help them build their confidence and to deeply understand their own strengths and weaknesses.		

Knowledge and Learning

Personal Critical Success Factors	Personal Objectives	Personal Performance Measures	Personal Targets	Personal Improvement Actions	Progress	
					In Progress	Reached My Target
Enjoy the freedom to develop and share knowledge	Enjoyment	Level of enjoyment	Increase by at least 30% in 2009	Publish 3 new books in the field of personal branding, PBSC, and TPS-Lean Six Sigma.	X	
Be full of initiative, accept challenges continuously, and keep on learning	Be innovative	Number of new successful initiatives	At least four per month	Invest more in learning about future trends. Effectively translate creative ideas into business results. Share more.		X

(continued)

TABLE 4.2 (CONTINUED)

Hubert Rapersad's Personal Balanced Scorecard

Knowledge and Learning

Personal Critical Success Factors	Personal Objectives	Personal Performance Measures	Personal Targets	Personal Improvement Actions	In Progress	Reached My Target
Learn something new every day and always be a scholar	Improved listening skills	Number of times positive feedback received from others regarding my listening skills	At least 1 per week	Build effective TPS-partnerships across Asia. Explore opportunities for professional development in my field. Initiate new initiatives due to the launch of my new Personal & Company Branding and TPS-Lean Six Sigma book.		X
	Improved language skills	Time spent on learning Spanish language	At least 30 minutes per day during first quarter	Genuinely listen to others with more respect. Invest in ongoing personal development. Listen more patiently; become a supportive listener. Follow a Spanish language course. Read and speak Spanish more frequently.	X	

Financial

Personal Critical Success Factors	Personal Objectives	Personal Performance Measures	Personal Targets	Personal Improvement Actions	Progress	
					In Progress	Reached My Target
Financial security	Improved asset management	ROI stock portfolio	At least 8% per year	Pursue proven investment strategies		X
	Become financially healthy	Revenues TPS International Inc.	20% increase in 2 years	Develop a network in North America. Invest in promoting my Personal Brand, launch PBSC and Personal Branding software. Take decisive actions regarding brand promotion activities. Act more proactively by being attentive of trends and developments in my target market. Effectively anticipate on future opportunities.	X	X
	Manage expenditures	Income and expense ratio	Increase of minimum 10% per year	Be more costs conscious		

Before this can change, organizations must accept the facts and seize the opportunity, instead of rationalizing away the poor results.

Employee satisfaction means employees enjoy their work, feel personally fulfilled due to work accomplishment, and enjoy effective working relationships between themselves and their peers and between themselves and management. The most important factor is that employees feel connected to the work they are doing and see the value to it. When this happens, connections are made, the lifeblood of the corporation pumps strongly and rhythmically throughout, and employees feel valued and respected. This feeling is contagious. It spreads throughout the corporation. This is when the magic happens for the corporation.

NOTES

1. Mary Kay Ash, *Brainy Quotes*, http://www.brainyquote.com/quotes/authors/m/mary_kay_ash.html (retrieved July 7, 2009).
2. David Sirota, Louis A. Mischkind, and Michael Irwin Meltzer, *The Enthusiastic Employee: How Companies Profit by Giving Workers What They Want* (New York: Wharton School, 2005).
3. *Webster's New World College Dictionary* (Cleveland: Wiley , 2004), s.v. "satisfaction."
4. Hubert K. Rampersad, *Personal Balanced Scorecard: The Way to Individual Happiness, Personal Integrity, and Organizational Effectiveness* (Charlotte, NC: Information Age, 2006).
5. Feodor Dostoyevsky, *The Brothers Karamazov*, trans. Constance Garnett, p. 658, available at http://books.google.com/ (retrieved July 7, 2009).

5

Becoming Lean: Trimming the Fat

Time waste differs from material waste in that there can be no salvage. The easiest of all wastes and the hardest to correct is the waste of time, because wasted time does not litter the floor like wasted material.

Henry Ford
Founder of Ford Motor Company

If you ask any physician to identify the first thing a person should do to become healthy, the response often is to adapt a healthy lifestyle — eat nutritious foods, exercise, and lose weight. Losing weight increases a person's energy, reduces aches and pain, improves mobility and zest for life, and prevents many diseases. Lean manufacturing is very similar to a healthy lifestyle, in that its function is to trim the fat and to make organizations become much fitter, faster, and more competitive. The main objective of Lean initiatives in any company is to eliminate waste, such as excess inventory, overproduction, and excessive equipment setup times.

Studies show that the benefits of Lean manufacturing make it well worth the effort, just as a healthy lifestyle benefits the human body. Some of the benefits are

- Responding quickly to customer needs, promoting better satisfaction
- Reducing inventory and increasing cash flow
- Understanding and simplifying the value stream to reduce allocated cost structures
- Solving problems sooner to reduce quality defects
- Reducing cycle time by more efficient process flow
- Increasing capacity throughout to avoid additional capital expenditures
- Reducing waste significantly and taking cost out of the bottom line

- Eliminating bottlenecks with improved scheduling
- Extending the life of machines and equipment

In a healthy diet, objectives are achieved by limiting portion sizes and balancing the food groups consumed. Similarly, Lean forces companies to measure business goals. These measures must be visible throughout various functions, including manufacturing operations and supply chain. The visibility of these measures makes it possible to attack inefficiencies, to align improvement with business objectives, and to integrate the business environment so that it supports improvement of business objectives. Therefore, implementing Lean can create superior financial and operational results.

Many companies are turning to Lean manufacturing in an effort to become more profitable. Lean is a management system for satisfying customers on delivery, quality, and price. Lean also leads to improved employee satisfaction, as employees are involved in the effort and benefit from improved work conditions. To succeed, Lean manufacturing must become a way of life for the organization.

5.1 BRIEF HISTORY OF LEAN

In the mid-1940s, Toyota Motor Company recognized that American automakers had a tenfold productivity advantage. Toyota knew that they could not compete with other industrialized economies on cost, volume, or quality by using typical mass production techniques.

Most companies in Japan had limited resources, especially after the devastation of World War II. They had very little capital to build modern factories or to buy modern equipment. Many Japanese manufacturers had to "make do" with what little they had. These limitations actually promoted and created the ideal environment for Lean. In order to compete with American automakers, Japanese leaders such as Kiichiro Toyoda, Shigeo Shingo, and Taiichi Ohno (considered the fathers of many Lean operational methods) devised a new, disciplined, process-oriented system, which is known today as the "Toyota Production System" (TPS) or "Lean manufacturing."

Their pioneering thinking with a focus on low-tech, pull systems became the foundation of the Toyota Production System. The basic ideas behind the Lean manufacturing system are waste elimination, cost reduction, and employee empowerment. The term "Lean" denotes a system that utilizes less, in term of all inputs, to create the same outputs as those created by a traditional mass production system, while contributing more variety for the end customer.

Taiichi Ohno, who was given the task of developing a system that would enhance productivity at Toyota, is generally considered the originator of TPS and the primary force behind it. Ohno drew upon ideas from the West and particularly from Henry Ford's book *Today and Tomorrow*. Ford's moving assembly line of continuously flowing material formed the basis for TPS, which, after some experimentation, was developed and refined between 1945 and 1970, and is still growing all over the world. The basic underlying idea of this system is to minimize the consumption of resources that add no value to a product. The Lean manufacturing discipline is to work in every facet of the value stream by eliminating waste in order to reduce cost, generate capital, bring in more sales, and remain competitive in a growing global market.

For many years, Toyota has proven the success of this system by producing quality products and promoting cost-reduction activities. A further study of Toyota will reveal that the foundation of Lean is derived from a combination of different tools and techniques.

Some generic names for Lean production are cellular, flexible, one-by-one, agile, synchronous, demand-flow manufacturing, and pull manufacturing. Most common, however, are the terms *just in time* and *kaizen*. Since the mid-1980s, large Western automobile manufacturers have adopted many of the basic principles of Lean manufacturing. By that time, many of the Lean principles had been covered in the book *World Class Manufacturing*, by Richard J. Schonberger.[1] The term "Lean manufacturing" first appeared in *The Machine That Changed the World* by James Womack, Daniel Jones, and Daniel Ross, which was the result of a study conducted at the Massachusetts Institute of Technology regarding the movement from mass production toward Lean manufacturing. The study outlined the great success Toyota had at New United Motor Manufacturing Inc. (NUMMI) and showed how Toyota eliminated the huge productivity gap that had existed between the Japanese and Western automotive industries. As a result of the success at Toyota producing and distributing products with half or less human effort, capital investment, floor space, tools, materials, time, and overall expense, many of the Lean principles and tools were adopted by U.S. companies.

In a subsequent book, *Lean Thinking*, James Womack and Daniel Jones revealed to a wider audience the benefits of Lean thinking, which, although it had its roots in manufacturing, could be applied by anyone championing a Lean transformation.[2] Readers discovered that Lean thinking could help to solve their business problems with a simple use of five dynamic steps beginning with the critical starting point of defining value. Womack and Jones believe that value can only be defined by the ultimate customer and is only meaningful when expressed in terms of a specific product (a good or a service, or both at once), which must also meet the customer's needs at a specific price at a specific time.

> There are so many men who can figure costs, and so few who can measure values.
>
> **Author Unknown**

After value come value stream, flow, pull, and perfection:

1. Specify the *value* desired by the customer, what the customer is willing to pay for.
2. Identify the *value stream* for each product that provides value and challenge all wasted steps (generally nine out of ten) currently necessary to provide it. Eliminate those steps that do not create value to the customer.
3. Make the product *flow* continuously through the remaining, value-added steps at the rate of customer demand. Make sure the value-creating steps occur in tight sequence to provide smooth flow to the customer without disruption.
4. Introduce *pull* between all steps where continuous flow is possible. Customers pull value from the next upstream activity.
5. Manage toward *perfection* so that the number of steps and the amount of time and information needed to serve the customer continually falls.

Lean thinking is the next generation of Lean; it was heavily promoted by Womack and Jones. Their book provided a call to action for managers at all levels. They point out that many business leaders have lost sight of what true value is for their customer and challenge all leaders to consider these five basic steps to increase the value added to their customers. Although basic, these are powerful concepts and embody a new way of thinking. Lean thinking has been proven (the book provides examples of companies that incorporated Lean and succeeded) and can be a groundbreaking method for those who are willing to try it. Where applied correctly, Lean thinking has revolutionized today's business world. Industries, including services and nonprofits, have successfully adopted some form of a Lean strategy.

Among the strategies include a "Quick Lube" for your automobile, a "once and done" for the help desk, streamlined aid to disaster zones, and "made-to-order" computer systems shipped directly to your home. Leaders who understand the value to the customer and implement a Lean system that beats their competitors have led their companies to sustainable growth and higher profits. After decades of downsizing and reengineering, many companies have successfully embraced this new way of thinking.

5.2 ELIMINATION OF WASTE

Eliminating waste (or *muda*) from processes is a core concept of Lean. The Japanese word *muda* is often used because Japanese tends to be three-dimensional and its words tend to paint pictures or tell stories. In Japanese, *muda* is much more than just waste. Its literal translation is "to flog a dead horse; go on a fool's errand; uselessness, pointlessness, vain efforts, and to waste money on." Many U.S. companies use *muda* because it sends a stronger vision of how wasteful the activity really is.

Many have learned seven types of waste. However, the challenge is to spot these wastes on the shop floor or in the office environment because they are often hidden by a common symptom (excess inventory), which often is accepted as norm in the workplace. It takes a trained eye to recognize this symptom and to identify the true root cause of the waste that hides beneath. When recognized, the benefit is the elimination of the underlying waste and therefore the removal of the root cause. A number of problems lead companies to create and store excess goods, but these goods tie up valuable cash on a company's balance sheet that could be used for other important investments. Figure 5.1 illustrates how various symptoms of waste create a sea of inventory. As we eliminate wasteful activities, the water level is lowered and inventory problems are exposed.

The Toyota Production System classifies wastes in seven ways:

1. *Waste of Overproduction:* Producing more than the exact amount of goods the customer (internal or external) requires. This challenges the Western premise of the Economic Order Quantity (EOQ), which is based on the concept of fixed ordering costs, built around setup time, and thus the need to spread these fixed costs over large batches. To eliminate this type of waste, produce the exact quantity that customers need when they need it.

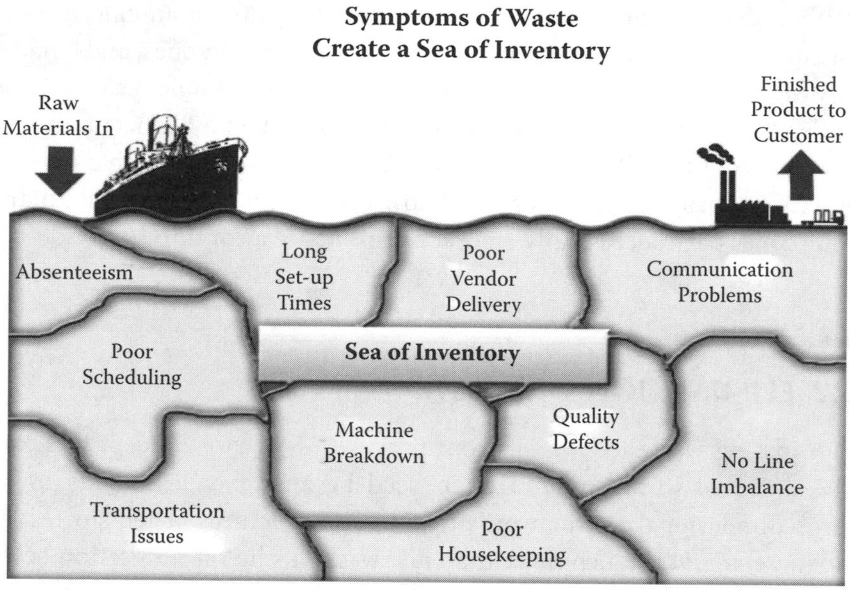

Symptoms of Waste
Create a Sea of Inventory

FIGURE 5.1
Symptoms of waste.

2. *Waste of Inventory:* Any type of material (raw, work in process, finished goods) and any level of stock can hide problems. Work-in-process and finished parts inventories do not add value to a product and should be eliminated or reduced. To eliminate this type of waste, keep a constant flow to the customer and do not have idle material. Reduce setup time and then production lot sizes to make the cost per unit constant. When inventory is reduced, other sources of waste are reduced too. For example, space that was used to store inventory can be utilized for other things such as facility capacity.

If we reduce batch sizes by half, we also reduce by half the time it will take to process a batch. That means we reduce queue and wait by half as well. Reduce those by half, and we reduce by about half the total time parts spend in the plant. Reduce the time parts spend in the plant and our total lead time condenses. And with faster turn-around on orders, customers get their orders faster.

Eliyahu M. Goldratt
Author, The Goal

3. *Waste of Defects:* Anything more than the ideal state of zero defects is waste. The simplest form of waste is components or products that do not meet specifications. To eliminate this type of waste, make every effort to reduce defects. Total Productive Maintenance (TPM) is one way to eliminate defects and scrap.

4. *Waste of Motion:* All unnecessary operations, movement, and steps are waste. Workers spending time moving around the plant is wasteful, as is the time a machine operator takes walking to the tool room or the stores for a fixture or a component. To eliminate this type of waste, avoid excessive bending or stretching and time spent searching for frequently lost items.

5. *Waste of Waiting:* Delays and downtime because of machines or people is waste. Time is not being used effectively, thus incurring the cost of wages and all the fixed overhead costs. To eliminate this type of waste, avoid long setups, delays, and unexpected machine downtime.

6. *Waste of Transportation:* Movement of material and the repeated handling of the same parts through the factory is waste. Moving things around incurs a cost such as the electricity absorbed by a forklift truck. To eliminate this type of waste, stop transporting materials and information that does not add value to the product. One way to do this is to utilize a cellular manufacturing layout to ensure a continuous flow of the product. This also helps eliminate another source of waste, energy. When machines and people are grouped into cells, unproductive operations can be minimized because a group of people can be fully dedicated to that cell. This avoids excess human utilization.

7. *Waste of Overprocessing:* Working a product more than necessary throughout its manufacturing cycle is waste. The most obvious example is overpackaging. To eliminate this type of waste, remove unnecessary steps in the process. Make it simple.

Overproduction is known as the root cause of the other forms of *muda*. Think about what happens when a process overproduces. People are busy making or doing things that nobody ordered — waste of motion. Unneeded finished goods must be moved to storage warehouses — waste of transportation. Overproduction creates unnecessary raw materials, parts, and works in progress — waste of inventory. Additionally, over-processing occurs when organizations build in more complexity or specifications than are required by the customer. These are several examples of extra costs that result from overproduction. Overproduction, referred to as the batch and queue mode of operation, is a source of waste for most firms.

This large-batch processing mode is an outdated paradigm. The main problem with large batches is that there is no connection between the pace of production and the pace of demand. Lean tools can help with reduced lot sizes with quick setup capability. These are the new paradigms of the twenty-first century. Producing various models in small lots improves responsiveness to customers and flexibility to changes in demand. The smaller the lot, the smoother the process flow is. Lean manufacturing views continuous, one-piece flow as the ideal and emphasizes the optimization and integration of systems into machines, materials, people, and facilities. Continuous flow follows the concept of producing one-by-one as efficiently as possible.

An eighth waste has recently emerged and is getting much attention. *People waste*, the waste of human capital, can arise from failing to harness the potential that exists in all work groups. Value is lost when management and employees at all levels are not consistently aligned to address critical issues. Problems are not resolved because resources are focused or aligned on different priorities. This type of waste is considered more important than the other wastes, and companies are just starting to recognize the huge potential. Peter Drucker said, "The first sign of decline of an industry is loss of appeal to qualified, able, and ambitious people."[3]

Examples of people waste include institutional knowledge from change implementations such as Lean, robust information systems, introducing or designing a new product, and making continuous improvement a way of life for every employee. The freeing up of employee creativity when other wastes are removed provides many benefits for companies from a larger source for new ideas, improved employee morale, lower turnover, and a culture of continual improvement.

There is no question that the elimination of waste is an essential ingredient for survival in today's manufacturing world. Companies must strive to create high-quality, low-cost products that can get to the customers in the shortest time possible.

5.3 LEAN PRINCIPLES

Value must be maximized in every facet of the value stream. Instilling the discipline to reduce costs and offering a fair market price will achieve maximum value. Typically, value-added activities are those that the customer is willing to pay for. Anything that the customer is *not* willing to pay for is non-value added or waste. For the most part, a value-added activity is one that changes the fit, form, or function of the product. For example, a customer is willing to pay for the actual time spent making the product but is not willing to pay for time spent waiting for supplies, rework, or repeated physical movement of the product without any real change to its appearance. Some non-value-added work is necessary, such as machine changeovers, tax accounting, and sales and marketing. The goal is to eliminate all forms of waste and to reduce non-value-added unnecessary work to achieve the most efficiency possible.

The value stream of a business is the sequence of steps that a company performs in order to satisfy a customer's need. This includes all value-added actions as well as non-value-added actions. The value stream is comprised of the people, tools and technologies, physical facilities, communication channels, and policies and procedures that are required to bring a product or a group of products from raw material to the customer.

Often it is difficult to envision the entire value-stream process because companies are more global, and product and information crisscross the globe either physically or virtually. Value-stream mapping is an enterprise improvement tool that is critical to visualizing the processes to realize a product — both physical flow (material movement and transformation) and information flow (data and communication). Value-stream mapping provides the graphical representation needed to allow full comprehension of how a company truly functions.

Once the value-stream map is complete, the main objective is to identify all types of waste in the value stream and to take steps to eliminate them. The graphical representation makes sense of the daily routine and often immediately draws attention to the frustrations faced by workers as they perform their tasks. By stepping back and looking at the value stream in its entirety, the new vantage point allows you to see and streamline the big picture instead of the traditional approach of focusing on the individual processes. The whole flow is streamlined, with focus given to bottlenecks. Value-stream mapping also creates a common language across all processes, improving communication between direct labor and office functions to facilitate thoughtful decisions to improve the value stream.

> All we are doing is looking at the time line, from the moment the customer gives us an order to the point when we collect the cash. And we are reducing the time line by reducing the non-value-adding wastes.
>
> **Taiichi Ohno**
> *Father of the Toyota Production System*

Documenting this allows activities to be evaluated through the customer's eyes, and actions can be taken to eliminate those steps that do not create value to the customer. Flow is promoted to ensure that the value-creating steps occur in the right sequence. To provide smooth flow, a number of processes must be linked together to provide customers with little or no disruption.

One-piece flow is the most popular choice for Lean manufacturing experts. This concept allows products to flow at the rate at which customers are buying them, often called "*takt* time." The word *Takt* is the German word for the baton that an orchestra conductor uses to regulate the speed, beat, or timing at which musicians play. Therefore, *takt* time is "beat time," "rate time," or "heartbeat." Throughout the value stream, customers pull value from the next upstream activity, which in turn authorizes the process responsible to build another one. When necessary, the customer may need to pull from prepositioned inventory stock locations. Ideally, these locations are close to the customer and are only used as a countermeasure until flow is established. The pursuit of the perfect value stream is the ultimate objective.

Lean is a fundamental enterprise conversion that must be approached as a *total organizational and cultural transformation*. An important step that a company must take to change a value stream is to determine its Lean status. Value-stream mapping is a good tool that will train leaders to find waste in the system.

Once waste is identified, the root cause of the waste must be examined in order to implement proper countermeasures. Value streams typically include the study of cycle and lead times. They also document the total number of people needed, tools, technologies, and information loops.

When mapped out, the information and material flow of the business is clearly seen. Each step on the map includes a data box with all the specifics associated with that step in the process. These numbers provide a quantitative means of measuring the magnitude of the waste and the success of the countermeasures in driving the numbers from the current state to the future state.

Once opportunities are identified, plans are laid out to close the gap between the current and future state maps. Typically, there are large numbers of activities in a strategic plan, which should include both long- and short-term actions. Many project-planning tools can help manage the improvement activities. The ultimate goal is to keep it simple to manage and to use it.

The value-stream map is a technique that enables leaders to see the waste in the system. This pictorial representation of material and information flow differs from process mapping, which tends to represent only material flow.

In a process, many things happen concurrently. The value-stream map gives you a picture that shows the various process levels within the whole value chain. Standard icons are used to create a common language that all can understand. This allows the map to be read by anyone familiar with the icons and to be used as a communication tool across organizations to share current-state situations. Additionally, the future-state vision and the countermeasure plans are also shared with any functional teams associated with the value stream. A very good reference for developing current- and future-state value-stream maps is in the book *Learning to See*.[4]

Nature does constant value-stream mapping — it's called evolution.

Carrie Latet
Poet

In summary, value-stream mapping is a good starting point for any enterprise that wants to be Lean (see Figure 5.2). Value-stream mapping:

- Helps you visualize the entire process flow
- Helps you see not only wasteful activities but also their source in the value stream
- Provides a common language for talking about manufacturing processes
- Helps you design how the entire door-to-door process should flow. Value-stream maps become a blueprint for Lean implementation.

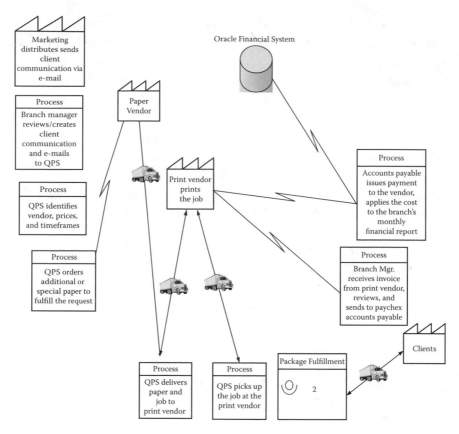

FIGURE 5.2
Value-stream map.

5.4 LEAN AS A BUSINESS SYSTEM

Lean principles works together to create a business system. Understanding the current state of the material and information flow is the starting point. When you have stable, predictable, and repeatable processes, you can begin to focus on speed and quality improvements, which should always be done with the customer in mind. The goal is to ensure that the elements of the system, including the tools and the people, are working together. At times, Lean leaders must teach others how to think with a continuous improvement mind-set. The resulting culture and climate brings change for the better when improvements are sustained.

Critical to thinking Lean is making every decision with an understanding of its impact on the customer. The goal is to create processes in the least

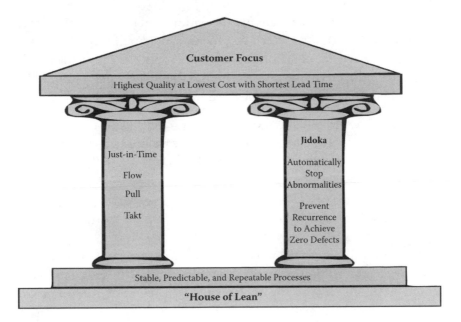

FIGURE 5.3
Model business system for the House of Lean.

wasteful way. Steps that add value from the end customer's perspective do this. By focusing on the customer's needs and wants, we can clearly determine what the value-adding steps are. Figure 5.3 shows a model business system. The House of Lean rests on two important pillars, the Just-in-Time and the *Jidoka* (Japanese for "automation"). The Just-in-Time (JIT) pillar directly links output to customer consumption so that there is little or no inventory. This should be the future state of any manufacturing company. Remember, inventory is simply a countermeasure to ensure perfect flow to your customer; the ideal is to achieve a "make to order" system. JIT production is the backbone of Lean manufacturing. Just-in-time production is about not having more raw materials, work in process, or products than what is required for smooth operation.

JIT utilizes what a "pull system." Customer demand, seen by the generation of the order, sends the first signal to production, and the product is *pulled* out of the assembly process. The final assembly line goes to the preceding process and pulls or withdraws the necessary parts in the necessary quantity at the necessary time. At each stage, the needed parts are pulled from the preceding process further upstream.

The whole process is coordinated using a *kanban*, an information system that is used to control the number of parts produced in every process. The most common types of kanbans are the withdrawal kanban, which specifies the quantity that the succeeding process should pull from the preceding process, and the production kanban, which specifies the quantity to be produced by the preceding process. In this fashion, shipments under JIT are small but frequent. A kanban is used to manage these shipments.

> Kanban is like the milkman. Mom didn't give the milkman a schedule. Mom didn't use MRP [manufacturing resource planning]. She simply put the empties on the front steps and the milkman replenished them. That is the essence of a pull system.
>
> **Ernie Smith**
> *Lean facilitator*

The *Jidoka* pillar typically represents the quality side of the house. The kanji ideographs for Ji, Do, and Ka roughly translate to auto, move, and action, or automation; at Toyota, *Jidoka* is referred to as *Ninben-no-aru Jidoka*, meaning "automation with a human touch." In practice, this means that each item is automatically inspected after it is produced. When there are defects, the process automatically stops to prevent additional defects from occurring and the worker is notified in creative ways that a defect was detected. For example, when a defect is detected during a manufacturing process, a red light goes off, indicating a problem; in a nonmanufacturing process, when Accounts Payable processes an invoice that does not match the amount on the purchase order, the computer system "warns" the operator, triggering additional review before the invoice can be processed. JIT and *Jidoka* must work together to satisfy customers.

5.5 OTHER ESSENTIAL LEAN TOOLS

Other important tools used in Lean applications include cellular manufacturing, production smoothing, standardized work, and Total Productive Maintenance (TPM). The proper use of these tools is necessary to ensure Lean implementation success.

5.5.1 Cellular Manufacturing

Cellular manufacturing is generally defined as "linking manual and machine operations into the most efficient combination to maximize value-added content while minimizing waste." Cellular manufacturing, one of the cornerstones of Lean, is a concept that increases the mix of products with the least waste possible. A cell consists of equipment and workstations arranged so that a smooth flow of materials and components is maintained throughout the process. (One of the major constraints to the flow of production through the factory is the way it is laid out.) Qualified and trained operators are assigned to work at that cell. In the ideal state, anyone should be able to follow the flow of production visually, from incoming components and raw materials through the packaging of the finished product, with little or no physical blockages to the flow.

Arranging people and equipment into cells is a great advantage in terms of achieving Lean goals. Just as one of the advantages of cells is the one-piece flow concept, which states that each product moves through the process one unit at a time without sudden interruption and at a pace determined by the customer's need, extending the product mix is another advantage of cellular manufacturing. When customers demand a wide variety of products as well as faster delivery rates, it is important to have flexibility in the process to accommodate their needs. This flexibility can be achieved by grouping similar products into families that can be processed on the same equipment in the same sequence. This will also shorten the time required for changeover between products, which will encourage production in smaller lots. Other benefits associated with cellular manufacturing include the following:

- Inventory (especially work in process) reduction
- Reduced transport, material handling, and minimizing travel distance
- Better space utilization
- Reduced lead times
- Identification of causes of defects and machine problems
- Improved productivity
- Enhanced teamwork and communication
- High visibility of the flow

The cellular concept can be applied in the office environment and other nonmanufacturing areas, such as service or administrative activities, for example, in order processing. The process usually involves people from different departments. An office cell groups people involved in the process together and makes them responsible for handling it.

5.5.2 Production Smoothing

In a Lean manufacturing system, it is important to move to a higher degree of process control in order to reduce waste. Another tool to accomplish this is *Heijunka*, the Japanese word for production smoothing, which is where manufacturers try to keep the production level as constant as possible from day to day. *Heijunka* is also a concept adapted from TPS, where in order to decrease production cost it was necessary to build no more cars and parts than could be sold. To accomplish this, the production schedule had to be smooth in order to effectively produce the right quantity of parts and efficiently utilize labor. If the production level is not constant, the result is waste (such as work-in-process inventory) at the workplace.

Many companies are using the *Heijunka* concept in the service sector to level consumer demand; for example, patients are given specific times for doctor appointments, or the price of airline tickets is reduced during off-peak times when there are few business travelers. A common example of smoothing workflow can be seen in "help desk" activities across a global team. Utilization of a shared e-mail address for an IT group allows routing of work requests to the next available person, whether the team member is in India or the United States, allowing a smooth workflow.

5.5.3 Standardized Work

Standardized work is defined as work in which the sequence of job elements has been efficiently organized and is repeatedly followed by a team member. A very important principle of waste elimination is the standardization of worker actions. Standardized work ensures that each job is organized and is carried out in the most effective manner. No matter who is doing the job, the same level of quality should be achieved.

> Without a standard, there can be no improvement.
>
> **Taiichi Ohno**
> *Father of the Toyota Production System*

Without standardized work, continuous improvement activities are not manageable because any improvement would be just another variation occasionally used and often ignored. Standardized work makes abnormalities visible. Sometimes, it is called the secret weapon in becoming Lean.

To standardize a method is to choose out of the many methods the best one, and use it. Standardization means nothing unless it means standardizing upward. Today's standardization, instead of being a barricade against improvement, is the necessary foundation on which tomorrow's improvement will be based. If you think of "standardization" as the best that you know today, but which is to be improved tomorrow — you get somewhere. But if you think of standards as confining, then progress stops.

Henry Ford
Founder of Ford Motor Company

At Toyota, every worker follows the same processing steps all the time. This includes the time needed to finish a job, the sequence to follow for each job, and the parts on hand. By doing this, line balancing is achieved, unwarranted work-in-process inventory is minimized, and non-value-added activities are reduced. *Takt* time, or how often to produce a part in a product family based on the actual customer demand, is used to standardize work. The target is to produce at a pace no higher than the *takt*. *Takt* time is calculated based on the following formula:

$$Takt \text{ time(TT)} = \frac{\text{Net time available for production}}{\text{Customer demand}}$$

The *takt* time formula can also be used in nonmanufacturing applications; for example, the emergency room in a hospital must keep pace with patient demand. In this case, dividing available time by patient demand determines the *takt* time. Another example can be seen in grocery stores that track the number of items scanned per minute during customer checkout.

5.5.4 Total Productive Maintenance (TPM)

TPM is a process that maximizes the productivity of equipment for its entire life. It fosters an environment where improvement efforts in safety, quality, cost, delivery, and creativity are encouraged through the participation of all employees. Figure 5.4 describes the objectives of TPM, which includes developing the people who usually operate the equipment, creating well-engineered equipment, creating an environment where enthusiasm and creativity flourish, and maximizing overall equipment effectiveness.

Machine breakdown is one of the most important issues that concern the people on the shop floor. The reliability of the equipment is very important

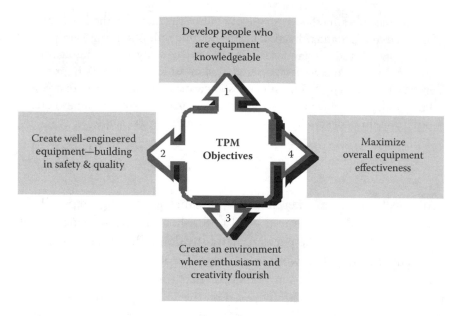

FIGURE 5.4
TPM objectives.

since, if one machine breaks down, the entire production line could go down. Seventy-five percent of machine breakdowns have two major causes: contamination and improper lubrication. TPM reduces equipment breakdown, stabilizes the equipment failure interval, lengthens equipment life, periodically reverses deterioration, and assists in predicting equipment life.

In almost any Lean environment, a TPM program is very important. There are two main components of a TPM program: preventive maintenance and corrective maintenance.

Preventive maintenance traditionally is managed through regular planned maintenance on all equipment rather than random checks. Workers have to carry out regular equipment maintenance to detect any anomalies as they occur. By doing so, sudden machine breakdowns can be prevented, which leads to improvement in the throughput of each machine. Progressive companies have expanded the idea to include predictive maintenance techniques in the preventive maintenance program. This approach allows evaluation of the condition of in-service equipment to predict when maintenance will be needed. This approach is more cost effective than time-based preventive maintenance, because tasks are performed only when needed.

Corrective maintenance deals with decisions such as whether to fix or buy new equipment. If a machine is always down because its components are always breaking down, it is better to replace those parts with newer ones. The machine will last longer and its uptime will be higher.

Maintenance prevention has to do with buying the right machine. If a machine is hard to maintain (for example, hard to lubricate or bolts are hard to tighten), then workers will be reluctant to maintain the machine on a regular basis, which will result in a huge amount of lost money invested in that machine.

5.6 BUSINESS PHILOSOPHY FOR LEAN

As a system, Lean becomes a philosophy for how to run a business. It is comprised of many tools and techniques. Without a picture of the entire value chain, people tend to apply the tools and the techniques with no real goal in mind. A current- and future-state map allows clear plans to be developed. Process checks can be used as tools to monitor the successful implementation of these techniques. Applied in the proper order and at the right points in the chain, minimizing the waste and maximizing the value to the customer is achievable. Other areas that benefit from Lean include cost, quality, delivery, safety, and morale.

As a Lean business system, success comes when all members of the organization understand and practice the philosophy as they go about their daily jobs. The system promotes the involvement of individuals and teams in looking for waste and suggesting better ways. Success often comes from how people are treated and thought about in the Lean journey. Promoting a "no-blame" environment in which employees' suggestions and ideas are heard and all participate is essential. This requires that employees at all levels look for ways to eliminate waste daily. Identifying opportunities is critical as you begin to train yourself and others to "see" waste.

However, this is just the start; the ability to execute change is the true test. Lean cultures engage everyone in identifying and implementing improvements every day. These improvements are more than continuous improvement, they are *Kaizen* (a Japanese word, where *Kai* means to take apart and make new, and *Zen* means to do so in a way that helps others); therefore, they not only eliminate the waste, but they also make the person's work better.

The reason many organizations fail to implement Lean is the result of "tool shopping." Rather than designing a systematic implementation strategy, they attempt to pick low-hanging fruit. For example, kanbans and lot-size reductions always reduce inventory, but they often generate more waste of waiting unless standardized work is followed. In addition, error-proofing efforts eliminate only a small portion of waste such as defective goods. Setup-reduction procedures will dramatically reduce machine downtime and increase capacity in any traditional plant. The economic benefit is the cash savings resulting from reduced inventory levels by installed kanbans and work leveling. Simply stated, the full profit and quality impacts of Lean are achievable by implementing Lean as a *total* business systems approach.

Lean success depends upon more than just tools. Lean tools are not the same as Lean thinking. It is the thinking, not the tools, that promotes waste elimination and increases the value of flow to the customer. Tools such as value-stream alignment and production-flow cells are neither a means nor an end. While these tools are easy to understand and apply, in any specific instance that is not the Lean challenge. Tools fix problems here and there, but are not effective for any length of time without structure and ownership.

Tools will not create a new culture of Lean. That is why there are so few world-class organizations. In order to create a Lean culture that will apply appropriate tools when necessary over the long term, a leadership team must provide focus, structure, and ownership at *all* levels of the organization, every day. For organizations in the manufacturing and operations arena, there is no alternative to Lean for long-term survival and success. Every successful plant or site in the world is, or will be, implementing some form of Lean methods and approaches as needed for survival. Organizations that understand Lean thinking and improve their cultural interrelationships will be the best in their industries.

5.7 OTHER RESOURCES

Our goal in this chapter was to provide an overview of Lean principles and some ideas about how to use them to help you and your organization succeed. There are a number of books on Lean.

Many who have read the book *Lean Thinking* consider it the foundations of Lean. If you were to stop by a Toyota plant, people there might reference the book Henry Ford's *Today & Tomorrow*.[5] The concepts are thought provoking because Lean challenges the traditional ideas behind mass manufacturing. Creating a strong vision such as Henry Ford's conceptualization of the idea of mining ore on Monday, then melting, processing, and forming it for use in a car assembly plant on Thursday is clearly Lean thinking. Other successful companies such as the Wiremold Company of West Hartford, Connecticut, featured in *Lean Thinking* realized that it is not about the tools, it is a way of thinking. It is a value or belief system by which a business is led and decisions are made. A Lean strategy then is a strategic value system.

We believe Lean's philosophical approach is an effective path because its emphasis is more about the people and less about the tools and techniques. Implementing a Lean strategy is primarily about changing the way people think about business processes, specifically about the status quo. Successful Lean companies who have adapted and survived "backsliding" have learned to think with their hearts, minds, and hands before their checkbooks.

NOTES

1. Richard J. Schonberger, *World Class Manufacturing* (New York: Free Press, 2008).
2. D. T. Jones and James Womack, *Lean Thinking: Banish Waste and Create Wealth in Your Corporation* (New York: Simon & Schuster, 2003).
3. Peter F. Drucker, *The Essential Drucker: The Best of Sixty Years of Peter Drucker's Essential Writings on Management* (New York: Collins Business, 2007), 27.
4. Mike Rother and John Shook, *Learning to See: Value Stream Mapping to Add Value and Eliminate Muda* (Cambridge, MA: Lean Enterprise Institute, 1999).
5. Henry Ford, *Today & Tomorrow* (1926; repr., New York: Productivity Press, 1988).

6

Six Sigma Protocol: The Medicine

Six Sigma is the only program I've ever seen where customers win, employees are engaged in and satisfied by, and shareholders are rewarded — everybody who touches it wins.

Jack Welch
Former Chairman and CEO of General Electric

People typically go to doctors when they have a health problem or when they experience signs of symptoms of an illness. Doctors usually check the patient and, based on their findings, prescribe a medication and determine if any additional tests or visits to a specialist are needed, or if the patient needs hospitalization or surgery. Any of these may cure the person or not. Doctors encourage regular visits to identify any concerns early on.

Just like patients, companies need regular health checkups, but their leaders tend to wait until the illness has grabbed hold. The Six Sigma experts play the role of doctors in corporations. They conduct routine tests to determine if there is a sign of any illness — in this case, a poorly performing process. Depending on the illness, they recommend and administer medication in the form of intervention to improve or cure the ailing process. Six Sigma tools play the role of the medicine.

In this chapter, after a brief history of Six Sigma, we describe its methods, tools, and the building blocks required to make a successful Six Sigma program.

6.1 BRIEF HISTORY OF SIX SIGMA

In the 1980s, Motorola was struggling to compete with foreign manufacturers, especially Japanese companies. This struggle became apparent after an executive meeting held in Chicago, chaired by Robert Galvin, Motorola's president. At the end, Senior Sales Vice President Art Sundry stood up in front of 75 executives and admitted, "Motorola's quality stinks." The recognition of their need to improve the quality of their products forced Motorola to benchmark other companies. Robert Galvin challenged his people to improve the quality level tenfold. Six Sigma was the method these executives chose to meet his challenge. Bill Smith, a quality engineer at Motorola, called the father of Six Sigma, first introduced a Six Sigma statistical approach aimed at increasing profitability by reducing defects. Mikel Harry and Richard Schroeder later took this concept and transformed it into an enterprise-wide strategy. By combining change management and data-driven techniques, they transformed Six Sigma from a simple quality measurement tool to a breakthrough business-excellence methodology.

In 1986, Six Sigma implementation began at Motorola with a plan to close the quality gap. Goals were set to achieve a tenfold quality improvement in two years, a hundredfold quality improvements in four years, and to obtain a Six Sigma quality level in six years. To achieve a Six Sigma quality level, a process can have only 3.4 defects or errors per 1 million produced or processed (see Section 6.2 for more details). Initially, Motorola used Six Sigma as a process-improvement method primarily in manufacturing. Motorola's position in the global market today demonstrates the benefits of the Six Sigma methodology.

Since those early days, Six Sigma has been shown to be beneficial in a wide range of nonmanufacturing settings. Today, it is used in all company functions — for example, purchasing and IT — in many industries. It has also demonstrated powerful results in service industries as diverse as financial services, software development, and health care, to mention a few. It has become a business initiative used to grow market share, improve customer satisfaction, develop new products and services, accelerate innovation, and manage ever-changing customer needs. Six Sigma has changed the definition of quality to mean that both the organization and its customers benefit from it. Most earlier quality-improvement programs addressed quality only insofar as it affected the customer. They did not address the business aspect of it.

After the success that Six Sigma demonstrated at Motorola, three other companies adopted it. They were Eastman Kodak Company, Allied Signal, and Texas Instruments. Larry Bossidy, Allied Signal's former CEO, introduced Six Sigma to Jack Welch, General Electric's former CEO. Welch convinced Bossidy, who was an ex-GE senior executive, to talk to GE's leadership team about Six Sigma initiatives, the successes achieved at his company, and how this approach would benefit GE as it transformed itself. The GE leadership team was convinced that Six Sigma was the tool needed to improve its business, and in 1995, Welch directed the company to undertake Six Sigma as a corporate initiative with a corporate goal to be a Six Sigma company by the year 2000.

The success achieved by Motorola and GE through their Six Sigma programs has secured the popularity of this business-improvement methodology. Today, thousands of companies, including household names like American Express, DuPont, Eastman Kodak, Sony, Toshiba, and Xerox have used Six Sigma successfully.

6.2 WHAT IS SIX SIGMA?

Six Sigma's definition has evolved since the late 1980s. In addition, Six Sigma means different things to different people. Motorola University defines Six Sigma at three different levels: (1) as a metric, (2) as a methodology, and (3) as a management system. It is all three at the same time. For the purposes of this book, we define Six Sigma as a management driven, structured, data-based methodology for product and process improvement that provides breakthroughs in financial performance and customer satisfaction. It focuses on both strategic business goals and customer needs.

Six Sigma is based on a solid foundation of tools, methodologies, and infrastructure that is designed for success and for processes that are capable of meeting the business's and customers' needs. An organization that implements Six Sigma has a greater focus on the customer, involves the entire organization in the process, improves processes, empowers employees, and, as a result, retains loyal customers and increases profit margins. These are the building blocks of Six Sigma (see Figure 6.1). Without a strong foundation, the whole initiative will collapse.

6.3 DMAIC MODEL

The Six Sigma methodology is a structured process aimed at understanding customers' needs, identifying key processes linked to these needs, applying statistical and quality tools to reduce process variations of those key processes, and sustaining this improvement over time.

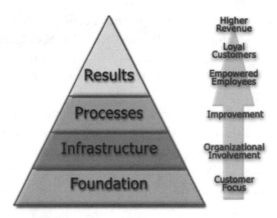

FIGURE 6.1
Building blocks of Six Sigma.

Every improvement project follows the Define, Measure, Analyze, Improve, and Control (DMAIC) model. In the Define phase, the team seeks to understand what the problem is. In the Measure phase, the team assesses the current process performance. In the Analyze phase, the team needs to find out the root cause of the unacceptable or undesired process performance. In the Improve phase, the team seeks solutions to better the process performance. In the Control phase, the team looks for ways to sustain process improvement achieved in the previous phase. The steps and activities for each phase are outlined in Figure 6.2.

6.3.1 Define Phase

The first step in the DMAIC model is for the improvement team to gather information in order to understand the voice of the customer (VOC — the process of gathering information about the customers' needs and wants), summarize and prioritize customer needs, and identify critical-to-quality (CTQ) characteristics to be measured, assessed, and improved. CTQ characteristics are physical, measurable responses that are linked directly to customer requirements. They are critical because they are the requirements that are most important to the customer. They are design requirements that the product *must* satisfy. To achieve these objectives, the team creates a charter in which it defines the problem (opportunity) and sets goals and benefits that are summarized in the team charter.

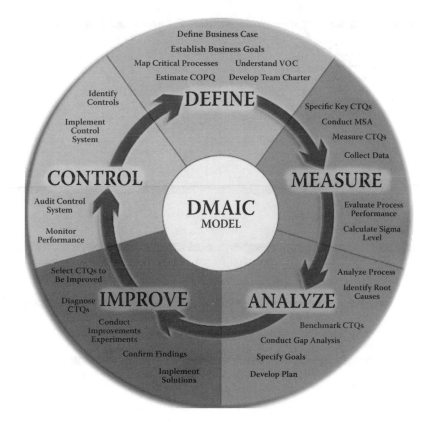

FIGURE 6.2
DMAIC model.

The Define phase includes the following steps:

1. Understand the voice of the customer (VOC).
2. Define the business case. The rationale for initiating the project must demonstrate how this project aligns with the corporate strategic business goals and estimate the financial and other benefits of the project.
3. Establish business goals using the Corporate Balanced Scorecard (see Chapter 3) to establish business goals.
4. Map critical processes using the value stream map (described in Chapter 5) to map the process to be improved.
5. Estimate the cost of poor quality (COPQ), an estimate of the costs associated with the deficiency in the process — usually the result of rework, waste, review, scrap, repair, and customer complaints.

PROJECT INFORMATION		PROJECT TEAM	
		TITLE / ROLE	NAME
Project No.:		Project Champion	
Project Name:		Master Black Belt	
Business Unit:		Finance Champion	
Location / Dept:		Process Owner	
Start Date:		Black Belt	
Target Completion Date:			
Estimated Project Savings:			

BUSINESS CASE (list problem, opportunity, strategic alignment, and impact on the business)

OBJECTIVE / GOALS (list business and financial objectives, include all metrics to be used)

SCOPE (list what part of the process will be investigated, what will be excluded, and if there are any limitations)

GATES

	ESTIMATED COMPLETION DATE	COMMENTS
DEFINE		
MEASURE		
ANALYZE		
IMPROVE		
CONTROL		

APPROVALS

	SIGNATURE	DATE
Project Champion:		
Master Black Belt:		
Black Belt:		
Finance Champion:		

FIGURE 6.3
Team charter.

6. Develop the team charter. The team charter (see Figure 6.3) includes
   Project information: States the project title and process definition.
   Team members: Lists all those who provide project support by attending meetings, collecting and analyzing data, and so on.
   Business case: Describes why the project is important to the customer and the business. Management should make it a priority to review, revise, and approve the business case to ensure that it aligns with business's strategic objectives before the team starts.

Problem statement: Describes what is wrong or not working and how bad the problem is. It should also describe when or under what conditions the problem occurs. A well-written problem statement will be specific and quantified.

Project objectives: States the project objectives and goals; it should be specific and measurable. The team defines the improvement they need to accomplish, and the focus of the goals should be on the results the team hopes to achieve.

Project scope: Specifies the resources available and the process boundaries on which the team members should focus their improvement. A well-defined scope is critical to the success of the project. A broadly defined scope may lead to ineffective solutions that address only part of the problem or attempt to address too many problems at once; too narrow a scope can produce limited solutions and results.

To ensure ongoing management support, the charter needs management approval. In addition, the team should set dates for project reviews with management. These reviews may cover resources allocated, the project scope, project effectiveness and progress, and alignment with the company's strategic objectives.

6.3.2 Measure Phase

The primary objectives of the Measure phase are to identify the types of measures needed to support (link to) customer requirements and to assess the measurement system for errors, bias, and stability. These measures and the related targets are included in the project information. If the measurement system is adequate, the team then develops data collection and sampling plans in order to assess the capability of the process. Process capability evaluates the process's ability to meet customer requirements and the specified project targets. The process variation is compared to customer's specifications. The process capability study is covered later in this chapter.

Measure phase steps include

1. *Specify critical-to-quality characteristics* (CTQs). Identify those things that are essential to achieving the key customer requirements after gathering the voice of the customer (VOC).

2. *Conduct a measurement systems analysis* (MSA). MSA assesses whether your measurement device is precise and adequate to measure the process to be improved.
3. *Collect data and measure* the CTQs.
4. *Evaluate process performance* to understand the ability of the process to meet customer requirements.
5. *Calculate the Sigma level.* This quality measure is described in detail in Section 6.5.

6.3.3 Analyze Phase

The Analyze phase involves the application of statistical tools to better understand the potential causes of poor process performance. In the Analyze phase, the project team analyzes past and current process performance data in order to determine if performance has met the targets. Hypotheses on possible cause–effect relationships are developed and tested. Appropriate statistical and graphical tools and techniques, such as process flow maps, value-stream maps, histograms, Pareto charts, box plots, scatter plots, correlation and regression analyses, hypothesis testing, and analysis of variance (ANOVA) are used.

Analyze phase steps include

1. *Conduct gap analysis* — a business resource assessment tool used to understand the difference between how a current process performs and the how you want it to perform.
2. *Specify goals* that the team is seeking to accomplish. These will define how success is measured.
3. *Develop project plans* and outline the activities needed to solve the problem including resources, milestones, and schedule for completion.
4. *Analyze the process* to identify what process variable might be causing the problem.
5. *Identify root causes* of the problem.
6. *Benchmark the CTQs* to understand what the best in class performance level is for these requirements.

6.3.4 Improve Phase

In the Improve phase, the team identifies, assesses, and implements effective solutions to the problem. They usually conduct a design of experiment

(DOE) to determine the relationship between process input variables (X_i) and process outputs (Y_i) or CTQ customer requirements. A DOE is a series of structured tests where deliberate, simultaneous changes are conducted on the process input variables — for example, temperature or pressure — to evaluate the effect of these changes on the process output variables or responses — for example, the strength of material. DOE helps the team develop a mathematical equation that describes the process. This equation is used to predict, improve, and optimize the process performance. For example, if the goal is to improve the gas mileage of a car, the input variables, called process inputs, would be the brand of gasoline used, driving speed, and temperature — all things that have a high influence on gas mileage — and therefore to improve gas mileage, you need to concentrate on the process inputs.

Improve phase steps include

1. Select CTQs to be implemented. Diagnose quality characteristics (CTQs).
2. Conduct improvement experiments (DOEs).
3. Confirm findings.
4. Implement solutions.

6.3.5 Control Phase

The objective of the Control phase is to sustain the improvement achieved in the previous phase by ensuring stable processes. The team usually implements the necessary controls and quality plans such as checks and balances on the process inputs that need to be controlled to maintain the improvements and ensure the problem does not resurface. Statistical process control (SPC), a statistical method for analyzing and controlling variation in a process, standardized work, and mistake proofing are some of the tools used.

Control phase steps include

1. Identify controls to be used.
2. Implement control system.
3. Audit control system.
4. Monitor performance.

6.4 PROCESS CAPABILITY STUDY

A major step in the DMAIC model is to assess the process capability. Process capability is a measure of process performance; in other words, it is the process's ability to meet customer requirements. A process is considered capable when its natural variation is equal to or less than the total tolerance of the specification. The study usually estimates the percentage of defective parts, evaluates new equipment purchases, predicts whether design tolerances can be met, tracks improvement of a process over time, and assesses suppliers' quality. It is used in the Measure phase to determine if the process meets customer requirements. Process capability studies help answer the following questions: Does the process need to be improved? How much improvement does it need? The capability of a process is most often expressed by two capability indices, C_p and C_{pk}:

C_p stands for capability of a process:

$$C_p = \frac{USL - LSL}{6S}$$

C_{pk} is an index that takes into account both the spread of the distribution and its location:

$$C_{pk} = \min\left(\frac{USL - mean}{3S}, \frac{mean - LSL}{3S} \right)$$

Figure 6.4 shows processes with different process capability. For companies to be healthy, their processes should operate at C_p equal to or greater than 2.

Figure 6.5 shows the results of a process capability study. The data is not centered within the specifications — the mean is shifted to the left of the target — and the process seems to be barely capable. It has $C_p = 1.16$ and $C_{pk} = 0.90$. A Six Sigma process must have C_p equal to or greater than 2 and C_{pk} equal to or greater than 1.5.

For a nonmanufacturing process or a process measure with attribute data such as number of defects or number of errors in a process, we use the defect per million opportunities (DPMO) to calculate the process capability. (DPMO calculation is explained in detail in Section 6.5.2.)

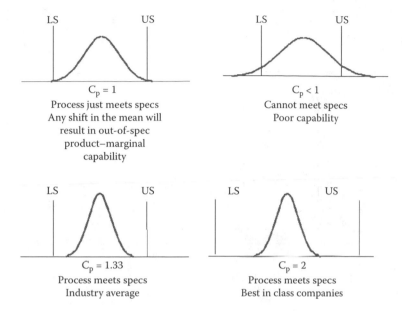

FIGURE 6.4
C_p for different processes.

6.5 SIX SIGMA METRICS

Six Sigma is a statistical unit of measurement that allows you to measure the quality of your products or services. The higher the Sigma level, the lower the number of defects in your product or services. Six Sigma quality level means that a product containing a single critical requirement is produced with only 3.4 defects per million opportunities (DPMO). An opportunity is an estimate of the number of chances to create a defect. Traditionally, the level of quality in most North American companies has been measured at the 3 (66,807 DPMO) or 4 Sigma level (6,210 DPMO).

Delivering innovative products or services without defects, when promised, at high value will satisfy customers. These criteria are met by reducing and eliminating defects in the process or, in other words, reducing process variation. To reduce process variation, the process must be centered, on target, and within customer specifications. As Figure 6.6 illustrates, a process with too much variation or that is off target can lead to excess defects. It is not until you use Six Sigma tools to reduce the variation and center the process about the mean that you will have a process that is capable and

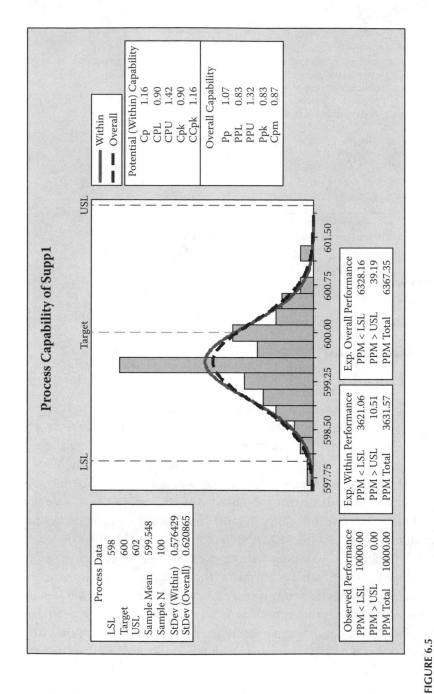

FIGURE 6.5
Example of a Process Capability Study (Source: Minitab).

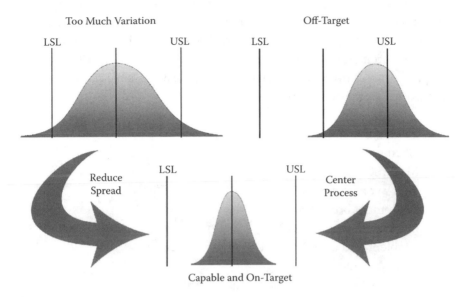

FIGURE 6.6
Reduce process variation and center process to create fewer defects.

on target. A process that is capable and on target is one that will meet the customer's needs.

6.5.1 Process Shift

Motorola's studies and other independent research suggest that a typical process shifts and drifts over time to the right or to the left of the target by about 1.5 Sigma (σ). A typical process spreads about 6 σ. Figure 6.7 shows

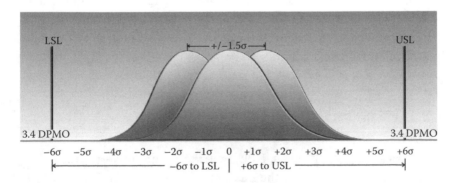

FIGURE 6.7
Typical process shift of 1.5 Sigma.

this process shift. The process should be well centered between the specifications with minimum variation in order to be capable of meeting customer requirements. This shift represents the average amount of change in a typical process over many cycles of that process. Possible causes, among many others, of process shift include

- Production shift changes
- Changing operators
- Machine life
- Tool wear over time
- Equipment breakdown or repairs
- Equipment calibration
- Ambient and operational temperature changes
- Humidity fluctuations
- Variation in quality of incoming material

6.5.2 Types of Metrics

Six Sigma has many types of metrics in its toolbox. Some metrics are specific to an organization; others are universal. When selecting metrics, ensure that they are well defined and understood, as these same metrics may have different meanings for different organizations. The following are some universal metrics used in Six Sigma.

6.5.2.1 Defect per Unit (DPU)

DPU is one of the most common Six Sigma metrics. A unit can be a component, piece of material, line of code, administrative form, timeframe, distance, and so forth. It reflects the average number of defects found during the manufacture of a unit.

$$DPU = \frac{\text{number of defects observed}}{\text{number of units}}$$

Motorola uses the product DPU metric as "the universal measure of quality," which means that the number of defects per unit found in the entire manufacturing process is directly proportional to delivered defects, average cycle time of the manufacturing process, and latent defects.

6.5.2.2 Rolled DPU

Rolled DPU is the total average number of defects for the product being produced; it includes the DPU for each process step across the entire flow.

$$\text{Rolled DPU} = \text{DPU1} + \text{DPU2} + \text{DPU3} + \cdots + \text{DPUlast}$$

6.5.2.3 Defect per Million Opportunities (DPMO)

DPMO reflects the average level of defects found during the manufacture of a product. An opportunity is an estimate of the number of chances to create a defect. Motorola defines an opportunity as any action performed or neglected during the creation of a unit of work, where it is possible to make a mistake that may ultimately result in customer dissatisfaction.

$$\text{DPMO} = \frac{\text{rolled DPU}}{\text{number of opportunities per unit}} \cdot 1{,}000{,}000$$

DPMO is normalized by using opportunities. It allows comparison of products or services of varying complexity. DPMO is converted to Sigma level using Table 6.1, which lists two types of Sigma levels. The first is the short-term Sigma (Sigma_{ST}), which is calculated based on data gathered over a few manufacturing cycles. The second is the long-term Sigma (Sigma_{LT}), which is calculated based on data gathered over many manufacturing cycles (three to six months, depending on the process).

To demonstrate how to convert DPMO to a Sigma level, let us use an example of a process to fill in an application form. The form has six sections that require information to be entered — for example, someone's name, address, birth date, social security number, phone number, and e-mail address. Thus, there are six opportunities to make a mistake when completing this form — one form and six opportunities.

Let us assume we made mistakes entering three sections. Here is what we have:

Unit = 1 form
Number of defects = 3
DPU = (3 defects)/(1 form) = 3
Since the number of opportunities = 6, the defect per opportunity (DPO) = 3/6 = 0.5
Defect per million opportunities (DPMO) = (DPO) · 1,000,000 = 0.5 · 1,000,000 = 500,000

TABLE 6.1

Sigma Level Conversion

DPMO	Sigma ST	Sigma LT
500000	1.50	0.00
300000	2.02	0.52
200000	2.34	0.84
150000	2.54	1.04
100000	2.78	1.28
68000	2.99	1.49
25000	3.46	1.96
10000	3.83	2.33
5000	4.08	2.58
1000	4.59	3.09
500	4.79	3.29
233	5.00	3.50
50	5.39	3.89
40	5.44	3.94
30	5.51	4.01
20	5.61	4.11
10	5.76	4.26
3.4	6.00	4.50
1	6.25	4.75
0.1	6.70	5.20

Using Table 6.1, the short-term Sigma level is equal to 1.5 and the long-term Sigma level is equal to zero (see Figure 6.8). This means that the process produces 500,000 defects or errors for every million parts produced or activities processed. (DPMO metrics play a major role in assessing Corporate Sigma, which will be discussed further in Chapters 8 and 11.)

6.5.3 Counting Opportunities

Counting process opportunities is a challenging task. The Six Sigma deployment team needs to agree on a universal method of counting opportunities prior to applying Six Sigma methodologies. For example, they could agree to count opportunity for each product delivered, each step in the process, or each activity performed.

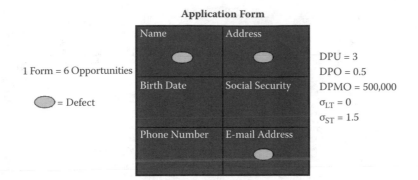

FIGURE 6.8
Converting DPMO to Sigma level.

Kodak, for example, defined three opportunities for each part or component assembled into a product:

- The part is "to spec" or "not to spec."
- The part is or is not assembled or installed properly.
- The part does or does not function in the product.

To calculate opportunity count in this case, multiply the complete bill of materials (BOM) by 3. Whatever method the company chooses, it must be simple and uniform throughout the organization.

6.6 SIX SIGMA INFRASTRUCTURE

Most experts agree that building an effective infrastructure to support a Six Sigma program is critical to successful Six Sigma deployment. An effective infrastructure must be in place before selecting the right projects and identifying the right people to lead projects and before any improvement activities are initiated. It lays the foundation to support all players to achieve their objectives. Project leads (typically "Black Belts") without a successful infrastructure to support their work are doomed to failure.

An organizational infrastructure must be comprised of two levels of players (see Figure 6.9). The first level includes the executive leadership, the champions, and the finance department. These are usually called the *Sponsors* and should be first trained in the Six Sigma concepts and

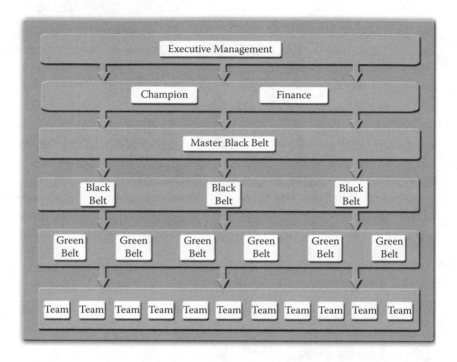

FIGURE 6.9
Typical organizational infrastructure.

philosophies before initiating the project. The second level includes Master Black Belts, who are the technical experts in Six Sigma tools and techniques; Black Belts; Green Belts, who also lead projects but smaller in scope than Black Belts; and project team members, called the *Doers*, who support the Black Belts and the Green Belts by attending meetings, completing assignments, and collecting and analyzing data. The roles and the responsibilities of each of the players are outlined below.

6.6.1 Role of Executive Management

Since Six Sigma is a top-down initiative, the role of the executive management/leadership team is vital. Again, without their active support and involvement, the whole process will lack the commitment and support needed, and Six Sigma might become another "program of the month." Their role depends on the size of the company. In large companies, there should be a leadership team at the corporate level, as well as a leadership team for each of the business units. The executive management/leadership team roles are to

- Create vision
- Set clear objectives
- Provide visible leadership support for Lean Six Sigma initiatives
- Demand solid measure of results
- Communicate results

6.6.2 Role of Champions

The success of Six Sigma initiatives lies in the hands of the Champions, who are often referred to as overall deployment leaders. They have the toughest and most important responsibilities. They are typically business unit managers and are responsible for the successful completion of the projects. The Champion's role is to

- Set rationale and goal
- Nominate and select Black Belts
- Nominate, screen, and select projects
- Allocate resources
- Assign teams to projects
- Review projects
- Tackle critical projects
- Remove barriers
- Help quantify the impact of Six Sigma efforts

6.6.3 Role of Finance

A well-understood financial system is necessary to track, report, and validate the benefits of Six Sigma initiatives. The Finance Department is a key participant in the improvement effort. Its members are actively involved in the financial evaluation of the project and its impact on the company prior to approval. Finance's role is to

- Help establish and validate estimated and actual project savings
- Incorporate actual project savings into revised budgets/standard costs
- Quantify the overall return on investment from Six Sigma initiatives

6.6.4 Role of Master Black Belts

Master Black Belts are individuals respected in the organization who embody strong leadership and technical skills. A Master Black Belt has more extensive training than a Black Belt does and has typically completed several Black Belt projects. The Master Black Belt provides training, coaching, and mentoring for Black Belts and Green Belts. The Master Black Belt role is to

- Train in Six Sigma tools and techniques
- Provide technical support and mentoring to Black Belts
- Review and approve Six Sigma projects
- Facilitate multiple projects led by Black Belts
- Provide consulting assistance to champions and executive management
- Devote 100% of his or her time to Lean Six Sigma initiatives
- Act as an internal consultant, trainer, and expert

6.6.5 Role of Black Belts

Black Belts are most often referred to as *change agents*. They are knowledgeable and highly skilled in the use of Six Sigma tools such as team facilitation, change management, and statistical techniques. They lead improvement projects to completion. The Black Belt role is to

- Lead Lean Six Sigma projects (minimum of four projects per year)
- Provide training in Lean Six Sigma tools and concepts
- Review and approve Lean Six Sigma team charters
- Manage full-time Black Belt resources

6.6.6 Role of Green Belts

Green Belts make up the largest population of trained belts in the workforce. Green Belts are the worker bees. They take their direction from the Black Belts. Green Belts are the ones who are hands-on, taking measurements, collecting data, and doing whatever else is necessary for the project. The Green Belt role is to

- Lead projects (minimum of two projects per year)
- Utilize statistical and quality techniques
- Support Lean Six Sigma project teams
- Implement the Lean Six Sigma philosophy in their daily jobs
- Train others in basic quality tools
- Identify project opportunities

6.6.7 Role of Project Team Members

Project team members are a cross-functional mix from throughout the organization assembled for the specific purpose of executing the specific Six Sigma project. While the team is comprised of a variety of "belts," including Black and Green Belts, other significant personnel may be needed to support the project. At a minimum, all team members will have Six Sigma overview training. The project team member's role is to

- Attend all meetings
- Complete assignments between meetings
- Actively participate and contribute expertise
- Listen to others' ideas
- Use Lean Six Sigma DMAIC process to solve problems

6.7 LEAN SIX SIGMA: A PERFECT MARRIAGE

Customers and shareholders are becoming increasingly demanding. As a result, companies must consistently deliver products and services that are of greater value. Many companies pursue either Lean or Six Sigma as a means to meet these challenges. Individually, Lean and Six Sigma fill important needs. Both are based on improvement. However, using one or the other alone has limitations. Six Sigma reduces scrap rates and quality defects by focusing on measurement systems, as well as capability or process quality variation; however, it does not optimize process flow. Lean does not dramatically improve process capabilities but it does target cycle times, wastes, and other process costs. Used together, these methods complement and reinforce each other.

If your company has excess inventory, lack of space or lead time issues, Lean tools are applied to attack these problems. If your company has reject, scrap, overall yield issues, or service errors, Six Sigma tools are used to define, measure, analyze, improve, and control (DMAIC) these issues. Thereafter, both methodologies, Lean and Six Sigma, are applied continually in tandem to sustain the realized improvements and allow a continuous improvement program to take hold within your enterprise. Companies can expect to see greater speed, less process variation, and more bottom-line impact by focusing the use of statistical tools and establishing baseline performance levels.

Lean Six Sigma combines the speed and power of both Lean and Six Sigma to achieve process optimization. Speed, quality, and cost are the components that drive the success of any organization. Lean Six Sigma works on all three simultaneously because it blends Lean, with its primary focus on process speed, and Six Sigma, with its primary focus on process quality, within a proven organizational framework for superior execution. Both are necessary pillars of any continuous improvement process. Integrating Lean (making work faster) and Six Sigma (making work better) helps an organization move quickly with higher quality and lower cost; thus, by incorporating both concepts — Lean and Six Sigma — we create "speed" by eliminating waste, and we create "quality" by eliminating variation.

7

Systems Thinking: The Prescription for Corporate Arrhythmias

Systems thinking is a discipline for seeing wholes. It is a framework for seeing interrelationships rather than things, for seeing patterns of change rather than static "snapshots." It is a set of general principles.

Peter Senge
Author, The Fifth Discipline

A corporation is a living organism; it has to continue to shed its skin. Methods have to change. Focus has to change. Values have to change. The sum total of those changes is transformation.

Andrew Grove
Founder, Intel Corporation

Businesses are complex organisms created to achieve goals. The paths leading to these goals are not scenic trails or paved roads; rather, they are a complex web of local and global interdependencies comparable to the neural structure of our brain. Organizations learn and grow by consuming and reacting to endless flows of information, events, and dynamic forces involving individual and group thought processes, emotions, and indelible cultural rhythms. Periods of poor and stellar performance wax and wane seemingly independent of rewarded accomplishments. Nevertheless, we attempt control by prescribing policies, improvement projects, and personal performance assessments in response to events and symptoms of corporate ill health, hoping to have an immediate measurable impact and sustained cure in the face of a steady stream of unexpected or recurring problems. If success or survival means knowing why we are getting the results we are getting, then what part do we play in creating and sustaining such arrhythmia (an irregular beat)?

In his book *The Fifth Discipline*, Peter Senge describes our natural tendency to react to events before seeing the bigger picture.[1] Organizations need to be aware of this tendency because seeing events as "the problem" leads us to attack only the symptom. Short-term relief is rewarded but the underlying cause of the problem is never understood or cured.

When we see life as a series of independent events and problems, we overlook the longer-term patterns we learn to tolerate as part of the cultural rhythm. However, we can learn by doing only if we can see the results of what we do. Yet, because of the complex web of interdependencies over time and space, the effects of our actions may not be tangible or immediate. Detectable change may not be seen in the fiscal quarter or year when companies assess performance. After the symptoms subside, we believe that we have taken charge and that we have learned something from our actions. We repeatedly fail to see the role we play in sustaining the arrhythmia, although it is the essence of the self-imposed learning disorders that exist in all companies. If your organization's learning disorders are less than your competitor's, you will rule the road.

Evolving from fragmented problem solving (immediate time and space) to systemic problem solving (broader time and space) is essential if corporate organizations are to understand how they contribute to unforeseen and recurring problems. Only then can they take proactive steps toward avoiding or eliminating harmful arrhythmias that may eventually lead to the demise of the business. Imagine organizations adopting a policy of rewarding its members for raising difficult questions about corporate policies and operating procedures in the same way it rewards those solving urgent problems. The role of such a policy is analogous to the role of our immune system.

7.1 SYSTEMS THINKING: A BETTER SOLUTION

Systems thinking is any process used to estimate or infer how local policies, actions, or changes influence the health of the system's neighbors by identifying and interacting with the intrinsic but hidden system structure. Our personal beliefs about what-causes-what are mostly a product of living in a constantly changing environment. We are all "system thinkers" whether

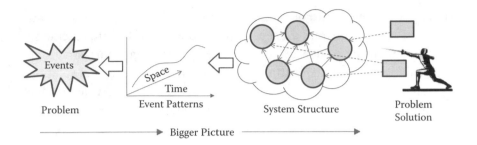

FIGURE 7.1a
Systems thinking: Identifying and interacting with system structure to solve problems.

we know it or not. We seek to understand events that affect us because our survival and success depend on learning from what happens to us.

Reacting to an emergency to minimize injury is certainly the right thing to do. However, it is not a solution to the problem unless the system is addressed and modified to minimize or eliminate recurrence. The bigger picture emerges when we look deeper into events and event patterns and expose the system structure that created them. Revealing and understanding system structure is the key distinction between system thinkers and non-system thinkers and enables a proactive rather than reactive approach to problem solving and policy development. Figure 7.1a and Figure 7.1b illustrate the difference between systems and non-systems thinking as well as how systems thinking allows us to see the bigger picture.

Events are local short-term snapshots of problems encountered in isolated areas or with certain people or groups in the organization; event patterns are the longer-term trends encountered throughout the organization, company, and beyond.

A systems thinking approach (Figure 7.1a) focuses on examining the responsible system structure. Unlike non-systems thinking (Figure 7.1b),

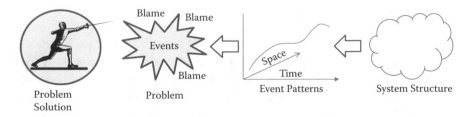

FIGURE 7.1b
Non-systems thinking: Reacting to events to solve problems.

systems thinking does not seek to assign blame. Seeing how the variables are related provides a deeper understanding of how to interact in harmony with the system to obtain a balance between short- and long-term solutions. The systems thinking approach also reveals that solutions to systemic problems may have seemingly unrelated project deliverables (rectangles). This is because they target different leverage variables within the system. Leverage variables are things we can change or control regardless of what is happening elsewhere in the system. For example, a company can raise the price of its service to increase profit but they cannot control competitors' sales, which also affect profit. In this case, price is a leverage variable in a system that drives profit. Project leaders or Champions will need to explain leverage variables to stakeholders and customers to help them clearly understand the project's purpose.

7.2 SYSTEMS THINKING AND STATISTICAL THINKING

When battling variation, *statistical thinking* prescribes appropriate inaction while *systems thinking* prescribes appropriate action. In other words, statistical thinking helps us detect patterns or events that vary over time, such as shifts, drifts, and outliers, and avoid reacting to random variation, or "noise." Systems thinking helps us react appropriately to the patterns and events detected by statistical thinking because it helps us see how our actions and policies have an impact on the broader business landscape. Together they are essential skills that change agents need to cure chronic corporate arrhythmias.

7.3 TYPES OF PROBLEMS SYSTEMS THINKING CAN HELP SOLVE

An increasingly critical and difficult task that organizations face is choosing the right projects in which to invest resources while focusing on the daily needs of customers, stakeholders, and employees. Determining the best leverage variables for sustaining desired results requires systems thinking because the causes of the symptoms and the changes needed to produce desired outcomes rarely share the same space and time, and the right projects might not be selected or developed to the degree needed.

Nowhere is this more important than when governmental institutions set policies or when companies start a Lean Six Sigma program. Selected projects may optimize locally but have negligible or unknown systemwide or corporate-wide impact. It is common to see projects improve local performance but have an overall negative impact across the broader business landscape. For example, overproduction and rework help a manufacturing organization meet production volume and schedule goals but can lead to potentially bigger problems associated with inventory, quality and reliability, opportunity risk, overtime, and higher cost of quality. The success of Lean Six Sigma programs is at the mercy of well-chosen projects and teams. Investing in more tools and training will be useless unless the right projects are applied to the right leverage variables in the system.

Systems thinking helps teams see and work with the complex invisible web of local and global interdependencies created by organizations on the path to achieving goals and fulfilling their purpose or mission. The path to success (or failure) is never scenic or without detours, delays, and dead-ends. Without knowledge of the latent system structure that creates these problems and inefficiencies, our efforts to mitigate their effect will be myopic, unsustainable, and likely to lead to poor business results.

The following questions illustrate the types of problems we can begin to address using systems thinking:

- What drives *defects*? How will the proposed Black Belt project stabilize and improve it? What deliverables from another project might play against mutual success?
- What drives *employee morale, productivity,* and *supervision quality*? What procedures and policies will likely instill lasting improvements?
- What drives the amount of time managers *waste* doing subordinate's duties? How can this be eliminated with a win-win solution?
- What drives *cycle time* for process change validation and verification in an FDA-regulated production line, and how can process engineering *morale* be improved in this area?
- What are the best leverage variables for projects aimed at improving global *market share*?
- What drives *sick-time utilization* and to what degree does it affect *morale* and *productivity*? What can be done to break these connections?
- How can we *stabilize profit* of a product line on the market when our competitor has a similar product?

7.4 SYSTEMS THINKING TOOLS AND LANGUAGE

The tools and language used by Six Sigma practitioners have evolved and expanded in many ways. Six Sigma tools and methods may already be in use in some organizations involved with continuous improvement efforts. For example, the information generated from the following set of tools is an excellent source of knowledge needed to create a causal loop diagram (see Figures 7.8a and 7.8b later in the chapter) model because they contain only facts (no theories or conjectures). In addition, they support the philosophy of examining the underlying system structure when problems arise and they help teams take steps toward exposing different aspects or pieces of the underlying cause.

These methods include cause–effect or fishbone diagrams, interrelationship digraphs, force field analysis, impact analysis, fault trees, and root cause analysis, among others. These tools will not be discussed here; however, the cause–effect diagram serves to highlight some common limitations. *Cause–effect* or *fishbone diagrams* are designed to organize variables associated with a problem. The treelike structure is useful for facilitating brainstorming for variable selection and later sorting theory from fact. Figure 7.2 shows a cause–effect diagram with categories from a manufacturing system. The smaller branches represent specific causes falling within the main branch category.

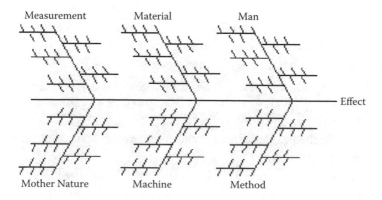

FIGURE 7.2
Cause–effect or fishbone diagram.

The terms "cause" and "effect" should not be taken literally, since the variables exposed by brainstorming tend to be a mix of facts and theories that need to be sorted out by experimentation. The cause–effect diagram groups similar concepts; however, this will not provide insight into the dynamics of the system generating the problem. This is true of the other tools mentioned above, which are all based on linear thinking involving lists, open-loop tree diagrams, and tables of related items. What is missing is a simple means of capturing and interpreting the *voice of the system* (that is, the latent yet predictable event patterns) and using it to see ways to create systemwide win-win change. This can be easily accomplished using a tool known as *causal loop diagrams* (CLDs).

CLDs help us capture the voice of the system and allow us to translate it into action for improvement. They are a simple, graphical, no-name approach to understanding and interacting with complex system structure and inferring dynamic behavior. They help us formulate solutions without having to learn new software and languages; they are also an aid or alternative to other tools used by Six Sigma practitioners. Like cause–effect diagrams, CLDs are easy to create. Unlike the other methods, they only involve known, causally related variables since there is no reason to include experimental variables in system models. When contrasting the information content of cause–effect diagrams with CLDs, think of the cause–effect diagram as the "fish's bones" while the CLD is the "swimming fish," representing a system alive with complex behavior and inviting us to tame and domesticate it to our advantage.

Those who are familiar with systems thinking are aware of the names given to system structures, known as *system archetypes*, which show up repeatedly. Archetypes are made up of substructures known as *balancing loops* and *reinforcing loops*. Although the intent of these classifications is to create an efficient systems-thinker language, the identification of common structures or archetypes and the names given to them has been a major source of confusion for both beginners and seasoned practitioners. Fortunately, this terminology is unnecessary since CLDs offer a simpler no-name approach that avoids the need to identify archetypes, which tend to fall severely short of representing the uniqueness of the system generating the problem of interest.

Once the CLD is created, it can be simulated in Microsoft Excel (or equivalent software), and then the dynamic event patterns can be interpreted directly in terms of the problem being solved. Furthermore, advanced systems dynamics software can generate detailed quantitative estimates in terms of dollars, scrap, defect, and labor hours, to name a few. These products introduce constructs called "stocks" and "flows," which are building blocks used to construct dynamic system models. A *stock* is like an account that holds a quantity of something — for example, dollars. Its level rises and falls because money flows into and out of the account. The *flows* are deposits and withdrawals to and from the account. Flow rates and time delays add dynamic detail and enable calibration to the time frame of the business. These elements are useful if the objective is to obtain quantitative forecasts over time and infer dynamic behavior in detail. Although impressive, these embellishments go far beyond inferring event patterns, which is the basic information needed to determine and assess solutions to systemic problems, and they come at the cost of additional training and software. Throughout this chapter, we will see more examples of how CLDs simplify modeling for systemic problem solving, thus improving the methods currently used in the field of systems thinking.

Causal loop diagrams predict event patterns. Event patterns have direct implications to systemic problems and solutions. For example, seeing that Account Balance Growth is high, unstable, or trending downward has the same actionable information as knowing the actual dollars in the account at any point. The difference is that account balance in dollars is the net accumulation of positive or negative account balance growth. The bottom line is that simulating "account balance" requires a "stock" and "flow" construct with special software while simulating "account balance growth" does not. CLDs are much easier to create and simulate. Dynamic event patterns are inferred using basic Excel functions and plotted on a trend chart. This will be demonstrated in Section 7.8.2, where simulation is discussed in detail.

That said, CLDs are a "best practice" for approaching systemic problems. The remainder of this chapter illustrates how to create and use CLDs for systemic problem solving. In the context of the Six Sigma DMAIC process, we will focus on the Analyze phase as highlighted in Figure 7.3.

Six Sigma tools that facilitate creation of CLDs:

- Current-state process maps (supply, input, process, output, customer diagram, or SIPOC)
- Interrelationship digraphs
- Root cause analysis
- Force field analysis
- Impact analysis

Define
-Create problem specification
    -Who (Who care and why – VOC)
    -Extent (Scope, COPQ, ROI)
    -What, Where, When (<u>Is</u> and <u>Is Not</u> for each)
-Create team
-Define target metrics

Measure -Gather baseline data for target metrics

Analyze
-Research & Development (operational thinking)
    -See Six Sigma tools that facilitate creation of CLDs
    -Brainstorming system variables using 5-Whys
    -Organize using cause–effect (fishbone) diagram
    -Separate causal facts from theories
    -Create expert causal loop diagram (CLD)
-Simulate (event pattern inference)
    -Determine leverage variables & policy types
    -Experiment & optimize target variable scores

Improve -Share with all stakeholders and adjust as needed -Execute policy design projects at optimal leverage points -Assess impact relative to baseline data
Control -Monitor target metrics, communicate, and audit

FIGURE 7.3
Systemic problem solving using DMAIC.

- Why trees
- Process failure mode and effects analysis (PFMEA)

7.5 CREATING CAUSAL LOOP DIAGRAMS

To understand causal loop diagrams and how to unlock and interpret their dynamic behavior (or event patterns), we need to understand the basic elements and how to use them. We begin with simple system models and then move on to larger ones and discuss leverage variables for installing policies to disrupt harmful patterns or arrhythmias.

7.5.1 CLD Elements

Causal loop diagrams have only three elements: *variables*, *connections*, and *signs*. Working with these elements, a team can create a mental model that captures the voice of the system and translate its dynamic patterns into a plan for corrective action.

7.5.2 Variables

A system is a set of two or more causally related variables. Variables are time-varying concepts or factors that communicate the content and scope of the system. They can be tangible, such as the circuits and components of a computer or the behavior of a certain animal species in an ecological food chain; or they can be intangible, such as thoughts, beliefs, emotions, policies, or events. System variables can represent any real or abstract entity. They can have measurable or observable quantitative or qualitative characteristics but this is not necessary for a variable to be real. The most important attribute of a system variable is its definition.

Variables must have simple, unambiguous, agreed-upon, written definitions. This makes interpretation of their dynamic event patterns succinct and actionable. In addition, since each variable has a pattern that changes over time and that will be plotted on a trend chart, the names given to system variables should make sense when plotted as increasing or decreasing degrees of strength over time. For example, "Employee Morale" is an intangible qualitative concept that can be plotted as a time varying pattern of increasing or decreasing degrees of strength. "Quality," "Productivity," "Stability" and "Alignment with Values" are other examples of variable names, as are "Costs" and "Profits." Some are measurable and some are not, but this is acceptable.

When naming a variable, use neutral or positive terms to avoid double negatives. The importance of this will become apparent when you try to interpret a variable's increasing or decreasing trend. For example, a negative moving trend for "Customer Dissatisfaction" is harder to grasp than a positive trend for "Customer Satisfaction"; both have the same meaning.

It is also important to avoid names such as "Account Balance," "Population Size," or "Inventory Level" because they imply accumulations of quantitative flows with defined rates of change (that is, "stocks" and "flows"). Instead, use "Account Balance Growth," "Population Growth," or "Inventory Growth." Both troubling arrhythmia and desired trends are adequately conveyed by patterns in the degree of strength of these variables and do not require stock–flow constructs to represent them.

Variable selection and definition is best done in a team setting consisting of subject matter experts and stakeholders. Their task is to pool their points of view and choose and define the variables involved ("expert opinion" is always better than "opinion of *an* expert").

Finally, systems may or may not have inputs or outputs. These are labels we assign in order to study or interact with systems and do not alter the system structure or definition of the variables. Variables such as "Profit," "Customer Satisfaction," or anything critical to the business can be labeled an output or "Target Variable." You can also think of "Policies" as inputs or as connections between system variables.

7.5.3 Connections

Once the team selects and defines the system variables, the team members need to agree on how they are related. This is done by adding *connection arrows*, which represents a causal link or relationship between two variables. Two variables are causally related when a change in one variable directly causes a change in another. For example, itching and scratching are causally related variables. If itching causes scratching, draw an arrow from the variable named "Itching" to the variable named "Scratching" to show the connection (see Figure 7.4 and Figure 7.5).

In addition, Figure 7.4 shows itching as the source of scratching and scratching as the destination for itching. (We will discuss "Source" and "Destination" later when we discuss simulation.)

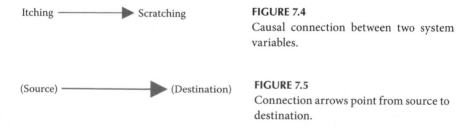

Itching ⟶ Scratching

FIGURE 7.4
Causal connection between two system variables.

(Source) ⟶ (Destination)

FIGURE 7.5
Connection arrows point from source to destination.

7.5.4 Signs

Signs communicate the *direction of change* between two variables. A plus sign (+) means that change is in the same direction and a minus sign (−) means that change is in the opposite direction. For example, if an *increase* in itching causes an *increase* in scratching, place a plus sign next to the arrow connecting the two variables. Conversely, a reduction in itching would cause a reduction in scratching. Thus, the direction of change for the destination variable is the same as for the source variable (see Figure 7.6).

FIGURE 7.6
Plus (+) sign indicating that a change in the source variable causes a change in destination variable in the *same* increasing or decreasing direction.

If an *increase* in one variable causes a *decrease* in another variable, place a minus sign (−) next to the connection arrow. Thus, the team may agree that an increase in scratching will cause a decrease in itching. Therefore, a connection arrow from scratching to itching is drawn and labeled with a minus (−) symbol to indicate that change is in the opposite direction when scratching is the source for itching, as shown in Figure 7.7. This illustrates circular causality, which, as we will soon see, is the rule rather than the exception. For this reason, cause–effect diagrams and other linear or checklist methods are limiting. Note: Another term for circular causality is feedback. All systems have feedback loops, which play a major role in creating and sustaining corporate arrhythmias as well as creating and sustaining a cure.

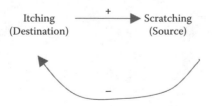

FIGURE 7.7
Minus (−) sign indicates that a change in the source variable causes a change in the destination variable in the *opposite* increasing or decreasing direction.

7.6 VOICE OF THE SYSTEM

Every day, we hear or read about what drives the rise or fall of the economy, terrorism, governments, companies, personal relationships, our health, and our planet's health. When someone describes how this led to that, which in turn caused something else, and so on, that is the voice of the system from that person's point of view, that person's mental model of how the world works. In this sense, everyone is a systems thinker. If the information offered from these points of view is correct, we can piece together the bigger picture using causal loop diagrams. Solving systemic problems requires us to gather and piece together the voice of the system from mental models of subject matter experts.

Figure 7.8(a) shows a simple system with two variables and the causal relationship between them. When we listen to the voice of this system, it says, "When Account Balance Growth increases, Interest Income also increases and when Interest Income increases, Account Balance Growth increases." You could assign a name to this system such as *Compound Interest* or *Reinforcing Feedback Loop*, but naming is unnecessary and may be confusing as you add more and more variables. A financial expert

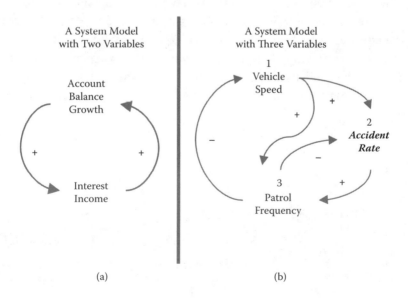

(a)   (b)

FIGURE 7.8

(a) Causal loop diagram, mental model. (b) Causal loop diagram, mental model.

is likely to ask, "Why not just use the equation for compound interest? It's simple and exact!" Although this is true, it is unnecessary. It is extra work and not everyone understands or speaks the language of math. CLDs speak to a much broader audience and adequately capture the voice of the system.

Figure 7.8(b) represents a three-variable system. Its voice is saying, "When vehicle speed increases, accident rate and patrol frequency increase. When patrol frequency increases, accident rate and vehicle speed decrease. When accident rate decreases, patrol frequency decreases." We suddenly get the sense that adding more variables is like verbally juggling more balls. This simple diagram captures the voice of the system without math and almost without words.

7.6.1 Modeling Hierarchy

With just a few basic elements (variables, connections, and signs), we can draw mental models of how our world works and capture the voice of the system. One advantage of CLDs is that subject matter experts only need to agree on these three elements. This is important because it draws the line at a level requiring relatively little time or investment in gathering and validating data. Knowledgeable people rarely disagree on the direction and sign of the arrows; however, determining and agreeing on the magnitude of the effect and the functional form of equations with constraints is an enormous barrier when there are many variables and experts involved. By looking at the modeling hierarchy shown in Figure 7.9, we can appreciate the advantage of CLD models and imagine the excessive amount of

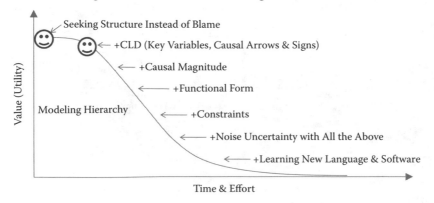

FIGURE 7.9
Modeling hierarchy.

time, resources, guesswork, and storming that could occur if the team slid below the CLD level.

In addition, more noise and uncertainty is a penalty paid for each level of complexity. Therefore, if the team avoids transcending to the lower, more complex, levels of the modeling hierarchy, higher certainty is the reward.

7.6.2 Knowledge Networking: The Big Picture

A broad selection of subject matter experts is important for anchoring confidence that the voice of the system is adequately captured. Each expert can create his or her own CLD remotely if needed. Once created, there is a straightforward procedure for combining individual CLDs into a single "Expert CLD," which can be causally linked to other Expert CLDs to include as many target variables as needed. This is illustrated in Figure 7.10 and Figure 7.11.

At this point, the CLD looks like a confusing pile of spaghetti; at the same time, it is packed with knowledge of the bigger picture. Looking for system archetypes and trying to identify balancing or reinforcing loops in order to prescribe solutions would be paddling upstream in search of a means of taking action. However, once the team is confident the voice of the system has been adequately captured by the CLD, it has in essence created an expert system that it can consult by formulating "what if" questions in the form of adding new variables and connections or removing existing ones. The answers to the questions will create time-varying patterns that can

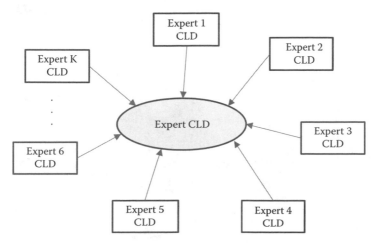

FIGURE 7.10
Expert CLD model.

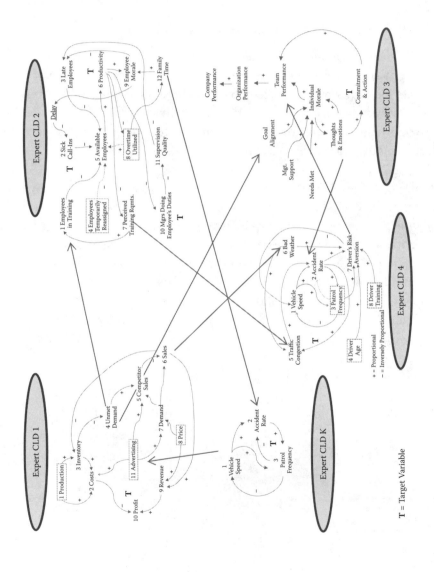

FIGURE 7.11
Expert CLD example.

be plotted on a trend chart. These patterns predict the future state of the system relative to the question asked; the answers naturally depend on the current conditions. CLDs also have the flexibility to vary the conditions or backdrop against which we ask our questions. We will see examples of all this after we learn how to take the next step toward seeing the voice of the system as dynamic patterns.

7.7 HOW TO CREATE A CONNECTION MATRIX

A *connection matrix* represents all the arrows or causal connections in a CLD. It is a template for all possible connections between the variables and policies. A connection matrix always has the same number of rows and columns (a square matrix), which is also equal to the number of concepts. The term *concept* is used here to represent any variable or policy that is part of the CLD.

In the accident rate example illustrated in Figure 7.8(b), the voice of the system is captured in a 3″ × 3″ connection matrix as shown in Figure 7.12. Each connection begins at a *source concept* and ends at a *destination concept*. The numbers entered into the matrix cells are –1, 0, or 1, where –1 represents an arrow with a minus sign, a 1 represents an arrow with a plus sign, and

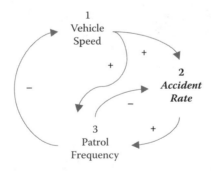

Connection Matrix

	Destination		
	1 Speed	2 Accident Rate	3 Patrol Freq.
Source 1 Speed	0	1	1
2 Accident Rate	0	0	1
3 Patrol Freq.	–1	–1	0

FIGURE 7.12
Accident Rate CLD and connection matrix.

a 0 represents no arrow or connection between the source and destination concepts.

An easy way to complete the matrix is to enter a zero (0) in each cell. Then begin with the source row for speed (concept #1), and, using the CLD, notice that vehicle speed (1) has two destinations, accident rate (2) and patrol frequency (3). Enter a 1 in these cells. Next, move on to the accident rate row. Here, the only destination is patrol frequency, so enter a 1 in that cell. Finally, move on to the patrol frequency row and identify its destination concepts, which are speed and accident rate. Enter a –1 in each of these cells. The connection matrix is now complete.

The main diagonal cells (running from top left to bottom right) are generally all 0 but could be 1 or –1, if the variable has a tendency to self-sustain or self-diminish respectively. For example, thinking negative thoughts (pessimism) or positive thoughts (optimism), or thinking both positively and negatively about the global economy have self-sustaining tendencies. The system structure responsible for each of these tendencies is associated only with that one variable and is usually beyond the chosen scope of the problem. A main diagonal matrix cell is a convenient way to exclude variables that are irrelevant to the main system. The system model the team devises should include only variables having ballpark influence on the target variables.

Using the example about itching and scratching, we can represent all variables that sustain itching (such as poison ivy or a complex biological system) as a concept connected to itself with a 1 in the top left cell of the connection matrix, as shown in the Figure 7.13.

Target variables (as determined in the DMAIC Define phase) should have zeros in their main diagonal cells. Remember, it is the team's job to

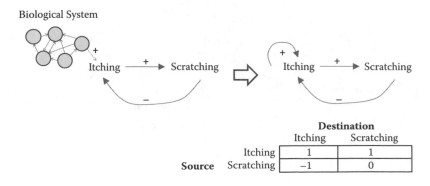

| | | **Destination** | |
		Itching	Scratching
Source	Itching	1	1
	Scratching	–1	0

FIGURE 7.13
Representation of self-sustaining variables.

adequately model the system structure so that it encompasses all the target variables. Therefore, if itching is a target variable and if the biological system that sustains itching contains target variables, then the CLD and its connection matrix should expand to include these structures as part of the problem scope. The resulting connection matrix will have zeros in the main diagonal cells for all target variables.

7.8 EVENT PATTERN INFERENCE

The Accident Rate CLD illustrated in Figure 7.8(b) represents one expert's opinion about what influences the accident rate along a certain section of highway.[2] We would like to minimize accident rate, so it will be designated a "target variable." The connection matrix, shown in Figure 7.12, captures all the knowledge contained in the CLD in matrix form; it then is used to simulate event patterns. CLD simulation produces event patterns plotted as time-varying trends on a trend chart as shown in Figure 7.14.

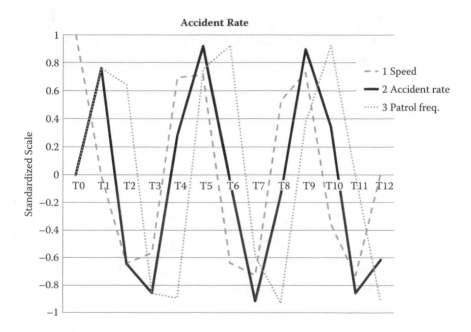

FIGURE 7.14
Event pattern inference for the three-variable accident rate problem.

(Appendix A shows how to use the connection matrix to simulate CLD event patterns using basic Microsoft Excel functions.)

This trend chart shows the Accident Rate (the target variable in solid line) cycling up and down periodically, as do the other two variables. In particular, we observe the reactive nature of Patrol Frequency (small dotted line), which is always lagging behind Accident Rate. As Accident Rate rises, Patrol Frequency follows, also rising. This arrhythmia continues without end. In the language of systems dynamics, this pattern is known as a "limit cycle." All systems have dynamic patterns. Some will have chaotic patterns, some will be random, and some will quickly settle down to a steady level.

Keep in mind that CLDs predict causal event patterns; they do not provide answers in units of miles per hour, hours per day, or accidents per year, so the *y*-axis scale is standardized to a range of −1 to +1, representing low to high strength of causal event occurrence respectively. The long-term steady-state patterns and the relative magnitude of each variable are the points of information requiring interpretation. The duration of one cycle — four time increments, in this example — has no meaning other than to indicate that the problem is a recurring one. We seek a solution or set of policies that will make all target variables settle down to a desired high or low fixed level, which, in the case of Accident Rate, is a relatively low steady level.

Additional concepts have surfaced from a brainstorming session among several experts as shown in Figure 7.15. Their challenge now is to agree on the causal connection arrows and signs.

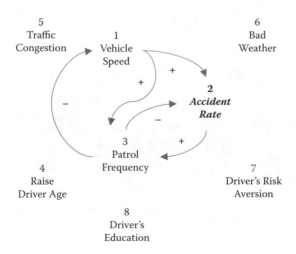

FIGURE 7.15
Accident Rate problem showing expanded scope.

The process of assigning connection arrows and signs is best facilitated by systematically beginning with concept #1 and asking a pair of "connection questions" relative to concept #2 and so on to the last concept. This process was used to arrive at the initial three-concept CLD; therefore, we will continue here with connecting concept #4 to the current CLD using the following "connection questions":

1. *Connection Arrow Question:* Will a change in the source concept directly cause a change in the destination concept?
   If *yes*, draw a solid arrow from the source concept to the destination concept.
   If *no*, do not draw an arrow.
   If *not sure*, draw a dashed arrow and return to the question when better information becomes available.
   Note: It is important to document the operational thinking or reasoning behind each connection so others can challenge it later as needed.
2. *Connection Arrow Sign Question:* If a *solid arrow* was drawn, will the change in the destination concept be in the same or opposite direction as the change in the source concept?
   If *the same*, assign a plus sign (+) to the arrow.
   If *the opposite*, assign a minus sign (–) to the arrow.
   If *not sure*, assign a question mark (?) and return to the question when better information becomes available.

Treating vehicle speed as the source concept, we state the first question as *"Will a change in speed directly cause a change in Raise Driver Age?"* If consensus is "Yes," a solid arrow is drawn from concept #1 to concept #4. If the consensus is "No," no connection arrow is drawn. If there is disagreement, a dashed arrow is drawn from #1 to #4, indicating that the team will need to return to the question and resolve the disagreement. In this example, the team's consensus is "No Arrow"; therefore, the secondary arrow-sign question does not apply.

The connection arrow question is repeated by treating Raise Driver Age as the source of change. We then ask, "Will a change in Raise Driver Age directly cause a change in speed?" Again, the arrow is solid, missing, or dashed, depending on the level of agreement. In this example, the consensus was "No," and therefore no connection arrows are drawn between concepts #1 and #4.

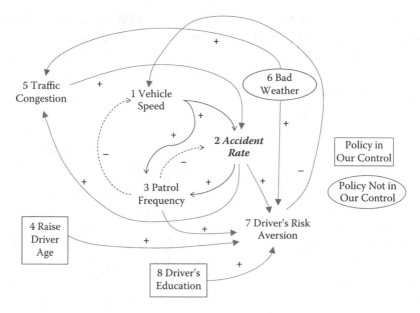

FIGURE 7.16
Accident Rate CLD illustrating controlled and uncontrolled policies.

This pair of connection questions is repeated for all concept pairs in both directions: #1 and #5, #1 and #6, #1 and #7, and #1 and #8; then continuing to #2 and #4, #2 and #5, and so forth. The final "expert CLD" is shown in Figure 7.16.

Note the appearance of dashed arrows from concept #3 to #2 and from #3 to #1. In Figure 7.8(b), they were solid arrows according to the expert who created it. However, they are being questioned by the larger pool of experts, who argue that Accident Rate (the target variable) is not directly affected by Patrol Frequency because there should be a mechanism by which Patrol Frequency acts in order to reduce the Accident Rate. The consensus is that this mechanism is Drivers' Risk Aversion. Drivers directly control Vehicle Speed and will lower their speed if they notice that traffic enforcement is present more often. Since this is the mechanism by which Patrol Frequency works to reduce the Accident Rate, the path is concept #3 to #7 to #1 to #2. The same argument holds for how Patrol Frequency reduces Vehicle Speed; it results from Drivers' Risk Aversion and not directly as originally conceived. This discovery has revealed a key system leverage variable.

7.8.1 Input and Connection Policies

Another important aspect Figure 7.16 illustrates is the emergence of *input policies*. Input policies are concepts that influence other variables. They are not influenced by other variables or other policies; therefore, there are no connection arrows pointing *to* them, only *away* from them. In other words, they are sources or system inputs.

Input policies are displayed with rectangular outlines if the source is in our control, oval outlines if the source is out of our control, or connection arrows if the organization has control over the causal relationship or link. Policies can emerge during the earlier brainstorming sessions or later after simulation and analysis. Both input and connection policies will be discussed in later examples.

7.8.2 Simulation

Once the subject matter experts agree the CLD is complete, they can begin policy evaluation through simulation with the connection matrix. The connection matrix represents a body of knowledge we can consult by asking explicit "what if" questions and specifying the conditions for which we would like to obtain answers. The math operations and graphing functions needed to obtain the answers are executed using a custom Microsoft Excel macro called CLD SIM (see Appendix A for details). We use this tool to lead us to action and improve the system's behavior by selecting leverage variables for policy evaluation. The connection matrix and trend chart are shown in Figure 7.17 for the updated Accident Rate CLD.

The simulation begins by shocking the system by setting the initial condition for one of the concepts to a value of either +1 or −1. This gets all the "causal juices" flowing. All other initial conditions can be arbitrarily set to zero. The trend chart in Figure 7.18 represents the system with the initial condition for speed set to 1. Changing an initial condition from 0 to 1 is analogous to asking the question "What if vehicle speed is initially high?" Shocking the system is like hitting a bell with a hammer; in the case of a CLD, we hear the voice of the system.

The event pattern for this system is a "limit cycle." Accident Rate (thick solid line) is the target variable, which has a long-term steady-state cycle with a peak-to-peak period of eight time increments. Like the y axis, the x axis timescale is also unitless so the temporal information to focus on

		Destination						
		1 Speed	2 Accident Rate	3 Patrol Freq.	4 Raise Driver Age	5 Traffic Congestion	6 Bad Weather	7 Driver's Risk Aversion	8 Driver's Education
Source	1 Speed	0	1	1	0	0	0	0	0
	2 Accident Rate	0	0	1	0	1	0	1	0
	3 Patrol Freq.	0	0	0	0	0	0	1	0
	4 Raise Driver Age	0	0	0	0	0	0	1	0
	5 Traffic Congestion	0	1	0	0	0	0		0
	6 Bad Weather	0	0	0	0	1	0	1	0
	7 Driver's Risk Aversion	-1	0	0	0	0	0		0
	8 Driver's Education	0	0	0	0	0	0	1	0

FIGURE 7.17
Connection matrix for the accident rate CLD.

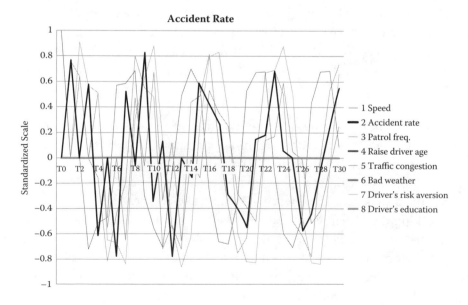

FIGURE 7.18
Event pattern inference for the expanded Accident Rate problem.

are patterns, periods, and delays (lead or lag). This pattern represents the Accident Rate pattern on any highway where these variables exist. In general, the same cycling and relative leads or lags between variables would be common to all systems with this structure. In order to reduce and stabilize the Accident Rate, we need to link the right policy into the system at the right leverage variable.

7.8.3 Policy Status

In CLD simulation, input and connection policies are either active or inactive, on or off, enforced or not. Once implemented, policies stay on until turned off. The status of input policies can be switched "on" with a constant 1 or "off" with a constant 0. Figure 7.19 illustrates the off-on status of an input policy using a trend chart.

Connection policies are a causal connection between system variables if the organization has direct control of that connection. For example, a connection between Inventory Growth and Order Activity is controlled by the manufacturing organization. In simulation, connection policies are turned on and off at the connection matrix. The connection is removed by entering a zero (0) into the appropriate cell and turned on by adding a 1 or –1 into the cell. Figure 7.20 illustrates turning a connection policy on and off.

In the itching and scratching example, we can control scratching; therefore, it is a connection policy with a pair of connections that can be turned on and off as shown in Figure 7.21.

Since scratching can lead to other problems, it may be a more stable lower-cost system if we learn to tolerate itching or find a solution that interrupts the tendency for itching to sustain itself (Figure 7.22).

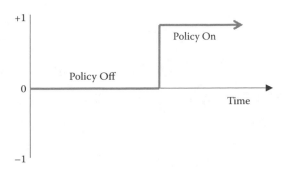

FIGURE 7.19
Trend chart showing input policy status.

FIGURE 7.20
Arrow signs showing connection policy on/off status.

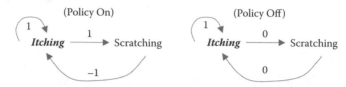

FIGURE 7.21
Connection policy status.

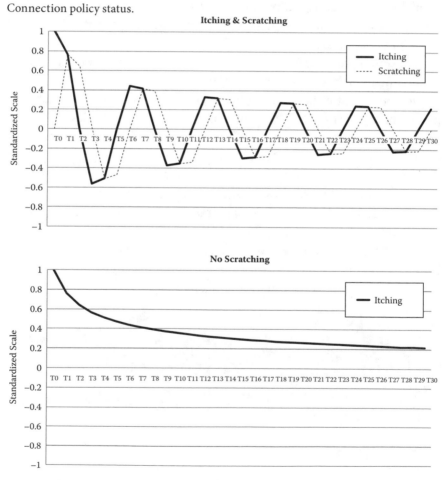

FIGURE 7.22
Scratching policy turned on and off (no scratching).

7.9 LEVERAGE VARIABLES

Leverage variables are system features that policies directly influence or cause to change. They can be any variable the policy has a direct causal effect on, including *target variables*. Variables that connect with many other variables or have more arrows leaving than arriving are potential *high-leverage variables* (HLV), meaning the policy will have a large (good or bad) effect on the behavior of the system. An example of a high-leverage variable is shown in Figure 7.23.

Policies that connect to multiple variables are high-leverage policies (HLPs), which offer more solution options. High-leverage policies allow us to run experiments and determine the combination of connections that co-optimize the largest number of target variables. Multiple policies offer options as well; however, each individual policy requires additional resources to implement and maintain it. Therefore, cost is of more concern when assessing solution options with multiple policies. Examples of multiple and high-leverage policies are shown in Figure 7.24.

CLDs provide an easy way to test drive and experiment to see if policies interact by reinforcing or reducing harmful arrhythmias for the target variables.

In the Accident Rate problem, Drivers' Risk Aversion (concept #7) is a leverage variable for the three input policies that emerged from the brainstorming session. This leverage variable has three system connections (that is, two arrows entering and one leaving) and three policy connections, as shown in Figure 7.16. We can use simulation to assess the impact each policy has on the target variable and determine the best combination for the policies we can control.

Raising Driver Age (#4) is a policy we can test by shocking the system by turning the policy off and then turning it on halfway through the simulation

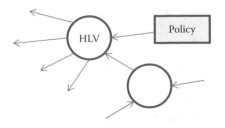

FIGURE 7.23
High-leverage variable (HLV).

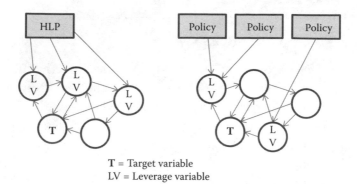

T = Target variable
LV = Leverage variable

FIGURE 7.24
A high leverage policy and multiple policies.

run. This is illustrated in Figure 7.25 where the time scale begins at time label T0 and ends at T30.

Expert opinion supports the theory that older (more experienced) drivers are more risk averse than young (inexperienced) drivers. If this is true, the simulation predicts that the Accident Rate will be significantly reduced, although the long-term cycling will persist. If we enable Driver's

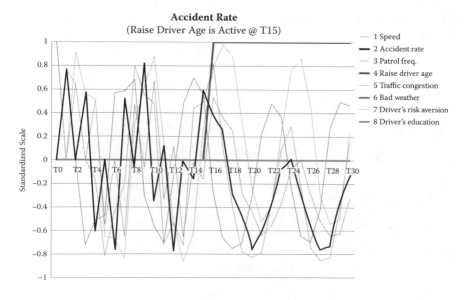

FIGURE 7.25
Accident Rate CLD simulation with Raise Driver Age policy activated

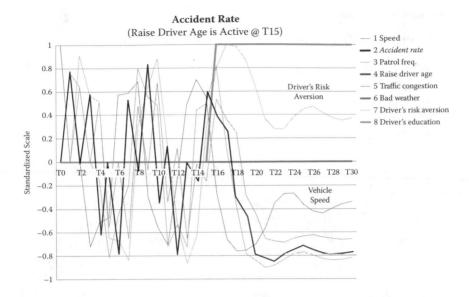

FIGURE 7.26

Accident Rate CLD simulation with Raise Driver Age and Driver's Education policies activated.

Education as well, we might be able to eliminate the cycling, as show in the Figure 7.26. Here, both Raise Driver Age and Driver's Education policies are enabled. The Accident Rate (target variable represented by the thick line) is sustained at a low level. Note the relative levels of Accident Rate, Driver's Risk Aversion (the leverage variable), and Vehicle Speed. This is the voice of the system. Ask the system a question and you get a qualitative answer in the form of event patterns.

Summarizing, according to expert opinion, policy implementation should link directly to Driver's Risk Aversion. Specifically, if the age and education of the driver can be sustained at a high level, Accident Rate can be minimized in the long term. The actual definitions and parameters for these policies were drafted by the team during the brainstorming session and will need to be further developed as part of the Analyze and Improve phases of the DMAIC process.

By using simulation, the spaghetti-like CLD has rendered a plausible solution to the systemic problem of cycling Accident Rate. Again, archetypes and sophisticated software were not part of the simulation or policy assessment process. The level of confidence is high because the model is derived from the highest levels of the modeling hierarchy (see Figure 7.9) and is based on expert opinion rather than the opinion of one expert.

7.10 PRACTICAL APPLICATION OF CLD MODELS

In the rest of this chapter, we examine CLD models involving business problems with policy impact evaluation.

7.10.1 Product Line Profit

Figure 7.27 is a team's model for the profit of a product line. These 11 variables are typical for all businesses competing for market share. The CLD shows Profit as the only target variable. Although there are no *input policies*, a few *connection policies* are apparent and designated by the thicker arrows.

The simulation results shown in the trend chart illustrated in Figure 7.28 reveal that Profit has a widely varying steady-state cycle, an arrhythmia many companies experience. An experiment can be conducted to find the optimal combination of connection policies that produces a more stable profit pattern. Such an experiment is shown in Figure 7.29 with numerical scores indicating the optimal combination of policies.

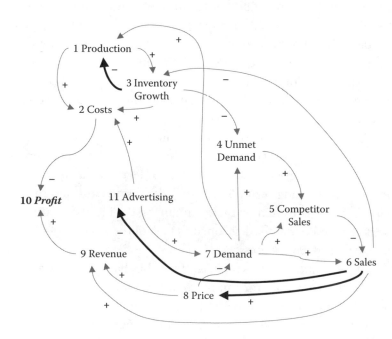

FIGURE 7.27
Product line profit CLD.

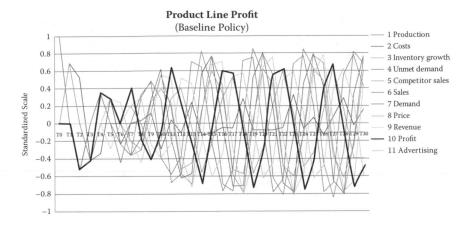

FIGURE 7.28
Product line profit CLD simulation.

7.10.2 Policy Evaluation (Policy Scores)

When evaluating the potential impact of a policy, there are two scoring metrics for each target variable in the evaluation experiment, *MScore(SS)* and *VScore*.

MScore(SS) is the steady-state mean difference between the CLD representing the current system (status quo or baseline) and the same system under an experimental combination of new policies. Positive values represent improvement in long-term direction of the target variable. This metric is a percentage of the standardized range –1 to 1.

VScore is the variance ratio of the event patterns for current and experimental systems. The variance of the current system is in the numerator thus values greater than one (>1) represent an improvement in the target variable's stability.

	Connection Policy			Target Variable = Profit		
Run	3-1(-)	6-11(-)	6-8(+)	MScore(SS)	VScore	
1	Not Active	Not Active	Not Active	1.4%	10.57	<Optimal
2	Active	Not Active	Not Active	2.3%	8.25	
3	Not Active	Active	Not Active	1.4%	5.03	
4	Active	Active	Not Active	0.3%	1.90	
5	Not Active	Not Active	Active	1.4%	5.04	
6	Active	Not Active	Active	0.6%	2.05	
7	Not Active	Active	Active	0.6%	1.00	
8 Baseline	Active	Active	Active	0.0%	1.00	

FIGURE 7.29
Profit CLD Simulation Experiment.

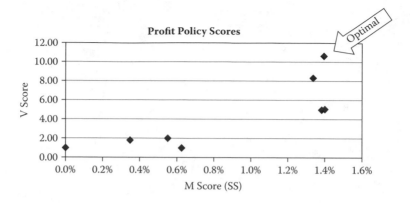

FIGURE 7.30
Optimal policy score for profit stability.

The optimal combination is where both scores are maximized, which means that the combination of active and inactive policies leads the system to a better long-term event pattern or state relative to the current or chosen baseline system. An MScore vs. VScore plot (Figure 7.30) is a convenient way to see the optimal combination, which always is a point in the upper right corner of the plot.

The simulation experiment reveals that the optimal policy combination is where all three connection policies are inactive. In other words, for the current system, the best strategy for stabilizing profit is not to drive production based on inventory growth (that is, when inventory is low do not react by making more product). Also, avoid advertising or pricing changes in reaction to sales (that is, if sales are slow, resist the temptation to lower the price and increase advertising); see Figure 7.27. The optimal system behavior is plotted on a trend chart in Figure 7.31. Keep in mind the *y*-axis scale is standardized so a steady-state level of zero represents normal status.

It is interesting to note that this same pattern occurs when the connection policy is removed from Inventory Growth (3) to Production (1) and by decreasing Advertising when sales are low. The Sales (6) to Price (8) connection is maintained. By changing the connection sign from Sales (6) to Advertising (11) from a (−) to a (+), we are testing the new policy of backing off on advertising when sales are low. This seems counterintuitive when we are event driven, yet from a systems-thinking perspective it has high potential to stabilize profits.

The resulting future-state CLD with the three connection policies removed is shown Figure 7.32. Here, Advertising and Price become input policies that need to be controlled by some other strategy or linked to

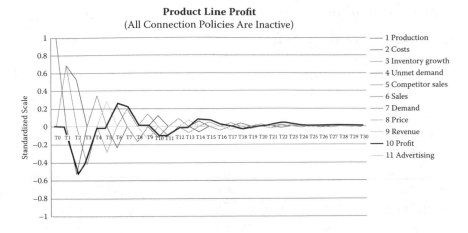

FIGURE 7.31

Product line profit simulation with optimal policy.

other CLD models in the knowledge network. If the team chooses this strategy, they will have more work to do since the organization will need some sort of activation logic if Price and Advertising are to be treated as controlled input policies.

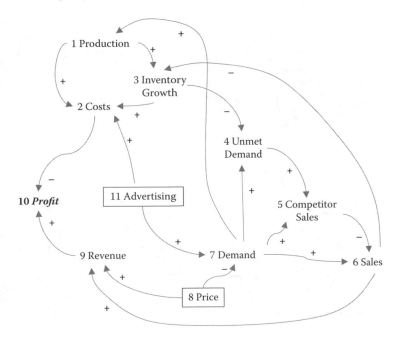

FIGURE 7.32

Product line profit CLD (future state).

7.10.3 Sick Call-In Reduction

This is a project to reduce the frequency of employees calling in sick, which has been on the rise for several months.

The CLD in Figure 7.33 has eight different policies (five *input policies* and three *connection policies*) to consider. Factorial experimentation is the tool of choice for optimizing the result, but it requires the aid of automation to score the 256 possible policy combinations. For now, we can quickly test the impact of the least invasive policy, which is to Evaluate ROI (return on investment; 17); which has a direct impact on Perceived Training Requirements (7). Note that Perceived Training Requirements is high when Productivity (6) is low. This is an example of non-systems thinking used by management in many organizations.

Although there are four target variables present (#2, #3, #9, and #10 in bold text), Sick Call-Ins (2) are critically affecting the workforce and productivity. Figure 7.34 shows the CLD predictions with the three connection policies active; this represents the status quo or baseline system. We can see that the predicted baseline event pattern for sick call-ins has an increasing trend, which matches the problem description and is a sign the CLD has adequately captured the voice of the system.

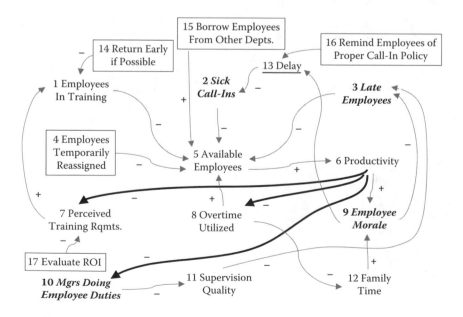

FIGURE 7.33
CLD for sick call-in problem.

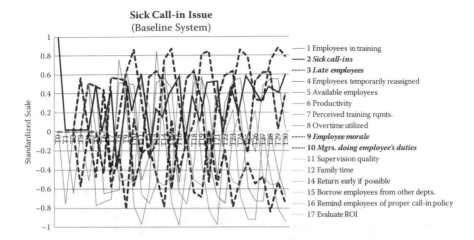

FIGURE 7.34
Sick call-in simulation for baseline system.

When the Evaluate ROI policy is activated, the simulation reveals that sick call-ins can be reduced over the long term and that the secondary target variables are also positively affected; in particular, Late Employees and Employee Morale both show a strong improvement relative to the baseline system pattern as shown in Figure 7.35 and the policy scoreboard (Figure 7.36).

Keep in mind that *MScore(SS)* is both a relative and qualitative indicator of change. A score of 48.6% is *not* to be interpreted as a 48.6%

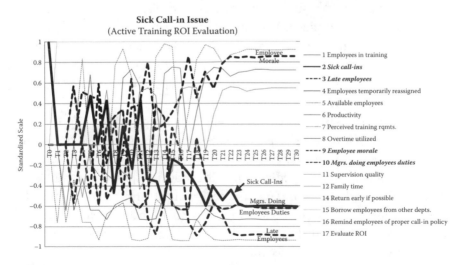

FIGURE 7.35
Sick call-in simulation with training ROI evaluation.

Target Variables

	2 Sick Call-ins	3 Late Employees	9 Employee Morale	10 Mgrs. Doing Employee Duties
MScore(SS)	48.6%	70.8%	69.6%	48.5%
VScore	0.52	0.57	.055	1.03

FIGURE 7.36
Training ROI evaluation scores.

improvement or reduction in sick call-ins; instead, a positive value simply means that the active policy is leading the system in the desired direction and that it has a greater impact on target variables with higher scores such as Late Employees and Employee Morale.

7.11 THINGS TO CONSIDER BEFORE ACTING

Don't just do something, sit there! Take the time to see what is really going on before jumping in to fix "the problem"; otherwise, the situation may get worse. Anticipation is better than surprise when the stakes are high.

Systems thinking and causal loop diagrams (CLDs) are powerful ways to share and question other people's mental models and to address controversial topics. Buried assumptions, beliefs, and biases can be brought to the surface and scrutinized. You can learn a great deal when you have an effective method to share, compare, test, and elevate our mental models. Anything that can offer new clarity around hot topics — usually the most perplexing and emotional — is worth a look, especially if it helps balance your perception when logic clashes with emotion.

Any informed layperson can generate new insights into any topic of interest. This approach lets us package our personal wisdom (or nonsense) into a picture of a piece of the world. As with all forecasting methods, the dynamic event patterns predicted by CLDs do not prove anything, but they can be validated with data. The techniques can be used to test the internal consistency of the person or group that created it. Just ask their CLD a question, and if the answer is consistent with their story line, at least you know they are consistent with themselves.

In his book *Fuzzy Thinking*, Bart Kosko asks us to imagine replacing opinion columns with CLDs. At first, the CLD will be an intriguing addendum to the article. We will begin accepting them as we check the causal links against the statements made and we will soon realize that the words argue for the CLD. In the future, the CLD will be the article and the words the addendum.

To be truly proactive, we need ways to see how solutions or reactions to past problems sustain the current problem or create the seeds of new problems. As stated earlier, we can only learn by doing if we can see the results of what we do. All too often, our solutions attack undesirable events and emotions, which can lead to other problems unless we learn to see and interact with the structure manifesting the problem. When it comes to solving problems, seeing and understanding the big picture or system that produced the problem is essential for creating sustained positive change. All companies have learning disorders. If your company's learning disorder is less than your competition's, then you have found a way to see the bigger picture and interact with the system in a truly proactive way.

Successful systems thinkers

- React to problems by getting the big picture
- Seek to understand how the current system works (operational thinking)
- Focus on structure, not events or blame
- Seek expert opinion, not the opinion of an expert (everyone is right from his or her point of view)
- Are aware that all events come from system structure, whether or not you can see it
- Know that there are both short- and long-term consequences of actions
- Create an "Expert CLD" and find the high-leverage variables and connections before trying to change the system
- Use simulation experiments to assess the impact each policy has on target variables and determine the optimal combination for sustained improvement
- Use the DMAIC process for systemic problem solving
- Keep it simple; lasting solutions reduce complexity

NOTES

1. Peter M. Senge, *The Fifth Discipline: The Art & Practice of the Learning Organization* (New York: Currency Doubleday, 1990).
2. The authors and publisher make no claims as to the correctness of the system models or the conclusions based on the simulation results.

8

The Corporate System

Perfection is not when there's nothing to add, but when there's nothing to take away.

Antoine de Saint-Exupéry
Author, Wind, Sand, and Stars

A corporate system, like the human body, is the whole organism. Ideally, its organs and subsystems function together in harmony and in constant change. *Systems engineering* (SE) is like holistic health, whose purpose is to create, nurture, and maintain the corporate system for an optimal life.

In this chapter, we identify characteristics of excellent companies, lay out the major steps followed when engineering a physical system, determine how to calculate and roll up two important metrics of system performance, apply systems engineering to a corporate system, and identify a few of the ways corporate systems can fail.

Excellent products and services come from excellent companies. Companies achieve excellence by having

- An accurate understanding of and the ability to adapt to the needs of their stakeholders.
- An organizational structure optimized to fulfill those needs.
- Capable, competent people (human capital) who are compensated fairly and are engaged in activities that fulfill stakeholder needs as well as their own needs.

SE can help a company excel in each of these areas. The major goals and steps of systems engineering as applied to physical systems (systems that primarily follow the laws of physics) can be applied to the engineering of corporate systems (systems that consist primarily of people executing activities as part of a complicated organizational structure).

The major goal of SE is the creation of a system optimized to adequately fulfill the needs of all its stakeholders. "Adequately" is the correct term because it is not possible to simultaneously and completely fulfill *all* the needs of *all* the stakeholders.

8.1 SYSTEMS ENGINEERING STEPS

To apply systems engineering to physical system, there are five major steps:

Step 1. Identify the stakeholders and elicit their needs.
Step 2. Translate the needs into a set of system requirements.
Step 3. Define the bounds of the system to be developed.
Step 4. Define the functions that the system must perform to transform inputs into outputs.
Step 5. Determine the "best" technology with which to implement the functions.

8.1.1 Step 1: Identify the Stakeholders and Elicit Their Needs

A stakeholder is defined as any person or entity that touches, or is touched by, the product or service. Stakeholders include functions such as engineering and agencies such as the FDA. A system has many stakeholders; they fall into two major classes, internal and external. This classification is usually with respect to the corporation producing the product or service. For our purpose, we will focus our discussion on a particular external stakeholder, the customer. Of course, fulfilling the customer's needs alone does not guarantee success. All stakeholder needs must be adequately fulfilled.

"Customers" primarily include the users of the product. Once you have identified the customers, you must elicit their needs, also known as the "voice of the customer" (VOC). "Elicit" is the appropriate word because it certainly is not a matter of simply asking "What do you need?" This approach cannot uncover the latent, unspoken needs that, when fulfilled, delight the customer. Yet it is delighting the customer that allows command of new markets or acquisition of significantly increased market share.

Ethnography, the study of human culture, is a powerful tool that is finding greater use in eliciting unspoken needs and getting to the "heart of the customer." Some companies (Xerox, for example) employ ethnographers for this purpose. The activities aimed at eliciting needs must occur continuously and must be sufficiently agile to react to, and even predict, changes in the customers' needs.

The customers and their needs must then be prioritized since, paraphrasing Abraham Lincoln, "You can't please all of the people all the time." Priorities must be set from the customer's perspective, not the company's assessment of what is important. If we set priorities on the customer's behalf, as is common, we must go back to the customer to confirm that the chosen priorities actually match those of the customer.

8.1.2 Step 2: Translate the Needs into a Set of System Requirements

No part of the delivery process is as critical or as difficult [as identifying system requirements] — because requirements map the human world to the technological world.

Jim Highsmith
Author

The voice of the customer should be embodied in statements of need, not the solutions that fulfill the needs. Some needs translate into input requirements and some into output requirements. For example, the need to use a system at home in the United States might translate into a system input requirement to run on 120V AC; the need to know when a system has completed its operation might translate into an output requirement to produce an audible "beep" of 30 DbA.

Initially, we are not concerned with how the requirements will be met; this is the concern of later steps. Our concerns at this point are

- What are the inputs and outputs?
- How do they link to the needs?
- What target values must they achieve to fulfill the needs?
- How will they be measured?

Let us begin with, What are the outputs? Typically, needs are stated in nontechnical terms. Consider a car door. A voiced customer need might be "I want the door to close nicely." A design team cannot design to "nicely." "Nicely" must be translated into a closing torque in Newton-meters, audible sound in decibels, spring force, and so on. A design team can design to these engineering quantities. If all these quantities simultaneously meet their target values, then "nicely" has been achieved and that particular customer need is fulfilled. We therefore measure how well we fulfill the needs by how well we fulfill the requirements. Accurate translation is, of course, crucial. The design team may meet the requirements perfectly, yet the product will fail in the marketplace if the translation is in error.

Next, how do the requirements link to the needs? We must understand which system outputs fulfill which needs. Tracing the system outputs to the prioritized needs allows us to determine which outputs are critical and which are merely important. Quality function deployment (QFD), a tool brought to the United States from Japan in the early 1980s, is a "best practice" used to establish this linkage and to determine which outputs are critical.

Criticality is based on whether the output has a weak, mild, or strong impact on fulfilling the needs to which it is linked. In the car door example, closing torque and audible sound are critical outputs because they have a strong impact on "closes nicely."

The critical inputs and outputs are the critical parameters of the system. Critical parameter management (CPM) begins when needs have been translated into system inputs and outputs. CPM ends when the system is retired but can continue into the development of the next member of the product family. CPM is a crucial tool in the system engineer's toolbox.[1]

Next, we must determine the target values that the outputs must achieve to fulfill the needs. Continuing with the car door example, the team must determine the minimum closing torque required to keep the door open on an incline and the maximum torque needed to close the door without excessive effort.

Next, we must determine how to measure the outputs. Capable measurement systems are crucial if we are to achieve the required system performance. We must quantify the amount of variation that the measurement system contributes to our measurements and compare it with the variation in what we are measuring. In general, a good measurement system's variation should be no more than 30% of the total variation. We can then be confident that design changes are in response to actual in system performance and not due to variation in our measurement systems.[2]

As development progresses, we continually assess the capability of the system by measuring the capability of its critical parameters. The parameters are of two basic types: attribute and continuous. Typical attribute parameters are pass/fail, good/better/best, and the number of defects detected. In physical systems, defects are typically the result of a system that has gone far awry; that is, they are lagging indicators of "physics gone wrong" and therefore not a preferred metric for assessing physical systems. They are, however, important for our discussion of corporate systems and so further discussion is therefore needed.

Defects per unit (DPU), defects per opportunity (DPO), and defects per million opportunities (DPMO) are common metrics applied to attribute parameters. These metrics are used when failures, defects, or errors are of prime importance — for example, in transactional and manufacturing systems. In this context, a defect might be an error on an electronic or paper form, a camera that fails a test on the production line, or an incorrect piece of data transferred from the Engineering Department to the Purchasing Department.

DPU simply compares the number of defective units to the total number of units. We must distinguish between defects and a defective unit. An order form could be a defective unit if it has at least one defect of any type or if it has n defects of a particular type. It may be defective if it has several defects of several types. For example, a form is defective if it contains at least one defect of any type. So, if 100 order forms were completed and 10 were found to be defective, then DPU = 10/100 = 0.1 or 10%.

DPU is more a measure of the number of defective units and less a measure of the capability of the process producing the units. For this reason, DPO and DPMO are preferred. DPO compares the number of defects found to the number of opportunities to produce a defect. Using the example above, if each order form has 20 fields, there are 20 opportunities for a defect per form. The total number of opportunities for a defect is therefore (20/form) × (100 forms) = 2000. If 10 defects were found on 100 order forms, DPO is calculated to be 10 defects per 2000 opportunities = 0.005 or 0.5%. DPMO normalizes DPO to a million opportunities. In our example, this is 5000 DPMO.

This is equivalent to an approximate yield of 99.53%. The process is performing at approximately a 4.1 Sigma level. See the table relating Sigma level, DPMO, and yield in Appendix B. The relationships in the table are true under the following assumptions; a normal distribution adequately describes the data and a 1.5 Sigma shift in the mean of the data is applied to simulate long-term variation in process performance.[3]

Keep in mind that DPO and DPMO measure process defect rates, not the number of defective units produced by the process. If a single defect causes a defective unit and if each defective unit contains only one defect, then DPMO equals the number of defective units, which can be translated into yield.

Also, keep in mind that DPO and DPMO can be considered sample statistics calculated from sample data and used as an estimate of the population failure rate. As with any statistic, its ability to estimate the population depends on how well the sample represents the population. We will make use of these metrics later when we apply SE to corporate systems.

As mentioned earlier, defect-based metrics are far removed from the physics of the system and are therefore not preferred for physical systems. Continuous parameters *are* closely tied to physics. They are the inputs and outputs of processes that perform physical functions such as a car's heating subsystem. This subsystem consists of a process whose function is to regulate the car's interior temperature. Failure occurs when the interior temperature has drifted above or below its desired limits. Let us look at an important metric used with continuous parameters.

C_p compares the limits of acceptable performance to the parameter's variability. The equation is

$$C_p = \frac{USL - LSL}{6\sigma} = \frac{\text{Tolerance}}{6\sigma}$$

The upper and lower specification limits (USL and LSL respectively) bound the limits of acceptable performance. The difference between the upper and lower limits is the tolerance. The tolerance should be determined from the amount of variability in performance that the customer will tolerate.

Parameter variability is quantified using the sample standard deviation, which provides an estimate of σ, the true population variation. The multiplier of 6 is used for several reasons. First, this is consistent with the ±3 Sigma control limits found on statistical process control charts made popular by W. Shewhart in the 1920s. Additionally, six standard deviations capture 99.73% of the parameter's variation (assuming a normal distribution).

Six Sigma performance is attained when $C_p = 2$ or, in other words, when there are 12 standard deviations (±6) within the tolerance. This is shown graphically in Figure 8.1. When this condition exists, using the table in the Appendix B, we can expect a DPMO of 3.4. The process will incorrectly perform its function three or four times for every million opportunities.

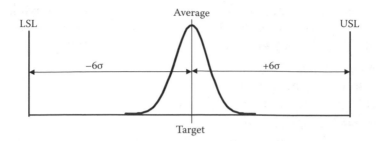

FIGURE 8.1
For Six Sigma performance, the upper and lower specification limits are each six standard deviations from the mean.

This assumes a 1.5 Sigma shift in the mean of the data to simulate long-term process variation.

A major difference between DPMO and C_p is that DPMO measures failures, while C_p measures physical performance that, if allowed to drift too far, will result in failure. Counting the number of failures does little to determine what caused them. However, it can tell us where to begin investigating. For example, a critical process with a high failure rate is a natural place to begin. Once the process is chosen, however, we will most likely need to measure the critical outputs of the physical functions carried out by the process to determine the root cause and thereby reduce the failure rate.

It is the accumulation of all these metrics — some continuous, some pass/fail — from the underlying subsystems, processes, and functions that provides a summary of the health of the entire system.

The "Holy Grail" of systems engineering is the roll-up of all the metrics of system performance into a single number, which we can then use to easily compare systems. While it is true that metrics of the same units can be rolled up into a summary number, the perfect method and the set of metrics has not yet been found for an entire system. Even the roll-up of metrics with the same units, such as the average, can be problematic. You may be familiar with the tale of the man who drowned in a lake whose average depth was half a meter. Details are hidden in the summary.

DPMO, however, is an enticing metric. Even though DPMO is a lagging indicator and is far removed from physics, it is a valuable metric for the roll-up of the underlying performance metrics. A property of DPMO is that, under certain conditions, a simple summation of the underlying processes' DPMOs provides an adequate estimate of the rolled-up DPMO.

Consider, for example, four serial processes, each at an approximate 3.1 Sigma level (~55,000 DPMO). The overall DPMO is then estimated to be (55,000) + (55,000) + (55,000) + (55,000) = 220,000 DPMO (a Sigma level of ~2.3).

The estimate is, however, conservative; that is, the estimated rolled-up DPMO is greater than the actual rolled-up DPMO. The actual DPMO is ~184,000 (a Sigma level of ~2.4), an overestimation of approximately 7%. The estimate degrades as the individual process failure rates increase and as the number of serial processes increases. In addition, most systems are comprised of serial and parallel subsystems. Because of this, we must understand how DPMO and yield combine for serial, parallel, and mixed configurations.

8.1.2.1 Serial Systems

Assume a system with two serial processes, P1 and P2 (Figure 8.2). This could model a manufacturing operation in which a part is assembled in P1 and then another part is assembled in P2. There are two possible outcomes of each process. The part can be assembled correctly or incorrectly. In this discussion, the outcome of P2 does not depend on the outcome of P1. This scenario could also model a corporation's human resource subsystem in which an offer is made to a candidate in P1 (accept/reject the offer) and his or her one-year performance is assessed in P2 (pass/fail the review).

In this example, we assume a 99.9% success rate for each process. This is approximately a 4.6 Sigma level and 1000 DPMO. We further assume that both processes must produce a good result for an overall good result. The

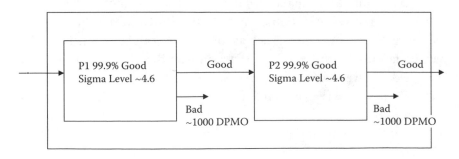

FIGURE 8.2
Two serial processes.

units that enter P2 are only the good ones from P1. The rolled-up DPMO of serial processes can be determined from the product of each.

Assume a system with n independent serial subsystems. Each subsystem's process has an individual success rate of $p_1, p_2, p_3, \ldots, p_n$. The rolled-up system success rate P is the product of the individual success rates. This can be written as

$$P = \prod_{i=1}^{n} p_i$$

The rolled-up system DPMO is then $(1 - P) \cdot (1,000,000)$. If each of the n processes has the same success rate, p, then the rolled-up system success rate is p^n. The rolled-up system DPMO is then $(1 - p^n)(1,000,000)$.

In our example, each subsystem's success rate is 99.9%. This is an approximate 4.6 Sigma level. The overall system success rate is then $(0.999 \cdot 0.999) = (0.999)^2 \sim 0.998$. Using the table in the Appendix B, this is equivalent to a 4.4 Sigma level and ~1866 DPMO. Notice that the overall system success rate is less than the success rate of the subsystems. The equivalent system is shown in Figure 8.3.

8.1.2.2 Parallel Systems

Now consider a system consisting of two parallel subsystems as shown in Figure 8.4.

Each subsystem has one process, P1 and P2. Two parallel assembly lines, each producing the same assembly, is an example of such a system. We can determine the likelihood of system success if we have a definition of success and if we know the success rates of P1 and P2.

Assume that p_1 and p_2 are the respective success rates of P1 and P2. There are four possible outcomes. They can be enumerated using a spanning tree diagram as shown in Figure 8.5.

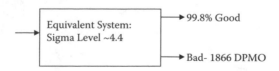

FIGURE 8.3
Equivalent system.

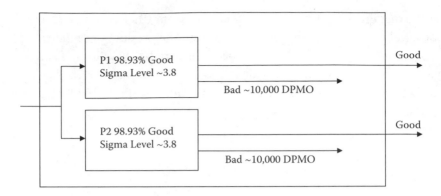

FIGURE 8.4
Two parallel subsystems.

The outcomes can also be enumerated using the binomial expansion $(p + f)^n$, where n is the number of parallel subsystems and f is the failure rate. In our example, $n = 2$ and $(p + f)^n = (p_1 + f_1) \cdot (p_2 + f_2) = p_1p_2 + p_1f_2 + f_1p_2 + f_1f_2$. Note that the probability of all these outcomes occurring must sum to unity since these are all the possible outcomes. So, $1 = p_1p_2 + p_1f_2 + f_1p_2 + f_1f_2$.

Now, assume in this example that at least one subsystem must succeed for the overall system to succeed. Therefore, system success is given by $P = p_1p_2 + p_1f_2 + f_1p_2$. So, $1 = P + f_1f_2$. Therefore, $P = 1 - f_1f_2$.

In this case, $P = p_1p_2 + p_1f_2 + f_1p_2 = .999886$. DPMO $= (1 - P)(1,000,000) = 114$, an approximate ~5.2 Sigma level. The success rate of the system is greater than the success rate of either of its subsystems. The equivalent subsystem is shown in Figure 8.6.

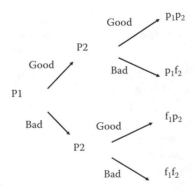

FIGURE 8.5
Spanning tree diagram.

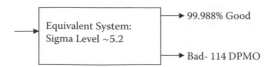

FIGURE 8.6
Equivalent subsystem.

8.1.2.3 Mixed Systems

We now know how to roll up the DPMO for systems consisting of parallel subsystems and those consisting of serial subsystems. How do we roll up a mixed system? We first convert the parallel subsystems into equivalent subsystems. The result is a system consisting of only serial subsystems. We then roll up the serial subsystems using the product rule given earlier for serial subsystems. This can be illustrated by combining the parallel system with the equivalent serial system from the previous two examples. This is shown in Figure 8.7.

The parallel system was converted into an equivalent system earlier. The intermediate equivalent system is shown in Figure 8.8.

The rule for combining serial subsystems is applied to the intermediate system to create the final equivalent system as shown in Figure 8.9.

Calculation of the rolled-up, system-level DPMO can be easily automated using custom software. Software intended for reliability calculations can also be used since the same methods are used to determine system reliability. Each equivalent subsystem's scorecard should contain its individual DPMO, yield, or Sigma level. These can be collected and combined, using the software to determine the overall system performance.

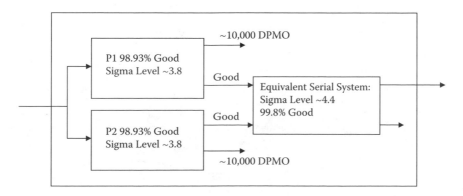

FIGURE 8.7
Mixed system.

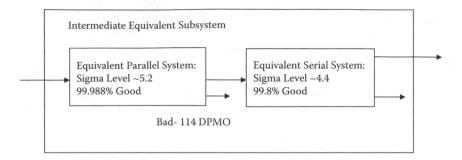

FIGURE 8.8
Intermediate equivalent system.

8.1.3 Step 3: Define the Bounds of the System to Be Developed

This sounds simple but can be difficult. We must decide all that *is* the system and all that *is not* the system. To help decide, we ask what mass, energy, and information will enter the system and what mass, energy, and information will exit the system. We must also be aware of whose perspective we take when answering this question. This is shown in Figure 8.10.

Typical examples of mass are raw materials such as plastic, steel, and a volume of air or water. Energy includes electrical, fluidic, thermal, and mechanical energy. Examples of information include control signals, fault enunciators, *andons* (Japanese for "light") signals, and the information that software systems act upon and produce.

8.1.4 Step 4: Define the Functions That the System Must Perform to Transform the Inputs into Outputs

For example, consider an automobile. This system's major physical function is mass translation, to move a mass from one point to another. Its

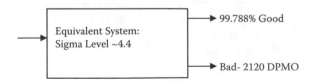

FIGURE 8.9
Final equivalent system.

FIGURE 8.10
System inputs and outputs.

motive subsystem, its engine, contains a process whose function is to convert input energy into torque. For the automobile, chemical energy in the form of gasoline is still the most common form of input energy. This system is shown in Figure 8.11.

We continue identifying all the system and subsystem functions and the processes within each subsystem that will carry out those functions. All of the subsystems exist to either directly support the system, support other subsystems, or both.

Once all the subsystems, processes, and functions have been identified, the system and subsystem inputs and outputs are interconnected with all the subsystems within the system. We search for a system architecture that optimizes system performance through reduced complexity. Complexity is reduced by decreasing the number of interfaces between subsystems and reducing the amount and types of mass, energy, and information flowing on each interface. This effort is called system architecting and optimization. The architecture is seen as a multitude of interconnected subsystems, an example of which is shown in Figure 8.12.

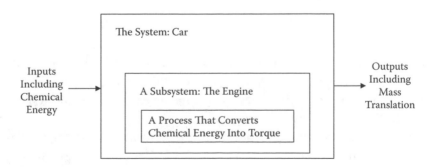

FIGURE 8.11
System view of a car and one of its major subsystems.

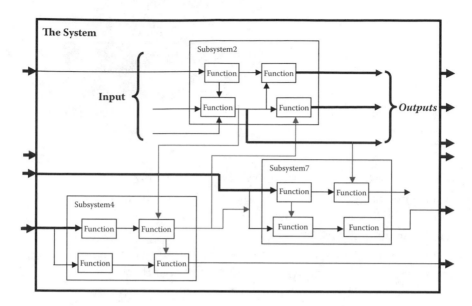

FIGURE 8.12
System architecture.

8.1.5 Step 5: Determine the "Best" Technology with Which to Implement the Functions

"Best" is in quotes because the choice is an "all things considered" trade-off. Each technology has its strengths and weaknesses given the environment in which it will be used and its application. The desired technology performs its functions with as little wasted mass, energy, and information as possible. The final choice has the fewest weaknesses and the most strength. It is almost never "the perfect choice."

In general, technology's purpose is to implement physical functions. For example, an electric motor is technology whose function is to convert electrical energy into mechanical energy. A light bulb converts electrical energy into light energy. Later, we will extend this concept to intellectual property, which can be thought of as technology that converts one set of thoughts into another set of thoughts.

Unfortunately, technology does not only perform intended functions, it performs unintended functions as well. A motor and a light bulb both produce unintended heat energy as they carry out their intended functions. This is waste. A major goal of technology development is to find ways to maximize the efficiency of the intended functions by minimizing the unintended functions. A goal of the systems engineer is to use imperfect technology as efficiently as possible by ensuring that the unintended functions do the least harm.

8.2 SYSTEMS ENGINEERING APPLIED TO HUMAN SYSTEMS

Knowing how systems engineering is applied to physical systems helps us understand how to apply it to a corporate system. The rigorous and disciplined methodology and metrics of systems engineering provides great value when applied to corporate systems, and in particular to the methodology and framework for structuring, tracking, and optimizing what otherwise might be a hopelessly complex and unmanageable beast.

That said, there are many similarities in the application of systems engineering to physical and corporate systems. There are also many important differences since people are *the* major component of the corporate system. People can be a corporation's greatest strength and its greatest weakness. People — indeed, a single person — can lead a company to greatness or disaster.

People do not follow physical laws, nor do they behave as predictably as physical systems. A person can take the same input and produce wildly varying output, or even no output. Emotions, moods, and physical ailments, for example, all influence a person's performance at work. Mission statements, standard operating procedures, method sheets, and so on are tools used to help reduce human variability and errors. They do so, however, only when followed. Therefore, it is important to apply each of the SE steps to the corporate system to optimize the corporate system.

8.2.1 Step 1: An Intense Focus on Identifying the Stakeholders and Eliciting Their Needs

Many corporations begin because one or a few founders believe that certain needs exist and that they have the ability to fulfill them. Fulfillment comes though the expenditure of physical and intellectual work in some area of expertise that, if successful, brings personal satisfaction and profit to these individuals.

John Bausch, an optician, and Henry Lomb, a financier, successfully fulfilled the need for low-cost, durable eyeglass frames. The need arose because gold and English horn, the materials then in use, were becoming expensive and difficult to obtain.

Initially, the stakeholders were limited to eyeglass wearers and those who provided the money for the venture. The needs to be fulfilled were those of eyeglass wearers for low-cost, durable eyeglasses and the financier's need to get his money back plus a profit. Bausch and Lomb's solution was to make eyeglass frames from vulcanite rubber. Rubber was cheaper, more durable, and more readily available than English horn. Successful fulfillment of the eyeglass wearer's need allowed the financiers to do well — so well that Bausch & Lomb (B&L) Inc. was founded in 1853 in Rochester, New York, and is now a multibillion-dollar eye-care corporation.

B&L has been able to remain in business for over 150 years by keeping a continuous focus on stakeholder needs and fulfilling needs that are consistent with B&L's mission statement, "Perfecting Vision. Enhancing Life." B&L has also been sufficiently agile in its reaction to and even prediction of changes in the stakeholders and their needs over the years. Thus, B&L's stakeholders have since been expanded beyond eyeglass wearers. Cataract patients, ophthalmologists, optometrists, opticians, contact lens wearers, sufferers of various ophthalmic diseases, the FDA, and until recently, Wall Street are some of B&L's external stakeholders.

Of course, B&L must prioritize the stakeholders and their needs, which cannot be equally satisfied. Prioritization drives the creation of a product/service portfolio, and each product or service in the portfolio is designed to fulfill a unique combination of stakeholder needs at just the right time.

An intense focus on the stakeholders and their needs is, by the way, consistent with Lean's focus. Lean identifies waste as any activity that does not add value to the customer. We therefore must know what the customer values to ensure all waste has been eliminated.

Once we have identified the stakeholders, we can use a cause-and-effect diagram (see Figure 8.13) to concisely display who they are, how they relate to each other, and their representatives within the corporation.

Once the stakeholders are identified, you must determine their needs. Ethnography, which we discussed earlier, is a powerful tool used to elicit stakeholder needs. It can be applied to both internal and external stakeholders, although it is most typically applied to a special class of external stakeholder, the customer.

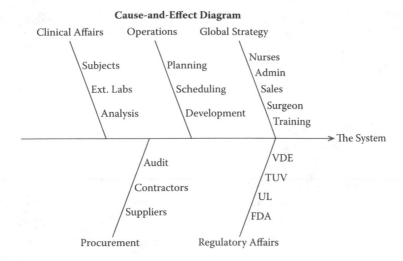

FIGURE 8.13
Cause-and-effect diagram.

Ethnography and a host of other needs-gathering techniques comprise the technology of the inbound marketing processes whose function is to identify and gather information about stakeholders and their needs. This process must be continually active for a company to thrive over the long term. This is the domain of the "Marketing for Six Sigma" tool set.

8.2.2 Step 2: Translate the Needs into a Set of Overall Corporate-Level Output Requirements

For public companies, Wall Street's needs drive specific critical outputs — most notably, stock prices and dividends. The financial health of the company is assessed using critical parameters typically listed in a company's balance sheet, including assets such as cash, net receivables, inventories, and fixed assets, and liabilities such as accounts payable and short- and long-term debt as well as shareholder equity in preferred and common stock.

The customer drives the parameters used to measure how well their needs are being fulfilled. Typical measures of customer satisfaction include complaint rates, quantity of goods returned, and sales volume (number of units sold, dollar amount, or percent of market share).

It is crucial that the parameters accurately reflect the corporation's underlying health. It is also crucial that the parameters do not lag excessively, causing action to come too late.

So far, we have not concerned ourselves with how the critical outputs will be met. Our concerns at this point are to define what the outputs are, to show how the outputs link to the needs, to establish the target values that they must achieve, and to determine how they will be measured.

We have listed several system-level outputs that are of prime importance since they fulfill the needs of two key external stakeholders, the customer and the investors. As with physical systems, we must trace the outputs to the prioritized stakeholder needs to determine which are critical and which are merely important. We must set target values for these output parameters. We can then measure how well we fulfill the stakeholder needs by how accurately and precisely the outputs hit their targets. As is the case for physical systems, it is crucial that we have capable measurement systems if the corporation is to accurately and precisely monitor its health and react to real changes in performance and not to random measurement system variation.

8.2.3 Step 3: Define the Bounds of the Corporation

We must decide all that *is* the corporation and all that *is not* the corporation. Worldwide partnering with other companies and individuals creates an extended enterprise whose boundary can become blurred. Is inventory from a supplier our company's inventory after it enters our receiving dock or after we've paid for it? Is our supplier's quality our quality? Are outsourced service personnel our personnel if we are their sole client? The answers depend on our perspective and agreed policies. However, keep in mind that the customer is blind to where or how we get our parts or whose quality, or poor quality, is responsible for the overall product's level of quality.

We must ensure that the system consists of the minimum and sufficient set of subsystems, processes, functions, mass, energy, and information to fulfill its stakeholder needs. Subsystems that are not considered part of the corporation — an external design house, for example — must be considered part of an extended enterprise with which the corporation interfaces through carefully engineered, monitored, and controlled interfaces.

A new form of "energy" exists in the corporate system that does not exist in physical systems. While people expend energy in ways traditionally thought of as work, such as lifting boxes or packaging products, "energy" can now be expended in the form of intellectual labor. We must consider the intellectual property that *is* and *is not* part of the system. This system component creates true differentiation between companies because this is the energy that fuels innovation.

8.2.4 Step 4: Define the Functions That the System Must Perform to Transform the Inputs into Outputs

Recall the process discussed earlier used to identify the stakeholders and to determine their needs. What corporate subsystem is responsible for keeping this process continually active? Where do its inputs come from and where do its outputs connect? What metrics allow us to monitor and track whether the process is working correctly and efficiently?

Typical names for the corporate subsystem that answers these questions are marketing, inbound marketing, strategy, commercial, and so on. Its inputs come from the global marketplace, competitive benchmarking, and lateral industries. Its outputs connect to the strategic product portfolio, strategic technology development, and product development. This is illustrated in Figure 8.14.

The decomposition of systems-level functions into a multitude of interconnected subsystems continues until all outputs are addressed. The result is a corporate architecture that depicts the subsystems and their interconnections, commonly known as the corporate organization (org.) chart.

The corporate architecture must be optimized to minimize its complexity. This is done by ensuring that only a minimum yet sufficient number of subsystems exists, and that minimum amounts of mass, energy, and

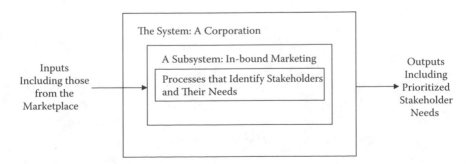

FIGURE 8.14
Input/output diagram for the inbound marketing subsystem.

information flow on the interconnections. Optimization continues within each subsystem by ensuring that each process implements its function with the least amount of waste and the fewest unintended functions. This is achieved by choosing the best technology for each process.

8.2.5 Step 5: Determine the "Best" Technology with Which to Implement the Functions

As with physical systems, "best" is in quotes because the choice is an "all things considered" trade-off. Each technology has its strengths and weaknesses given the environment and application. The final choice has the fewest weaknesses and the most strengths, and is almost never a "perfect" solution.

The term *technology*, however, can now be extended to include more than the computers, motors, and automated processes commonly thought of as technology. It can now include intellectual functions. In doing so, we capture the most crucial component of the corporate system: its people, its human capital.

The best human capital for a subsystem consists of those people who can best operate its processes. People not only operate the process, they are also a major component of the process itself. These are the professionals, regardless of their education level, who possess the expertise, experience, and knowledge needed to continually improve the process so that its functions are performed with the least amount of waste and fewest unintended functions.

8.3 SYSTEMS ENGINEERING A HEALTHY COMPANY

Systems engineering provides a methodology and tool set for structuring, tracking, and optimizing the corporate system. The corporation's structure is based on the minimum and sufficient functions, processes, and subsystems required to fulfill its internal and external stakeholder needs. Optimization is achieved by minimizing the system's complexity and by using the best technology, including human capital, to implement processes that carry out their functions with the least amount of waste. A roll-up of metrics that are based on the Sigma level, yield, and DMPO of the system's underlying subsystems are used to track results. The metrics are periodically measured and compared to their required target values.

In the chapters that follow, we describe a corporation's major subsystems and some of the engines of growth common to all the subsystems of a corporation, such as innovation. Later, we discuss how to assess the health of the subsystems using the corporate CAT scan and the proper actions to be taken to remedy the ailing subsystems.

NOTES

1. Clyde M. Creveling, Jeff Slutsky, and Dave Antis, *Design for Six Sigma* (Upper Saddle River, NJ: Prentice Hall, 2003), 251.
2. Creveling, Slutsky, and Antis, *Design for Six Sigma*, 495.
3. Creveling, Slutsky, and Antis, *Design for Six Sigma*, 507.

9

Conception and Development

An organization's reason for being, like that of any organism, is to help the parts that are in relationship to each other, to be able to deal with change in the environment.

Kevin Kelly
Executive editor, Wired

The human body is organized into a system consisting of a coordinated arrangement of organs and tissues combined to perform the complex functions needed for life. Each organ can be considered a subsystem, comprised of billions of microscopic parts, each with its own identity, working together in an organized manner for the benefit of the total being.

These systems are interconnected and dependent on each other. Our heart, which is part of our circulatory subsystem, is controlled by the brain which is part of our nervous subsystem through the vagus nerve. Our skeletal subsystem depends on our digestive system for nutrients. Our muscular subsystem needs our respiratory and circulatory subsystems to supply energy, in the form of oxygen and nutrients, and carry away carbon dioxide. It takes all the subsystems for human growth and development to occur. Each subsystem must be working for the success of the entire body. So too are corporations composed of subsystems. Each organization or department must work well within itself and interface with other organizations and departments while providing information and responding to change.

The optimization of corporate functions has been addressed in detail in other writings, and will not be repeated here. We stress here, though, that Six Sigma is a powerful method by which to achieve optimization. We have seen that some organizations are not amenable to Six Sigma methodology. We believe that when leadership creates the environment, all subsystems will benefit from the application of Six Sigma. In this chapter, we discuss some of these neglected subsystems to stimulate that creative thinking in your organization.

9.1 INBOUND MARKETING — THE EARS OF THE ORGANIZATION

A major subsystem of the corporate system is inbound marketing. This subsystem "listens" to the current state of the market, "hears" the voice of the customer (VOC), and predicts the future based on trends observed in the data. The processes and human capital contained within this subsystem perform two major functions: tracking/predicting the trajectory of the marketplace and identifying clusters of need that, if successfully fulfilled, result in profitable products and services. Inputs to the process include data from current customers, lost customers, competitor benchmarking, emerging markets, and regulatory changes such as changing reimbursement policies for health care.

Outputs of this process feed the product portfolio, product development, and technology development subsystems. The tools used to perform the functions within this process include the Marketing for Six Sigma (MFSS) tool set.

This process must be continually active. If it is used only when a new product development effort begins, the result will be a lackluster product portfolio. In fact, the output of this process helps justify initiating a product development effort. The process must continue in parallel with the development effort so that the features and functions of the product under development remain current with the changing stakeholder needs. It also allows the creation of multigenerational plans (MGP). An MGP determines which features and functions a product will and will not contain in its current version and subsequent versions. This helps to reduce the frequency and magnitude of distracting redirections of the development team, thereby improving the predictability in time, resources, and money required for product development.

9.1.1 Identify the Stakeholders

A stakeholder is anyone who touches or is touched by the product or service. "Anyone" includes individual customers, government agencies, service groups, manufacturers, and so on. As far back as 29 c.e., sufferers of

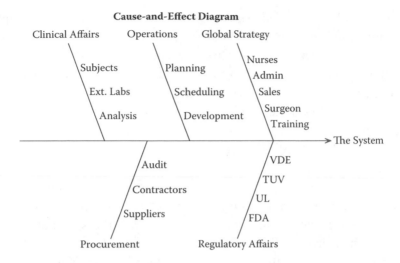

FIGURE 9.1
Cause-and-effect diagram.

poor vision were identified as key stakeholders of a technique to remove cataracts. "Needling" was used to surgically break the cataract lens into small pieces, allowing it to be slowly absorbed by the body.[1] Since then, the types of stakeholders with regard to cataracts have grown; among them are investors, the Food and Drug Administration (FDA), and surgeons, in addition to the sufferers from different types of cataracts.

Typically, there are many stakeholders and a cause-and-effect diagram, as shown in Figure 9.1, can be used to concisely list and organize the stakeholders. Fortunately, the stakeholders remain relatively constant within a given product and industry, allowing the diagram to be reused with little modification on the next development effort.

9.1.2 Elicit the Stakeholder Needs

Once the stakeholders are identified, the next step is to elicit their needs. Identifying the needs is a major function of the inbound marketing process. Consider the needs of cataract sufferers. A cataract is a hardening and opacity of the natural lens. The result is diminished ability to accommodate (near/far vision), reduced light, and reduced color intensity. Simply stated, the needs are for safe, long-lasting relief from these symptoms without serious side effects. However, many needs underlying these high-level needs must be identified.

Several tools can be used to identify the underlying needs. Ethnography, outcome-based inquiry, contextual inquiry, value chain analysis, focus groups, surveys, and interviews are some of the tools. Eliciting needs is not simply a matter of asking, "What do you need?" which mainly gathers the needs for which more or less is better — for example, "I need it to go faster," "I need less noise," and "I need increased mileage." Stakeholders freely describe these needs, sometimes without even being asked. These needs are fulfilled by product features and functions, called linear satisfiers.

An extremely powerful tool that can elicit needs beyond those fulfilled by linear satisfiers is ethnography. Ethnography is based on the techniques of anthropology where an investigator lives with the stakeholders and learns what their daily lives are like. Once identified, the needs must be grouped into common themes. Jiro Kawakita, a Japanese anthropologist, devised a method for grouping the artifacts uncovered at an archeological site to form a "picture" of what life was like at the site.[2] Large amounts of seemingly unrelated information are organized into common themes. The technique is called *affinity diagramming*, and it can be used to group stakeholder needs into themes. What emerges is a "picture" of the major types of need that the product or service must fulfill. David Garvin[3] identified eight dimensions of quality forming eight common (but not the only) themes into which needs may be grouped:

- *Performance*: primary operating characteristics
- *Features*: secondary characteristics of a product or service
- *Reliability*: frequency with which a product or service fails
- *Conformance*: adherence to specifications or standards
- *Durability*: how long the product is intended to last
- *Service (ability)*: speed, competence or ease of service
- *Aesthetics*: fit and finish
- *Perceived quality*: reputation, technical competence

Once the needs are identified and grouped into themes, they must be categorized based on type and the expected difficulty to fulfill each need. The needs can be grouped into three types of needs: basic, linear, and delighters. Basic needs are needs that must be met to gain entry into the marketplace, but even if these needs are met, the stakeholder does not feel satisfied. This is because the stakeholder strongly assumes that these basic needs will be met. However, if basic needs are not met, the stakeholder feels strongly dissatisfied. Imagine that you have purchased a new car and it arrives with no scratches. You are not impressed. You may not even be aware of this because it is so strongly expected. However, if there is one scratch on the new vehicle, you are extremely dissatisfied. Basic needs can be difficult to determine since they are not usually verbalized. This is due to the strong, almost subconscious, assumption that the basic need will be met.

Linear needs are those for which more or less is better. Examples for a contact lens include greater visual acuity, less sting upon insertion, and a lowered price. Linear needs are relatively easy to determine since the stakeholder is usually well aware of them. Fulfilling linear needs enables a company to remain in the marketplace.

Delighters are product features and functions that fulfill the needs that a stakeholder did not know he or she had or believed could ever be fulfilled. Not too many years ago, the thought of going home within a few hours after having cataract surgery was ludicrous. It is now common. Delighters can be difficult to determine since they are usually not verbalized. Fulfilling this type of need enables a company to take significant market share and to enter new markets.

The types of needs described above are part of the Kano model of quality, which includes a familiar phenomenon: Today's delighters will later become linear satisfiers and eventually basic satisfiers.[4] This is partly why the inbound marketing process must be continually active, constantly looking for new delighters that will lead to increased market share and entry into new markets.

We must also categorize the needs based on the difficulty we expect in fulfilling the needs. We can use the New, Unique, Difficult (NUD) model for this.[5] NUD categorizes the needs as

- *New* to the world or your industry
- *Unique,* that is, a competitor may currently be fulfilling the need but you are not
- *Difficult* in that the need may be commonly filled but it is difficult to do

It is helpful to plot this information in a "needs bar graph" to visualize the relative number of needs that are basic, linear, delighters, new, unique, and difficult. Note that the categories are not mutually exclusive. For example, a need can be both basic and difficult. Two examples of a needs bar graph are shown in Figure 9.2 and Figure 9.3. Figure 9.2 is characteristic

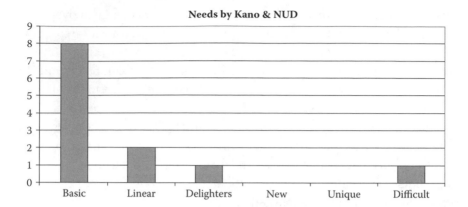

FIGURE 9.2
Needs bar graph characteristic of an "entry-level" product or service.

of an "entry-level" product or service. It is entry level in that it mostly fulfills basic needs. The organization is expected to have mild difficulty developing the product. The questions to be asked here are: "Why develop this product?" "Are we to be a close follower?" "What would cause the customer to choose our product over our competitors?"

Figure 9.3 graphs a product that attempts to provide many delighters and therefore could take substantial existing or new market share but, for the same reason, has great development risk. There are needs that the industry has not fulfilled before, needs that the company has not previously fulfilled, and there are needs that are simply "hard to do." The questions to

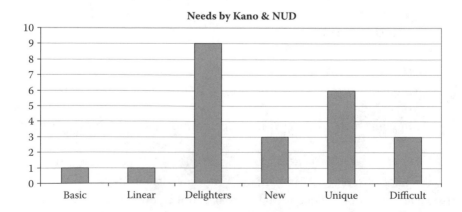

FIGURE 9.3
Needs bar graph characteristic of a product or service that could take substantial existing or new market share.

ask here are: "Is this effort worth the risk?" "How likely are we to succeed?" "Do we have the core competencies required for success?"

A business case can now be established using this and other information. The grouped, categorized, and prioritized needs — along with the business case information such as sales volume, price, and net present value — allow us to decide if the development effort should proceed. A business case also helps determine the corporation's product portfolio and the product's multigenerational plan. The needs drive the technology development process to create the technologies needed by product development to implement its designs. This is a good time to hold a gate review (a specific point in the schedule where the project is evaluated to ensure things are on track and to determine whether the work should continue). If the outcome of the gate review is to continue development, then the next major step can begin and the product development team can begin translating the stakeholders' needs into product requirements.

9.1.3 Opportunities for Success or Failure of Inbound Marketing

Failures of the inbound marketing subsystem may result from not identifying a basic, linear, or delighter need. Since these can be counted, they are candidates for the DPMO (defects per million opportunities) metric. Missed business-case projections that result in failure can also be translated into DPMO. For example, a projection is a failure if the first year's sales volume is more than 20% below the projected amount.

There are, however, some drawbacks to using DPMO for inbound marketing:

1. *DPMO might be excessive.* Unlike manufacturing processes or physical functions, "millions of opportunities," even for an entire industry, may not exist. A company that put ten new products on the market last year and missed four needs has a DPMO of 400,000.
2. *The time lag between successive updates to the metric might prohibit its use.* In all applications of DPMO, the process must produce an error to count an error. In the case of high-volume manufacturing, thousands of parts may be manufactured in one week. DPMO can change relatively rapidly. The opportunity to detect the effect of a process improvement therefore occurs frequently. This is not the case for inbound marketing. For products with long development times, the next opportunity may not come for years.

Although defects produced by manufacturing are detrimental, the number of units affected is limited to the number of defects produced before the defect is discovered. An inbound marketing error can affect the viability of the entire product line. This is one reason why extreme attention and care is required to get this process right.

9.2 TECHNOLOGY DEVELOPMENT — CELLULAR GROWTH

Technology development (Tech-Dev) is a critical subsystem within the corporate system. Its major function is just-in-time creation of technology that is certified as "safe for use" in the company's products and manufacturing processes. "Safe for use" means that the technology is tunable, stable, and robust.

We must distinguish between Tech-Dev and basic research. They are not the same. Basic research asks the question, "How does the world work?" while Tech-Dev asks, "How can I make the world work the way I want?" Basic research should be continually active and operate in parallel with Tech-Dev. Basic research delivers to Tech-Dev the "science" needed for its safe technology.

Technology consists of the human-made objects that carry out physical or intellectual functions; examples include a motor that converts electrical energy into mechanical energy, a light-emitting diode (LED) that converts electrical energy into light energy, a capacitor that stores electrical energy, and an information compression algorithm that allows information to be reduced in quantity for storage or transmission and then reconstructed without appreciable loss of information. Technology is the "stuff" that makes products, manufacturing processes, and services possible.

The processes and human capital contained within the Tech-Dev subsystem use a rich and varied tool set to transform its inputs into its outputs. Inputs to the process include stakeholder needs from inbound marketing, the product portfolio strategy from the product portfolio creation/renewal subsystem, emerging technology trends in related and distant industries, and the needs of the product development subsystem.

The primary output of this process is safe technology to be used by the product development subsystem during product development. In this context, product development includes concurrent development of the manufacturing processes required to manufacture the product. The outputs of

Tech-Dev also help drive the product portfolio creation/renewal subsystem. It does so by providing information about new and emerging technology that can make previously unconsidered products possible. Outbound marketing also benefits from the technical information that Tech-Dev delivers, for example, to create sales and product collateral.

Tech-Dev operates simultaneously in two major modes: technology push and technology pull. From a Tech-Dev perspective, "pull" equates to needs looking for solutions, and "push" equates to solutions looking for needs. The push and pull modes can operate simultaneously between subsystems. For example, technology push and pull occurs between Tech-Dev and the product development process. Product development *pulls* for the safe technologies it needs to implement product features and functions. Tech-Dev can *push* technology to enable the features and functions previously considered impossible by the product development community. Similarly, inbound marketing and product portfolio development can *pull* for the technology to be used in future products. Tech-Dev can *push* technology to these areas, allowing fulfillment of needs previously thought unable to be fulfilled. This multi-input/multi-output "push/pull" arrangement is illustrated in Figure 9.4.

Similar to the inbound marketing and product portfolio processes, the Tech-Dev process must be continually active, not just when a new product development effort begins. The output of this process helps justify initiating a product development effort by increasing the technical feasibility

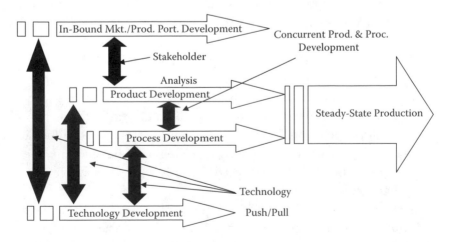

FIGURE 9.4
Multi-input/multi-output "push/pull" arrangement.

of the development effort. Tech-Dev improves the concept generation/ selection process by providing more options for consideration during concept creation. It also helps to reduce the amount of invention and discovery required during the product development effort. Excessive invention and discovery during product development severely erodes the predictability of the product development process and is indicative of a prematurely started development effort.

9.2.1 Technology Development for Six Sigma

Technology Development for Six Sigma (TDFSS) is a methodology that contains tools used for Tech-Dev. The tools have been mapped to a process called Invention/Innovation — Develop — Optimize — Verify (I^2DOV).[6]

I^2DOV begins with Innovation and Invention. This is driven by many sources, including the needs identified by inbound marketing and current and future products in the product portfolio. Innovation and invention during Tech-Dev takes the discoveries of basic research and converts them into technology that is certified safe for use. The output at this stage consists of the early analysis, simulations, and perhaps prototypes of the "ways" to carry out physical or intellectual functions determined during basic research. TRIZ, the Russian methodology for inventive problem solving, is a powerful tool to be used during this stage of Tech-Dev.

The next step in the I^2DOV process is to Develop the details of the technology, including defining its system and subsystem requirements and architecture. The Optimize stage includes the activities and tools used to make the technology robust to the generic noises to which it will be subjected when used in a product. The technique of robust design is used to achieve adequate robustness to the generic noises. The outcome of the Optimize stage is "technology-certified safe."

As we have seen, technology must be tunable, meaning that it can be used over a range of operating conditions. This allows a platform of products to be developed from a single Tech-Dev effort. Figure 9.5 illustrates tunable technology where an input signal causes a predictable and repeatable change in an output. A five-speed motor is a simple example of tunable technology.

Figure 9.6 is a graph illustrating technology that is not tunable. The signal factor appears to change the output. However, note that the output levels overlap at adjacent signal factor levels. The output at signal factor levels 1 and 5 are different. However, the output levels at signal factor levels 1

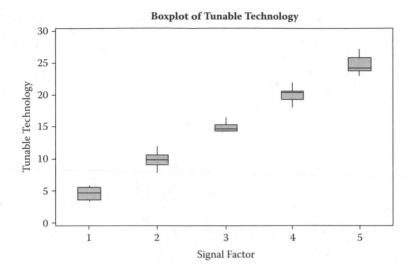

FIGURE 9.5
Tunable technology.

and 2 are not different. The same is true at signal factor levels 3 and 4. The input signal factor does not cause distinct changes in output levels.

Technology must also be stable. Technology is stable if the mean, variance, and distribution of its critical responses remain relatively constant.

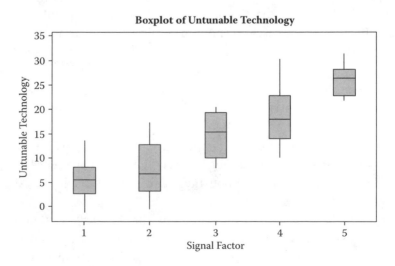

FIGURE 9.6
Technology that is not tunable.

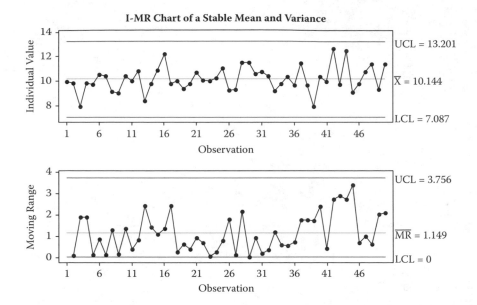

FIGURE 9.7

Statistical process control (SPC) chart for motor speed.

A statistical process control (SPC) chart can be used to demonstrate stability. Figure 9.7 is an example in which one critical response has been measured — in this case, the speed of a blender's motor when operating at a set point of ten revolutions per second.

The individual value chart (top) indicates that the mean motor speed is stable. The moving range chart (bottom) indicates that variation in motor speed is also stable. This is indicated by the fact that the observations remain within their respective upper and lower control limits in both graphs. Together, the graphs indicate that the technology is stable.

The technology must be robust. Technology is robust if the mean and variance of its critical responses are adequately insensitive to generic noises, which includes altitude, temperature, humidity, and aging. These are common noises, which almost all products will experience in their intended-use environments. Robustness can also be displayed using an SPC chart.

Figure 9.8 is an SPC chart of technology that is sensitive to noise and therefore may not be robust. In this example, a response was measured twenty-five times with the noises turned off and twenty-five times with the noises turned on. The SPC chart indicates a decrease in the mean and an increase in the variance when the noise is "on" compared to when the

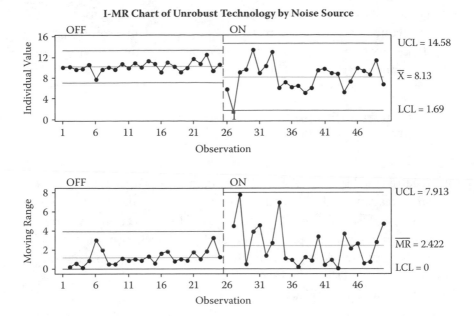

FIGURE 9.8
Unrobust, noise-sensitive technology.

noise is "off." If this change exceeds acceptable levels, then the technology is not robust. Consider a motor set to ten revolutions per second under a no-noise condition. A noise, in the form of increased load, is then applied. The result is decreased motor speed and increased variability in motor speed. If this motor is used in a blender, its performance will be sensitive to load (food added to the blender), and customers will perceive it as inferior if the motor slows by too much.

Verify is the final I²DOV step. Verification of stability, tunability, and robustness to generic noises occurs during this stage. The outcome is the data-based proof that the technology is "safe for use" in a product or manufacturing process development.

Creating safe technology is necessary but not sufficient. True product/process-directed Tech-Dev must be timed so that the safe technology is in the "technology warehouse" for immediate or near-immediate use in the product development effort. This allows the product developers to "shop" the warehouse for technology that is certified safe for use under conditions similar to those of the product they intend to develop.

The "product-preceding" technology cannot remain on the warehouse shelf too long or it will become stale and spoil. It can be "leapfrogged" by revolutionary and disruptive technology if it sits on the shelf too long. The timing requires the close coordination of inbound marketing, product portfolio development, product development, and manufacturing, which is orchestrated by the overall business strategy.

9.2.2 Opportunities for Success or Failure of Technology Development

Tech-Dev can fail to deliver its deliverables on time, on budget, and with the required quality. A lack of adequate planning and project management is mainly responsible for missed deliverables in terms of time and money. The saying, "If we fail to plan, we plan to fail" in connection with product development is equally applicable to Tech-Dev. However, product development and Tech-Dev do differ. One difference is the invention and innovation stage of Tech-Dev. Invention and innovation are difficult to accurately plan. The technique of probabilistic planning described in Section 9.3 is of great benefit in planning Tech-Dev. Probabilistic planning factors in realistic variability and uncertainty, which are common in the early stages of Tech-Dev, and allows for the creation of confidence intervals around milestones. Therefore, one form of failure is completing a milestone or spending money beyond the limits of its confidence interval.

Quality can be measured in a manner similar to that used for product and manufacturing process development. Critical parameter management using C_{pk}, P_{pk}, and the capability growth index (CGI) are good metrics by which to measure technology robustness if specification limits are available. If specification limits are not available, then deviations of the mean and/or variance from target values under noisy conditions can be used. A failure is a mean and/or variance that deviates beyond some limit when noise is applied. The failure rates can then be rolled up to the higher-level scorecards of the corporation's overall system performance.

9.3 PRODUCT DEVELOPMENT — THE DNA OF THE ORGANIZATION

Deoxyribonucleic acid (DNA) is a molecule consisting of thousands of base pairs aligned in a prescribed sequence. The sequence of base pairs determines how to create the proteins that the body needs to exist. The base-pair sequence is like the design created by product development. The design prescribes how to create the product. Manufacturing then executes the design to create the product.

The product development subsystem's inputs come from the inbound marketing subsystem. The inbound marketing subsystem must have previously identified and prioritized the major external stakeholders and their needs. Returning to an earlier example, the customers of a cataract surgical system include the surgeon, the patient, and the nurses, among others. Inputs also come from many other stakeholders, internal and external, who put constraints on how the needs are fulfilled. Government agencies, for example, may specify the minimum safety level required. Manufacturing may require that the new product be manufactured on existing manufacturing processes due to the cost and time required to create new processes.

The process for carrying out this subsystem's overall function typically follows a staged and gated structure in which a series of activities are conducted in each stage. These activities produce a predefined set of deliverables, after which a gate is reached that stops further progress to allow inspection of the current stage's deliverables. If the deliverables have been sufficiently met and if the risk of going forward is acceptable, then the gate opens and the next series of activities are conducted in the next stage. The next gate is reached and so on, until the development effort has been completed.

Most large corporations have a defined stage/gate product development process (PDP). Most, though, lack a defined set of tools mapped to their PDP. A PDP with mapped tools makes the product and manufacturing process development more predictable, repeatable, and controllable.

9.3.1 Design for Six Sigma

Design for Six Sigma (DFSS) is a product/process development methodology and tool set developed in the late 1990s. DFSS is an outgrowth of Six Sigma. Six Sigma, however, lacked the "fuzzy front end" tools needed for the creation of new products, processes, and services. Quality function deployment, concept creation methods, and the Pugh process for concept selection are important examples of the missing tools. These and other tools were brought together to create the DFSS tool set. Each tool was chosen for its ability to achieve product/process development excellence. The tools were then sequenced so that each tool's output provides the next tool's inputs.

Define, Measure, Analyze, Design, and Verify (DMADV) and Concept, Design, Optimize, and Verify (CDOV) are two generic frameworks to

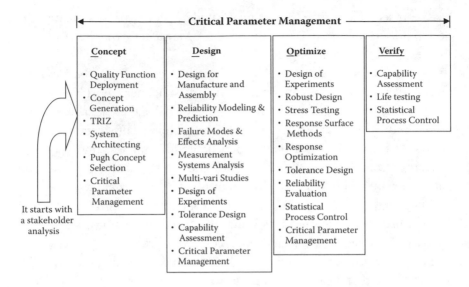

FIGURE 9.9
Mapping the DFSS tools to CDOV.

which the DFSS tools have been mapped.[7] Figure 9.9 depicts the CDOV process and shows how the major DFSS tools map to CDOV.

Notice the inclusion of critical parameter management (CPM) along the top of the figure. CPM is a crucial tool in the product developer's toolbox, and it begins when needs have been translated into system inputs and outputs. A major activity of CPM is to estimate the capability of the system's critical to function responses (CFRS) using C_{pk}, which is very much like C_p described in Chapters 6 and 8. The difference is that C_{pk} accounts for both average performance and variation while C_p only accounts for variation. Equation 9.1 shows the equation for C_p and C_{pk}. Notice the inclusion of the average in the equation for C_{pk}.

$$C_p = \frac{USL - LSL}{6\sigma_{short-term}}$$

$$C_{pk} = \min\left[\frac{USL - \bar{x}}{3\hat{\sigma}_{short-term}}, \frac{\bar{x} - LSL}{3\hat{\sigma}_{short-term}}\right]$$

(9.1)

x Also, note the inclusion of $\sigma_{short-term}$. C_{pk} and C_p both use estimates of variation measured under conditions of low variation called "short-term variation." Examples include measurements made using a single batch of material, over a short time frame, with no part-to-part variation or in a constant ambient environment. The result is a capability metric that is optimistic in that it estimates the processes' best performance. Note that, in this discussion, "process" refers to both manufacturing processes and to a product's functions.

P_p and P_{pk} differ from C_p and C_{pk} in that P_p and P_{pk} use estimates of variation measured under conditions of greater variation called "long-term variation." The equation is shown in Equation 9.2.

$$P_p = \frac{USL - LSL}{6\sigma_{long-term}}$$

$$P_p = \frac{USL - LSL}{6\sigma_{long-term}} \quad P_{pk} = \min\left[\frac{USL - \bar{x}}{3\hat{\sigma}_{long-term}}, \frac{\bar{x} - LSL}{3\hat{\sigma}_{long-term}}\right]$$

(9.2)

Note that the equations for P_p and P_{pk} and for C_p and C_{pk} are the same except for the conditions under which the estimates of variation are measured. P_p and P_{pk} are pessimistic but more realistic estimates of capability in that they estimate performance expected in the long run as material batches change, as part-to-part variation is introduced, and as ambient conditions change daily, weekly, monthly, or seasonally. C_p and C_{pk} are used to estimate how well the process can perform during short bursts of operation. P_p and P_{pk} are used to estimate how well the process performs over long periods of operation. We use C_p and C_{pk} to identify bursts of good performance and then determine what sources of variation are responsible for driving process performance away from the observed short-term capability.

The Capability Growth Index (CGI) is then used to roll up the capabilities of the underlying critical responses into a summary of overall capability called. The CGI is periodically reported, in bar graph form, by the development teams to the systems engineer and upper management. The CGI tracks the growth in capability, and therefore the robustness, of the developing product functions and the readiness of the development effort to enter its next stage. The equation for the CGI is shown in Equation 9.3.

$$CGI = \sum_i^n \left[\frac{100\%}{\text{number of CFRs}}\left(\frac{C_{pk_i}}{2}\right)\right]$$

(9.3)

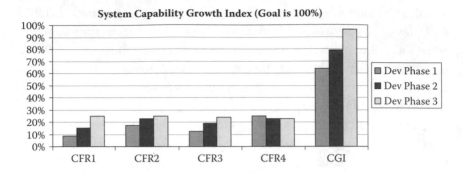

FIGURE 9.10
System Capability Growth Index (CGI).

Early in development, during the Concept stage of CDOV, few measureable quantities exist and the individual capabilities and CGI are both expected to be low (below 2). Later, during the Design stage, detailed design occurs and the CGI is expected to increase toward its target of 100 percent when measured under low-noise conditions.

Noise is then applied to stress the system. It is expected that the capabilities and CGI will decrease due to the sensitivity of the system to the noise. The techniques of robust design are then used to increase capability. Finally, at the end of the Optimize stage, the CGI is expected to once again increase toward its 100% when measured under noisy conditions.

Figure 9.10 is an example of a CGI bar graph where a subsystem of a product has four critical-to-function responses (CFRs), CFR_1, ..., CFR_4. CFR_1 might be the speed at which a memory device can be read. The CFRs were measured under low-noise conditions during the Concept stage (Dev Phase 1 in the figure), and the Design stage (Dev Phase 2) and under noisy conditions during the Optimize stage (Dev Phase 3 in the figure). We can see a steady growth in overall system capability as the development effort progresses. This continues until the product is fully designed and its CFRs, and therefore the CGI, have achieved their required levels.

9.3.2 Opportunities for Success or Failure of Product Development

In the context of product performance, a failure occurs when a CFR is outside its tolerance limits. The product in total may not have failed but the function producing the CFR has failed. If the process expecting the function is at a Six Sigma quality level ($C_{pk} = 2$), then the function will be performed incorrectly ~3.4 times per million opportunities. An opportunity for error exists every time the function is performed. For example, the function may be writing to memory in a computer. The process that carries out that function is primarily electrical and software related. Assume that the memory is written to every nanosecond (1×10^{-9} s). The function, therefore, is carried out 1,000,000,000 times per second. If this process performs at a Six Sigma level, then an incorrect write can occur ~3400 times per second. Obviously, computers perform this function well above a Six Sigma quality level.

We can relate C_{pk} to the expected functional failure rate in the same way we related Sigma level, failure rates, and yield in earlier chapters. Table 9.1 relates several capability levels to Sigma level and DPMO.

Now that we have considered a method to relate a product's functional performance to failure rates, it is time to consider the failures that the product development process itself can create.

Not producing its deliverables on time, on budget, and with the required quality are failures of this process. There are, however, many underlying reasons why one or all three of these failures might occur.

Quality might not be met if one or more critical parameters fail to meet their capability goals or if the product is missing a feature or function necessary to fulfill some stakeholder need. There are lagging quality failures such as the number of design changes after release to manufacturing or the number of design modifications installed during the product's first year in the field.

Budgetary failure includes poor cost estimation and control. Over- and underspending must be considered. It may seem that underspending is desirable while overspending is not, but this is not always true. For

TABLE 9.1

Relation of Sigma Level and DPMO

Sigma Level	Capability	Long-term DPMO
2	0.67	308,537
3	1	66,807
4	1.33	6,210
5	1.67	233
6	2	3.4

example, if a project is underspent, then the money was needlessly tied up and therefore unavailable for some other project.

Schedule failures include missing milestones, not having all the needed resources, or not having them when needed. Similar to variance to budget, it is not always best to be early. A deliverable produced too early runs the risk of needing rework or being scrapped if requirements change while it is waiting to be used. This is a precept of Lean: do things "just in time."

Usually, these types of failures are not independent. For example, it may be determined that to achieve on-time success we must reduce the product's feature set or increase the development budget.

If feature-set reduction is the compromise, then a multigenerational plan (MGP) should be created. A multigenerational plan is the result of conscious, data-based decision making as to what set of needs will be fulfilled in each version of the product and when each version will hit the market. This approach is far superior to attempting to develop a product that fulfills all the stakeholder needs but misses the market window.

Normalizing budgetary and scheduling failures to DPMO may not make sense, since for a particular company in a particular industry the development process will not be carried out millions of times.

An alternative approach is a metric that measures the process's predictability in terms of budget, schedule, and quality. CPM should be used to predict the product's functional quality. Budget and schedule predictability can be estimated using Monte Carlo simulation (MCS) of the project plan. MCS allows statements such as "We are 95% confident that the Concept stage will complete between June 5 and June 10," or "We are 80% confident that $100,000 will be spent on agency testing." Here is a simple example using MSProject and the software tool @Risk for Excel from Palisade Inc. A project manager is estimating the duration of the Concept stage of a CDOV-based product development effort. An MSProject plan was created for this portion of the development effort. The plan's major tasks are

- Analyze the stakeholder needs
- Translate the needs into product requirements
- Create/select the product's system-level concept
- Create/select the product's subsystem-level concepts

The key milestone in this portion of the plan is completion of the Concept stage, which occurs when these tasks have been completed. The typical approach to estimating this milestone is to obtain a single estimate of each task within the plan and determine the milestone's end date using the interim task estimates. The result is a single estimate of the milestone's end date. Estimates produced in this manner are usually wrong.

A more realistic approach is to use the program evaluation and review technique (PERT). PERT uses three estimates: optimistic, most likely, and pessimistic estimates of the duration of each interim task. The result is three end-date estimates — best case, most likely case, and worst case. A drawback of the PERT method is that we do not have an estimate of the likelihood of these three estimates.

The MCS method provides estimates of these likelihoods. MCS is similar to PERT in that it uses three estimates interim task duration. However, it goes one step further, thereby more realistically modeling the plan. MCS uses an assumed distribution of task durations. Figure 9.11 provides an example of the assumed distribution of the duration for the task of brainstorming potential concepts.

The distribution is assumed to be a skewed triangle. The tenth percentile duration is three days (most optimistic), ten days is the most likely duration, and the ninetieth percentile is twelve days (most pessimistic).

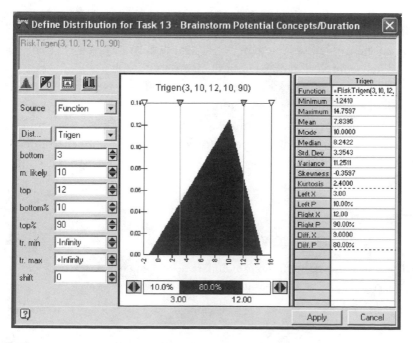

FIGURE 9.11
Assumed distribution for the duration of brainstorming potential concepts.

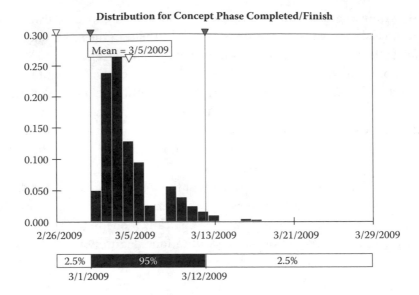

FIGURE 9.12
Ninety-five percent confidence interval for completion of the Concept phase using MCS.

Estimates of the duration of the other interim tasks were made in a similar manner. Using MCS, the result was calculated (Figure 9.12).

The simulation allows us to state that "We are 95% confident that the Concept phase will complete between March 1 and March 12, 2009." The most likely completion date is March 5, 2009.

MCS is not limited to estimating task duration. MCS can be applied to the plan's human resources and cost estimates. Those processes that simultaneously meet their confidence interval estimates for time and budget and meet their capability goals for product performance are deemed more predictable and therefore more desirable than those that do not.

9.4 INNOVATION: EVOLUTION

The Americans spent millions of dollars developing a pen that could write in zero gravity. The Russians gave their astronauts pencils.

Urban myth

Innovation is not a subsystem within the greater corporate system, it is the engine of growth required of all the subsystems. It is more like the mitochondria fuels in every cell within the body. The innovation engine can be revved up anywhere, at any time, by anyone. It can result in great leaps forward and significant competitive advantage or small, incremental improvements. Innovation should result in visibly cheaper, faster, more efficient, simpler, and cleverer ways to fulfill needs.

A member of a hotel's cleaning staff can be innovative in how he or she cleans a room for the next guest. An electrical engineer can design an innovative new electronic circuit. Members of the inbound marketing subsystem can innovate a new method to elicit the voice of the customer.

Innovation can occur spontaneously, a "Eureka!" moment, or through serendipitous discovery, a popularly held notion of how innovation occurs. The invention of the Post-it is a good example of this type of innovation.[8] In 1968, with no particular product in mind, Spencer F. Silver, a chemist at 3M, serendipitously discovered a "semi-glue." It was not until 1974 that Art Frey found a use for the glue as a removable bookmark, and not until 1980 — twelve years after the discovery of the glue — that the Post-it was launched in the United States. Despite these facts, the eureka version of the invention of the Post-it and its almost immediate market success survive. That it took twelve years from discovery to market for such a "low-tech" product is a clear indicator that a company should not base renewal of its product portfolio on this method of innovation. Yes, profits were huge, and a company should have some amount of this technology push method, but it is not a reliable or predictable way to generate top-line growth.

Innovation can and does occur methodically through the planned and disciplined use of a process and its tools. Two examples of methodical and planned innovation in the early stages of product development are described below.

During the early stages of product development, user needs must be analyzed and translated into product requirements, which then drive the creation and final selection of product concepts. Design for Six Sigma (DFSS) is a rigorous product development process and tool set that addresses these "fuzzy front-end" activities. Although it sounds counterintuitive, a rigorous process and tool set can encourage innovation.

In fact, DFSS, practiced properly, not only encourages but also requires innovation. For example, DFSS requires that the stakeholder needs be categorized against the Kano and NUD models. The Kano model categorizes needs into three types — basic, linear, and delighter (see Section 9.1.2 for a description of these needs). We must also categorize needs based on the difficulty we expect in fulfilling the needs, using the NUD model of new,

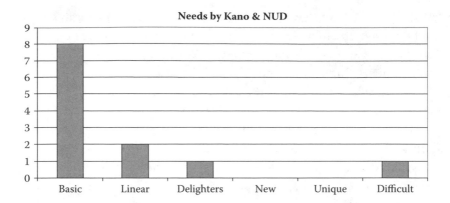

FIGURE 9.13
Tallied Kano and NUD categories.

unique, and difficult. These categories are not mutually exclusive and can be shown in a bar graph (see Figure 9.13). Analysis of this graph makes the need for innovation obvious.

Innovation is required to create the technology, used to fulfill the customer needs, but although this is necessary, it is not sufficient. The market considered in Figure 9.13 consists mainly of basic needs. If this is a new market in which there are few competitors and they are far behind in the required technology, then this is an opportunity to be first to market (F2M). F2M is a monumental advantage in terms of market share, return on investment, and iconic stature.[10]

Eventually, the company's competitors will gain the required technology. They may also identify some delighters, quickly take market share, and erode the F2M benefits that the first company has been enjoying. The technology must therefore also be innovative in its ability to block the competition from using the most robust and cost-effective technologies. This will further delay their entry into the market and compromise their cost competitiveness, even if they do identify delighters that allow them to "leapfrog" the competition.

The example above shows how the use of a methodical process can identify the need for innovation. In this example, it may be wise to postpone further product development until the competitor-restricting technology is developed. Alternatively, the effort might progress in the areas that do not require the technology. Here, the risk is that the technology may never arrive or that significant rework may be required, when it does arrive.

The nature of the innovation and how it comes about now resides within the technology development subsystem. This subsystem can use the I²DOV process for technology development, which itself contains tools that require innovation.

Another example of the DFSS process's need for innovation can be found during the concept creation and selection activities that occur during product development. DFSS prescribes the use of the Pugh process for concept selection.[11] The Pugh process is a method used to select the "all things considered best" concept to fulfill the product requirements. The Pugh process requires innovation in two key ways. First, the process requires several concepts to be compared to a datum or baseline concept. This forces the development team to create several concepts. Consideration of a single concept is not acceptable unless constraints are justifiably limiting and inherent risks have been assessed.

The Pugh Method requires a methodical and objective assessment of the pros and cons of each concept against a set of preselected criteria and a datum concept. The criteria are derived from internal and external stakeholder needs. As the Pugh process continues, the team members gain equal understanding of each concept. The pros and cons of each candidate concept are displayed for all to see together, at one time, and in one room or Webcast. The team must then attempt to synthesize a hybrid concept from the pros of each of the initial concepts studied.

The hybrid concept is usually far superior to any of the candidate concepts originally considered. The hybrid concept is also far less likely to emerge if the Pugh process had not been applied. The group and individual thinking applied to create the hybrid, even if unrealizable, can spark innovation that can eliminate a con in one of the initial concepts, making it the superior choice.

TRIZ ("trees"), an abbreviation from the Russian words for "the theory of inventive problem solving," is another major tool used during concept creation. TRIZ is a process specifically designed to identify the many ways in which physical conflicts have been solved. A common example of this conflict is that of strength and weight. Generally, strength is a "larger-the-better" requirement while weight is a "smaller-the-better" requirement. Generally, when you make something stronger, it becomes heavier. Thus, the conflict: to improve strength, we must degrade weight.

In this example, we would look up the conflict in a matrix that would contain solutions successfully applied in the past to the conflict. In this example, the matrix suggests changing from a uniform material to multiple materials or a composite material, or increasing the degree of fragmentation or segmentation. "Corrigation" is a common segmenting technique used to increase the strength of cardboard without substantially increasing its weight. Composite materials that have been engineered for increased strength and lighter weight are widely used in aviation.

We have seen two examples of how a disciplined process and tool set encourages and even requires innovation; now it is time to consider two common metrics of innovation: the rate of new product introduction and the number of patents, trade secrets, and records of inventions (ROIs) produced. These are sensible metrics, if applied properly. The rate of *successful* new product introduction is the more appropriate metric because the numbers of patents, trade secrets, and ROIs produced are only meaningful if they result in competitive advantage, and profit.

Finally, we must consider how innovation can "go wrong." First, it cannot occur at all. This is typical in corporations with an extreme focus on cost and end dates. While cost and end-date constraints are real and necessary. These pressures result in an approach to solving problems similar to the way they were solved in the past. Failure also occurs in corporations that follow processes that simply do not require innovation, as well as corporations that follow processes that require innovation but skip or "rationalize away" the required steps. This happens for a multitude of reasons, some good, and most bad.

Innovation can also "go wrong" when it produces results that do not benefit the company. At the beginning of this chapter, we said that innovation should result in visibly cheaper, faster, more efficient, simpler, and cleverer ways to fulfill need. Innovation resulting in patents, trade secrets, and records of invention that hang on the company's "Wall of Fame" are impressive, but they are of little value if they do not result in competitive advantage and profit.

One company allows its employees to spend 10% of their time on innovation. This can send an unintended message. For example, it can be interpreted as "I will only be innovative every Friday afternoon." It can be also be interpreted as "I have four hours to play in the lab to come up with something innovative." It discourages the idea that the potential to be innovative exists every minute of the day on every project.

As we have seen, these are not the best ways to drive innovation. Innovativeness is a response to unfulfilled needs and the need to get to "the next step." DFSS requires explicit identification of needs through a stakeholder analysis. DFSS itself is a process and, as its very name implies, a process is a series of connected "next steps." Methodology should constitute the majority of a company's approach to innovativeness, not "Eureka!" discoveries.

9.5 CORPORATE FUNCTIONS AND SIX SIGMA

These are just some of the areas often viewed as exempt from Six Sigma and quality improvements. As demonstrated, the application of Six Sigma to these areas allows leaders to drive the business results needed by providing better support to other subsystems in the organization.

There is a benefit to looking at things with a fresh perspective. There is a story we heard once about a gathering of people, including various experts, looking at an eighteen-wheeler that had become jammed under a highway overpass. The engineers were discussing how to raise the overpass so the truck could be removed. Others were discussing how to dismantle the truck to remove it. A little girl at the scene, who we imagine was at eye-level with the truck tires, said, "Daddy, why don't they just let the air out of the tires?" We often think of this story as experts explain how hard it is to do something, and we want to challenge them to look at things with a fresh perspective and to ask creative thinkers from other areas to work with them to solve a problem. This approach yields the best results, as the outside observer can clearly see overlooked problems. Ask yourself if the same is true of the overlooked organizations and processes in your corporation.

NOTES

1. "Cataract Surgery in Antiquity," *The Foundation of the American Academy of Ophthalmology, Ophthalmic Heritage and Museum of Vision*, http://www.faao.org/what/heritage/exhibits/online/cataract/antiquity.cfm (retrieved April 29, 2009).
2. Jiro Kawakita, a Japanese anthropologist, devised a method for extracting information from large amounts of seemingly unrelated non-numeric data found at an archeological site.

3. David Garvin David, *Managing Quality: The Strategic and Competitive Edge* (Tampa: Free Press, 1988).

4. Noriaki Kano, a professor at Tokyo University of Science in the late 1970s, created a two-dimensional view of quality.

5. Clyde M. Creveling, Jeff Slutsky, and Dave Antis, *Design for Six Sigma* (Upper Saddle River, NJ: Prentice Hall, 2003), 352.

6. Creveling, Slutsky, and Antis, *Design for Six Sigma*, 71.

7. Creveling, Slutsky, and Antis, *Design for Six Sigma*, 111.

8. Bethany Halford, Sticky Notes, *Chemical and Engineering News* 82, no. 14 (April 5, 2004): 64.

9. Creveling, Slutsky, and Antis, *Design for Six Sigma*, 352.

10. M. L. George, J. Works, K. Watson-Hemphill, and C. M. Christensen, *Fast Innovation* (New York: McGraw-Hill, 2004), 18.

11. Creveling, Slutsky, and Antis, *Design for Six Sigma*, 399.

10

Sensory Systems: The Critical Role of Information Technology and Human Resources

> I think it's fair to say that personal computers have become the most empowering tool we've ever created. They're tools of communication, they're tools of creativity, and they can be shaped by their user.
>
> **Bill Gates**
> *Founder of Microsoft*

The nervous system in the human body is an important function as it regulates and manages the information coming into the body. This information can arrive as visual cues through the eyes, as auditory signals through the ears, as touch through the skin, as olfaction or smell through the nose, and as taste through the tongue. This information can be pleasant, repugnant, or not noticeable. The amount of signals coming at the human body can be too little, leading to lethargy and stagnation of the brain or failure to develop properly, or it can be too much at once, overwhelming the system and causing undesired reactions. The nervous system needs to balance the signals it is receiving from all the regions of the body, process those signals, and react to it in the correct manner to ensure the well-being of the body. The role that Information Technology (IT) and Human Resources (HR) play in the corporation is to ensure that all areas are receiving the correct information at the right time in a manner that is understandable, allowing for proper reaction.

If you take the example further, think of what occurs when people are exposed to flashing lights. The stimulus creates varying reactions from an adrenaline rush and perhaps a desire to dance, to annoyance, and even to seizures. It depends on how the nervous system interprets and reacts to the situation. When the system is not working properly or when the system has an underlying condition, seizures — or in some rare cases, death — can occur. This is the same for the corporation. Some systems are able to process the information, and others react poorly to it. It is the role of IT and HR to ensure that everything is done to balance this out, and to ensure that unnecessary stimulus is blocked. When information is properly managed, it has people "dancing" to the rhythm; if not, it shuts people down. This chapter describes the role of both of these important functions in the corporation.

10.1 IT SIGMA: THE NERVOUS SYSTEM

IT's contribution to Corporate Sigma should be viewed from a systems perspective, which requires you to view the processes of the business and their resulting behaviors as a whole and not in the context of isolated parts. A change in one part of the system could have a dramatic impact on the rest of the system. Change can be good or bad.

With its portfolio of solutions and services, IT is uniquely positioned within an enterprise to provide a holistic view of the enterprise's system of business processes, collectively referred to as the business process system (BPS). IT can function as the nervous system of the BPS by helping to manage basic requirements of a BPS, including process interfaces among BPS functions such as finance, marketing, engineering, manufacturing, and so forth.

In this section, we

- Explore the role of IT in a Corporate Sigma environment
- Examine the characteristics of an IT Sigma organization and its relationship to an enterprise BPS
- Explain how the intersections of IT model-based assessments, Lean Six Sigma, and project portfolio management can empower an operationally efficient and effective BPS
- Offer suggestions and tools for transforming your IT organization into a fully functioning nervous system, a system that contributes to the health and maintenance of a BPS that adds value to product and service realization

10.1.1 Management Commitment to IT Sigma

Executive management must understand and believe that the application of Corporate Sigma in the IT organization, or IT Sigma, will produce a better BPS. The company's leadership team and IT must work together to

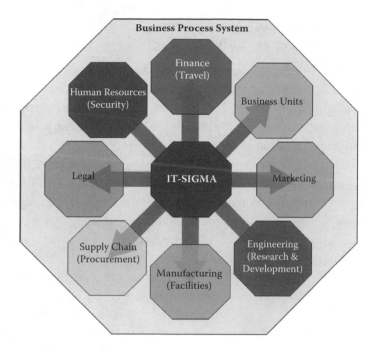

FIGURE 10.1
Business Process System (BPS) Functions.

establish and advance the IT Sigma agenda. IT Sigma has a value proposition of operational efficiency; it can turn lousy business processes into good processes that empower an operationally efficient BPS. IT, in turn, brings an operational efficiency value proposition to the BPS.

Figure 10.1 shows a BPS functional context diagram. In most organizations, IT maintains a portfolio of services and solutions in support of each function. Value-added IT portfolios are aligned with measurable goals and objectives (or the imperatives) of the enterprise itself. This alignment helps preclude, to some degree, the creation and maintenance of IT solutions that promote silo-based, self-optimizing functions at the expense of other BPS functions. Stove-piped (or siloed) capabilities tend to decouple efficient interface processes and create queues that can undermine the health of a BPS.

In an ideal IT Sigma environment, the IT organization functions as the nervous system supporting the overall BPS. It provides the leadership team with mechanisms to monitor and control BPS parts and supplies hard and soft data about the health of BPS processes. IT Sigma fosters a collaborative BPS environment by supporting the reception, storage, and transmission of information about business processes. Data-centric collaboration promotes fact-based decision making by BPS stakeholders.

10.1.2 IT Sigma Quality Management and Improvement Methodology

IT Sigma is a breakthrough quality management and improvement methodology that delivers value to both the IT organization and to the BPS. IT Sigma strategically orients the IT organization; it provides a methodology for selecting, prioritizing, and executing IT improvement projects supporting BPS optimization.

Breakthrough IT Sigma programs require knowledge of the enterprise's business imperatives and how IT Sigma seeks congruence with the imperatives. Along with this linkage, IT must understand its own strengths and weaknesses and its inherent capacity to carry out an IT Sigma agenda. Hence, the implementation of IT Sigma starts with a comprehensive assessment of the IT organization.

Table 10.1 provides a high-level synopsis of process frameworks that can be used to assess IT business environments. OPM3, CMMI, ITIL, and the APQC Process Classification Framework (PCF) are business excellence models that describe best practice requirements for core business and support processes.[1] IT Sigma stands independent of these models; the methodology can be used to improve the performance of planned BPS processes or ones that have already been introduced by the models.

When selecting a model for an IT assessment, consider the following when evaluating the fit of the model in meeting your organization's needs:

- The enterprise's business imperatives
- The current overall process context of the enterprise
- The process context of distinct BPS functions
- How these process contexts were created and maintained
- The potential return on investment from introducing the model based on the resource capabilities of the enterprise and the resulting value of the improvement efforts

A thorough assessment of IT capabilities, both inside and outside IT's organizational boundaries, can be instrumental in advancing the IT Sigma agenda. It can provide useful information about the haves and have-nots of IT best practices and how those practices, or absence of practices, allow or disallow a healthy BPS.

Assessments should not just focus on reports of best practice haves and have-nots. Key outputs of IT Sigma assessments should include generations of BPS functional decomposition and business systems context diagrams.

TABLE 10.1

Process Improvement Frameworks

	OPM3® (Project Management Institute)	CMMI® (Software Engineering Institute)	ITIL® (United Kingdom – Office of Government Commerce)	Process Classification Framework℠ (APQC)
Format	Model-Based	Model-Based	Model-Based	Model-Based
Appraisal Method	Assessment	Appraisal	Certification	Benchmark
Measurement	Maturity Continuum	Maturity/Capability Levels	Qualification Levels	Enterprise Level Categories
Implementation Guidance	Implementation Guidance	Institutionalization and Implementation Guidance	Implementation Guidance	Implementation Guidance
Application	Project Management	Product Development	IT Service Management	Enterprise

These diagrams serve as master blueprints for the IT nervous system. They help to identify the scope of the IT Sigma agenda and focus attention on important cross-functional issues. They should show areas of manual and process automation, trouble spots, and road maps for planned improvements. The diagrams can serve as source documents for the creation and maintenance of product and service realization value streams, which are basic constructs of Lean Six Sigma projects.

In the spirit of continuous improvement, the IT Sigma organization should strive to generate a balanced assessment program to provide timely and understandable information about IT processes and how they deliver value to the BPS. A nervous system itself must be strong to service the body. Symptoms of weakness should be identified and treated. Assessments of existing and planned introductions of new IT practices help identify weaknesses that can be fed forward into near- and long-term improvement opportunities. The improvements can then be prioritized to accelerate process efficiencies to BPS stakeholders when and where they are needed most.

10.1.3 IT Sigma Business Case

The IT Sigma business case must clearly demonstrate that the methodology can successfully support the achievement of business imperatives and prove that IT Sigma is doable from a resource perspective. Table 10.2 describes four typical areas of concern and the responses to overcome them and to help leadership understand and accept the IT Sigma initiatives.

TABLE 10.2

IT Sigma Business Case

Concern	Response
Alignment: "Don't we already have a quality management system?"	IT Sigma should be congruent with key BPS objectives and facilitate the optimization of core and support processes associated with the BPS product- and service-realization value streams. This linkage should be specific, explicit, and measurable. IT Sigma should be viewed as complementary and not competing with other quality and process improvement initiatives. IT Sigma should be used to make processes implemented by other initiatives more efficient and effective.
Governance: "Did Manufacturing review this Engineering process change?"	IT Sigma governance should include a BPS steering team (perhaps a subset of the leadership team) consisting of cross-functional BPS stakeholders. The BPS steering team steers (does not row) IT Sigma's role in BPS improvements. Decisions do not simply "come down from above" to BPS stakeholders; they are considered and balanced when resolving project portfolio priorities and issues.
Resources: "There are too many Six Sigma projects and not enough people to support them."	IT Sigma management should include an IT Sigma portfolio management team. This team is a highly visible, communicative, and collaborative group that uses best practices associated with portfolio management. The portfolio management team "rows" with the IT Sigma improvement teams and provides advice to the steering team. It works with improvement teams to ensure that the teams work seamlessly within the IT organization itself and among its IT BPS partners.
Communications: "I have never heard of IT Sigma."	IT Sigma communications should occur regularly and openly. Communicate the value of IT Sigma services and deliverables through written documents, presentations, marketing materials, and so forth. Never fail to announce the benefits of the initiative and be prepared to repeat basic messages of understanding. Trumpet the accomplishments of high-interest, cross-functional projects and initial projects seeding the IT Sigma methodology in a business function not previously scoped to the initiative. Develop a communications plan that includes message content, audience, medium, and frequency.

It is important to get leadership buy-in to the idea and purpose of an IT Sigma initiative. If you do not get leadership's buy-in, key BPS stakeholders may resist the effort. Other stakeholders may feel left out. A good way to garner support for IT Sigma is to involve the stakeholders in the early planning stages. This process helps to identify IT Sigma cheerleaders and naysayers. A balanced business case is a powerful planning device when inclusive of different voices and interests when scoping the IT Sigma initiative.

10.1.4 IT Sigma Project Selection

Once the leadership team approves the IT Sigma business case, selecting and prioritizing projects and resourcing those projects take top billing. Identifying and prioritizing IT Sigma projects should follow a structured process.

This process should be led by the IT Sigma portfolio management team because control and management of IT development and improvement projects demand an understanding of project portfolio management practices and principles. Today's rapidly changing, increasingly complex IT environments demand more than ever that quality time be dedicated to IT portfolio management. IT technologies are becoming increasingly pervasive, complex, and cross-functional. Effective portfolio management allows you to consolidate competing project ideas into an enterprise-wide initiative.

The following steps provide a list of activities that could be performed when selecting improvement projects.

10.1.4.1 Step 1: BPS Process Identification

Perform a systems look of the BPS, including the development of a master BPS product- and/or service-realization value stream (see the BPS systems context diagram in Figure 10.1). Examine how IT interacts with BPS functions and how the BPS functions interact with each other. Determine areas of process strengths and weaknesses. Compare the areas of strengths and weaknesses with the business imperatives of the organization to identify and record potential IT Sigma improvement targets.

10.1.4.2 Step 2: BPS Process Relationships

Perform a process interface look of the BPS, including the development of functional and cross-functional process relationship maps. Identify the core business processes and their issues. Determine the input and output relationships among the core processes, and evaluate the effectiveness of the process interfaces to deliver value to the BPS customer. Create a quantitative understanding of the business process by developing as-is and drafting to-be process maps, identifying process cycle times, work queues, and other areas of waste.

10.1.4.3 Step 3: IT Sigma Project Selection

Perform a focused process look of the BPS, including a project assessment. Establish the process boundaries associated with the core business process issues. Develop preliminary project purposes, goals, assumptions, constraints, deliverables, and projected benefits. Employ a structured project selection methodology (for example, cost-benefit analysis, net present value, payback period). Select the IT Sigma Project from this methodology.

As discussed, the IT Sigma portfolio management team should play a crucial role in the development of the IT Sigma business case and in the selection and prioritization of improvement projects. The team should continuously help monitor and control IT's value-added contribution to the BPS, including IT-related BPS investments and return on investment calculations. The team evaluates the IT Sigma project portfolio, balances the portfolio, and makes recommendations to the leadership team regarding the maintenance and improvement of the portfolio projects.

To energize and sustain the initiative, a comprehensive business case will identify the resource requirements, both human and equipment. Along with steering and portfolio management teams, distinct improvement projects should include, at minimum, qualified project managers, Lean Six Sigma Green or Black Belts, and targeted users of the new or modified system and/or process. If the process is to be seeded in another BPS function, a stakeholder from that function should be included on the project team. While performing a project assessment in Step 3, stakeholder analysis and project team selection are crucial activities. By virtue of their communicative behaviors, project team members function as IT Sigma neurons processing and transmitting the "goodness" of the initiative among BPS functions.

Some projects may be categorized as "go do it" or "low-hanging fruit" projects because they are commonsense projects and do not require the rigor described above. The above steps may need some degree of tailoring to ensure achievement of other projects' objectives. Nevertheless, they should still be tracked as part of the overall IT Sigma project portfolio because they may serve as building blocks to future projects and/or may quickly generate a sense of interest in the IT Sigma initiative.

10.1.5 IT Sigma Project Execution

The fundamental objective of the Lean Six Sigma methodology is the implementation of a measurement-based strategy that focuses on process improvement. Lean processes focus on the reduction of seven common wastes (transportation, inventory, motion, waiting, overproduction, processing, and defects) to improve product or service value in the eyes of the customer. The elimination of waste and queues increases productivity, reduces costs, and improves profits. That alone could be a leadership eye-catcher given today's economic challenges.

In addition, the Lean Six Sigma methodology is a natural fit for IT Sigma because of its customer-centric approach to resolving BPS problems. IT Sigma, with its reach throughout the enterprise, can serve as a centerpiece for excellence in project, program, and portfolio management, and in project execution. The IT Sigma approach allows the IT team to engage BPS functional customers in motivational efficiency, productivity, and innovative BPS gains. Engaging the users of a process in the development of that process can engineer user excitement and promote greater understanding and customer acceptance of the change initiative.

10.1.6 IT Sigma Playbook

A Six Sigma playbook is a good way to engage employees in IT Sigma and to ensure that optimal project management processes are followed. Playbooks can be used to help manage the project portfolio and to launch, direct, monitor, control, and close IT Sigma projects. They are tools that provide tactical guidance to projects. They record a project's essential information, and outline decision gates and options, and recommend activities and tools for those gates. They also serve to record project decisions, results of project activities, and the capabilities and assets to support those activities.

IT Sigma playbooks should be living documents which are regularly updated, and, at minimum, include the following work areas: Playbook Instructions, Project Charter, Method Area (for example, DMAIC), Milestone Schedule, Metrics, Risks/Issues/Action Items, and a Parking Lot for ideas or thoughts to be transferred to another group or worked by the team at a later date. A simple Microsoft Excel spreadsheet with seven workbooks can easily provide these partitions.

Table 10.3 is an example of a Method Work Area for DMAIC. Along with the completion of the project charter, the IT Sigma project team

TABLE 10.3

DMAIC Method Work Area

DEFINE Activities	MEASURE Activities	ANALYSE Activities	IMPROVE Activities	CONTROL Activities
Identify Problem	Identify Key Input, Process, and Output Metrics	Propose Critical Xs	Develop Potential Solutions	Develop SOP's, Training Plan & Process Control System
Complete Charter	Develop Operational Definitions	Prioritize Critical Xs	Develop Evaluation Criteria & Select Best Solutions	Implement Process Changes & Controls
Develop SIPOC Map	Develop Data Collection Plan	Conduct Root Cause Analysis on Critical Xs	Evaluate Solution for Risk	Monitor & Stabilize Process
Map Business Process	Validate Measurement System	Validate Critical Xs	Optimize Solution	Transition Project to Process Owner
Map Value Stream	Collect Baseline Data	Estimate the Impact of each X on Y	Develop "To-Be" Process Map	Identify Project Replication Opportunities
Gather Voice of the Customer & Business	Determine Process Capability	Quantify the Opportunity	Develop High-level Implementation Plan	Calculate Financial Benefits
Develop CCRs and CBRs	Validate Business Opportunity	Prioritize Root Causes	Develop Pilot Plan and Pilot Solution	
Finalize				

Tools	Tools	Tools	Tools	Tools
Project Selection Tools	Operational Definition	Pareto Chart	Brainstorming, Affinity	Check Sheets
Value Stream Map	Data Collection Plan	C&E Matrix	Benchmarking	Standard Operating Procedures (SOP's)
Financial Analysis (NPV, IRR, Cash Flows)	Pareto Chart	Fishbone Diagram	Process Improvement Techniques	Training Plan
Project Charter	Histogram	Brainstorming	Line Balancing	Communication Plan
Multi-Generation Plan	Box Plot	Detailed "As-Is" Process Map	Process Flow Improvement	Implementation Plan
Communication Plan	Statistical Sampling	Basic Statistical Tools	Constraint Identification	Visual Process Control
SIPOC Map	Measurement System Analysis (Gage R&R)	Supply Chain Accelerator Analysis	Replenishment Pull	Mistake-Proofing
High-Level Process Map	Setup Reduction	Non-Value Added Analysis	Sales & Operations Planning	Process Control Plans
Non-Value Added Analysis	Generic Pull (WIP Cap)	Hypothesis Testing	Poka-Yoke	Project Commissioning
VOC and Kano Analysis	Kaizen	Confidence Intervals	FMEA	Project Replication
QFD	Control Charts	FMEA	Solution Selection Matrix	Plan-Do-Check-Act Cycle
RACI Chart/Stakeholder Matrix	Process Capability, C_p & C_{pk}	Simple & Multiple Regression	"To-Be" Process Map	Project Lessons Learned
		ANOVA	Piloting & Simulation	Project Summary Briefing

selects activities it wants to perform by the DMAIC phase and the tools to support those activities. Projected completion dates of the activities can be added to a milestone schedule in a separate workbook. Metrics are collected and analyzed while the activities are executed and improvement ideas are generated from the analytical results. Action items and issues are maintained in the playbook, as are ideas or thoughts about future projects. Additional workbooks could be added to record the raw data associated with the activities and their subordinate tools.

Although operational and tactical in nature, Six Sigma project playbooks have strategic implications, especially when the projects are viewed in aggregate and oriented toward BPS solutions and business imperatives. One way to accomplish the aggregate view is to dashboard the portfolio as shown in Figure 10.2. The dashboard is a visual status of all open and closed projects.

The dashboard contains high-level summaries about the IT Sigma project portfolio. Essential elements can be extracted from the playbooks to populate the dashboard. The dashboard helps the IT Sigma and leadership teams monitor IT Sigma program performance and determine if performance improvement goals are being met. It also helps to communicate IT Sigma strategy, monitor and adjust that strategy, and communicate the benefits of IT Sigma involvement to all BPS stakeholders.

The IT organization is in the optimal position to function as a nervous system in support of an enterprise BPS. The BPS is a system, complete with formal and informal processes. A change in process in one part of the system, whether good or bad, can have a dramatic impact on the other parts of the system. It can render the BPS inefficient and ineffective.

IT Sigma engages the BPS with a structured, meaningful approach toward process improvement. It allows the IT organization to serve as a powerful, influential enterprise change agent. It provides leadership with information about the health of BPS processes. Just as a nervous system disease is cured by medicines assimilated by the body, IT Sigma provides medicinal benefits to BPS inefficiencies. IT Sigma is a quality management and improvement methodology that efficiently and effectively links and records the achievement of business imperatives through breakthroughs in BPS performance.

IT-Sigma Dashboard

Project name	Sponsor	Business Improvement	Affected Functions	D	M	A	I	C	Process Capability Baseline	Current Process Capability	Projected Process Capability	Cost Avoidance Opportunity	Work Code	Work Code Labor Cost	Total Cost Avoidance
Name #1															
Name #2															
Name #3															
					Complete										
					Current Effort										
					Limited Effort										
												$			$

ROI% = (Total Cost Avoidance − Labor Cost)/Labor Cost

Project Status (Activities Coded Yellow Require Status Statement)

Project Name #2 Conducted pilot training event on revised process

Project #3 Approved Initial Process Capability Baseline

FIGURE 10.2
IT Sigma Dashboard.

Notes: *Project Name:* Intuitive description of the project.

Sponsor: The actual name or the sponsoring team's name.

Business Imperative: Identifies relationship between the project and its business reason.

Affected Functions: Identifies the functional customers to benefit from the improvement.

DMAIC: Shown in figure in shaded areas; however, they are generally color colored to indicate status of improvement project by gate. The color green indicates that the gate is completed. The color yellow indicates that the gate is still open and in progress. The color red indicates that the gate is behind schedule.

Process Capability Baseline: Management approved process capability baseline.

Current Process Capability Baseline: Changes to the baseline resulting from improvements introduced as the project progresses.

Projected Process Capability: Projected process capability baseline at the completion of the project.

Cost Avoidance Opportunity: Projected savings at the completion of the project (may include savings).

Work Code: Self-explanatory (used to help calculate Return on Investment).

Work Code Labor Cost: Actual cost of labor as determined by the Work Code.

Total Cost Avoidance: Total benefits ($$$) realized at project completion or as the project progresses.

FIGURE 10.2
(Continued)

10.2 HR SIGMA: THE FIVE SENSES

Over the past decade, the role of Human Resources (HR) has increasingly emerged as that of a business partner and organizational strategist. Although the Human Resources Department is not typically large in terms of its headcount, its impact on the organization can be tremendous.

The purpose of Human Resources is to ensure that employees are utilized and deployed to meet organizational objectives and goals and that regulatory compliance of the organization to state and federal laws is met. To achieve this, HR must act as the corporation's five senses, not just the "eyes and ears" to ensure compliance to laws and policy but also by being sensitive to changes and picking up anything that may affect the corporation. HR must be tuned into the operations of the corporation using all senses available to them to detect any changes, problems, or opportunities. Just as humans need to adapt to changing climates, resource availability, illness, and growth opportunities, the corporation needs to be aware of both external and internal changes, and HR should be a key part of this process. HR should be the corporation's "early warning system" to enable flexibility and adaptation.

To do this, HR must link to three areas: strategic, operational, and administrative. HR provides a common thread running through the strategic and operational levels, where it is the organization's agent of change, and through the administrative functions, where it supports the performance of the organization. Six Sigma provides a framework for HR to communicate in a common business terminology throughout the corporation and to become a change agent that indeed affects the entire organization.

10.2.1 Strategic Planning

At the strategic level, HR has to ensure a good return on investment on human capital, which includes benefits, training, personal protective equipment (PPE), and so on. This implies that HR should participate in strategic planning efforts at the highest level of the corporation to ensure that projects are aligned with corporate initiatives and goals, develop and provide "metrics that matter" to support the company's strategic plan, and ensure that value-added factors are being reported and their effect on the business clarified. Often the first question any organization should ask is,

"How do we know that we are successful?" The answer will help define metrics that matter, and from there improvement opportunities for Six Sigma projects will become obvious.

Potential metrics of strategic planning include

- Return on investment
- Compliance of the workforce planning process with federal, state, and local laws (usually defined by law)
  - OSHA regulations (lost time)
  - HIPPA regulations (data privacy, integrity)
- Reporting structures in place and defined

10.2.2 Operations

On the operational level, HR must support leadership and departmental activities, provide feedback and information for analysis, ensure that effective and efficient systems are in place, address gaps in performance and policy, and act as an agent not only for the organization but for employees as well. For example, a successful HR program will balance the organization's financial needs while attracting and retaining the right talent at the right cost to the company at the right time in the company's maturity cycle. Unlike other forms of static capital, the variability of human capital makes it the most difficult to control and manage; it also presents the greatest realm of opportunity for an organization.

Potential operations metrics include

- Workforce planning, development, and retention
  - Recruitment time from requisition to hiring
  - Recruitment/retention costs
  - Skill set and minority/women hiring and percent of workforce goals met
  - Retention rates for key skill sets
  - On-board training time from hiring to fully utilized
  - Satisfaction management of new hires
  - Training/retraining effectiveness
- Rewards and recognition
  - Succession planning effectiveness
  - Employee satisfaction with total rewards system
  - Consistent and effective compensation policies and practices

- Benchmark salary structures, pay ranges, job grades, and salaries both internally and externally for equity
- Compensation and benefits administration
- Employee/labor relations
  - Skill set and minority/women hiring and percent of workforce goals met
  - Organizational demographics
  - Communication effectiveness
  - Performance review effectiveness
  - Employee satisfaction
  - Conflict/discipline effectiveness
  - Customer/internal client satisfaction with department and individuals
- Workplace health, safety, and security
  - Absenteeism and sickness rates
  - Safety and environmental audit results
  - Evacuation drills
- Workplace security (conflict rates, discipline rates, and theft rates)

10.2.3 Administrative

The administration of policies through consistent, predictable processes gives organizations the ability to achieve and maintain success. People need to know how the workplace functions and interacts, what the acceptable culture is, and how to push for change when problems arise. The last step of a Six Sigma project is "control." In HR, that means consistent processes as well as measures to ensure the processes remain in control.

Potential administrative metrics include

- Payroll errors DPMO (such as payment to terminated employees, overpayment to current employees, benefit deduction mistakes)
- Hit rate of the careers section of the company's Web site
- Timely performance reviews
- Training timeliness and effectiveness vs. cost
- Health, Safety, and Environment (HSE) compliance
- Time spent on administrative processes, with the goal of reduction

In the Six Sigma methodology, perfection is the absence of defects and the goal is to reduce defects that are important to the customer. In HR terms, customers include internal clients of the supported department.

Improving what the customer sees as "defects" and improving internal cost provides HR the opportunity to improve its management practices.

On the administrative level, Human Resources can find ways to improve efficiency and customer satisfaction in the actual performance of the department itself. Here, opportunities abound to implement Lean into processes to gain efficiencies, improve accuracy and, as a result, shift limited HR resources from administrative tasks to value-added activities.

Core Human Resource functions (rather than the perfunctory areas of responsibility often followed by Human Resource professionals) should include actions, such as those outlined above, that will significantly influence the growth and profitability of the company as well as take care of the welfare and morale of employees.

On any of the levels described, Human Resources is no different than any other area of a company in being able to deliver Six Sigma projects with significant financial impact. Projects are directed toward either Human Resource's own customers and colleagues (the business units they support) by providing its services faster, more efficiently, and more accurately, or toward the enterprise's external customers by HR's initiative and influence in driving and sustaining business results through the implementation of Six Sigma. When external customers are discontented, it is typically because one of the organization's internal processes is not functioning properly.

When you are "forced" to examine critically what you are doing and why you are doing it, you have the opportunity to step back and see if your current processes are

- Creating waste, including a waste of time
- Too administratively cumbersome and, as a result, creating a high chance of errors and inefficiency or contain redundant steps that, if changed, would reduce cycle times
- Obsolete, although new technology was available to relieve the administrative burden

Simply put, Human Resources must think and act more systematically and operationally.

Finally, Six Sigma is all about people and their influence on business outcomes. It is a philosophy, a metric, and a process. As such, it is a perfect match to Human Resources. The success of corporations and implementation of Six Sigma is not possible without the full embrace from top management to the floor. However, introducing Six Sigma is often met with fear either of losing people through better processes or simply of change and the resulting discomfort. It is here that HR's understanding of change and the resistance to it puts them in a position to influence the decision to deploy Six Sigma projects and support its successful implementation. HR professionals need to accept that this deployment not only applies to the organizations they support but also to their own internal processes.

The complexity of human capital has always been difficult to measure. Many of the metrics are viewed as "soft" or subjective and the difficulty relating the results to the bottom line call into question the accuracy of the measure. As Six Sigma initiatives are results oriented, working on critical process problems, they can aid in making that often-elusive connection. Six Sigma gives HR simple tools with which to translate company needs into metrics, hence contributing to the bottom line. Often, the HR metrics are those that measure the efficiency of the department (that is, reduction in time and cost to hire an employee without sacrificing quality).

Although many measures provide a good gauge for HR's own internal audit purposes, in order to link HR to corporate strategy, it is important to distinguish which metrics truly represent an added value to the organization. Workers' compensation and turnover are both areas of high cost to the enterprise and present impactful opportunities for HR. On the highest level, one can make the argument that Human Resource systems ultimately affect sales and EBITA (earnings before interest, tax, and amortization) and measure metrics such as revenue per employee.

Just as the nervous system links the systems of the human body to keep everything in sync, HR and IT play critical roles in linking a corporation's three key areas: strategic, operational, and administrative. Nervous systems are constantly at work to ensure that information is flowing so that decisions can be made. Just as the nervous system alerts the body about everything ranging from feeling cold (so put on a jacket) to hunger pains and light-headedness (eat something) to allowing you to assess whether an approaching person is friend or foe (greet or flee), the linkages in the corporation allow the system to make decisions about what is needed. If the information is moving correctly and the other systems are healthy, correct responses are achieved. This includes everything from alerting the system that inventory is low (order more parts) to "Department X is experiencing a jump in its absentee rate" (investigate reasons) to reviewing multiple product proposals to determine which fits the company strategy.

Not only are IT and HR critical to keeping information flowing, they also need to sound the warning if the system is not working. IT and HR need to move past simply being the "compliance officers" — the eyes and ears of the corporation — and develop the other senses needed to receive signals about other types of threats (internal or external) and develop new systems to meet new needs for the corporation. For example, is information accessible and meaningful to the user? Are employee satisfaction surveys being acted upon and is progress being communicated back to the employees? Just as the brain has learned to "flip" the image from the retina of the eye to be meaningful to the human brain, IT and HR need to ensure that the data received by management and employees can be interpreted and acted upon. Properly functioning HR and IT departments need to take a holistic approach and ensure that the corporate system encourages this type of information flow, or the system will fail.

NOTES

1. OPM3 is the Organizational Project Management Maturity Model. OPM3 is a registered trademark of the Project Management Institute. CMMI is the Capability Maturity Model Integration. CMMI is a registered trademark of Carnegie Mellon University. ITIL is a registered trademark of the Office of Government Commerce in the United Kingdom and other countries. APQC's Process Classification Framework (PCF) was developed by APQC and member companies as an open standard to facilitate improvement through process management and benchmarking regardless of industry, size, or geography. The PCF organizes operating and management processes into twelve enterprise-level categories, including process groups and over 1500 processes and associated activities. The PCF and associated measures and benchmarking surveys are available for download and completion at no charge at http://www.apqc.org/OSBCdatabase.

11

Corporate Wellness: The Physical

Without change, there is no innovation, creativity, or incentive for improvement. Those who initiate change will have a better opportunity to manage the inevitable change.

William Pollard
Chairman, The ServiceMaster Company

To stay healthy, people visit their doctors for regular physicals. This allows them to monitor and assess the function of vital organs and systems to ensure health and to identify any problems early on when intervention is easier. During a routine physical, the doctor discusses the patient's concerns and checks blood pressure, temperature, heart rate, responsiveness, and other basic vital signs. If, after these checks, any body functions are of concern, the physician recommends additional tests and an appropriate treatment. Regular physical checkups are necessary to evaluate wellness, and physicians view this as one of the most important steps we can take to ensure our health. Wellness is generally defined as achieving a balance between mind and body, or internal and external environments, which leads to a heightened state and feeling of peace. From the perspective of alternative medicine, wellness means much more than being disease free; it is a conscious choice to pursue a healthy lifestyle and balance of mind, body, and spirit.

The same is true for a corporation. In order for the corporation to be healthy, it needs to evaluate its wellness through constant assessment and monitoring of its vital functions. Review of profit and loss, customer satisfaction, employee satisfaction, and other metrics are common vitals that corporations need to check. If a department is not functioning well, an appropriate action should be executed to resolve the issue.

Evaluating corporate wellness is not an easy task. It is usually an ongoing and continuous struggle for most organizations. In this chapter, we use a holistic method of systems engineering to assess, monitor, and diagnose the overall corporate health in order to achieve business excellence. Once diagnosed, implementing a new method is not easy. It involves new attitudes and a new way of thinking. Note, too, that — like an exercise regimen — the process described in this chapter must be tailored to the needs of your specific organizational structure.

11.1 THE CORPORATE CAT SCAN

The term "computed axial tomography" (CAT) scan is a medical imaging procedure that uses x-ray and digital computer technology to create detailed two- or three-dimensional images. The CAT scan can "photograph" every type of body structure at once, including bone, blood vessels, and soft tissue. It assesses the body part's structure and shape along with the subsystems that make up the body part, and helps in the diagnosis of diseases, traumas, or injuries.

Just as a medical scan evaluates many items at the same time to find problems, the corporate CAT scan diagnoses problems in each department or subsystem by assessing the performance of the department and identifying improvement opportunities. The performance of the corporate business units or departments will determine the overall corporate performance or wellness.

Before we can begin scanning and interpreting data, we first need to understand the basic structure of the organization. Just as medical students first must study how the human body is "put together," we must first think about how the corporation and its goals are put together in order to develop a credible diagnosis of the organization.

The corporate structure begins with a vision. In Chapter 2, we described how to define and develop an effective corporate vision statement. The organizational vision is linked to critical success factors, objectives, targets, and improvement actions, which are then adjusted and fine-tuned to the related business units and teams. Using Corporate Balanced Scorecards, corporate requirements (or system requirements) are defined. These system requirements are then cascaded and communicated to business units or departments, and each department generates its own requirements (called subsystem requirements). Each subsystem requirement then is assigned a sponsor, a champion, and a team. The team defines its own requirements, known as component requirements. Each individual on the team will define his or her requirements, which are called process requirements. This process is illustrated in Figure 11.1, which shows how corporate requirements flow down throughout the organization.

This top-down and bottom-up process is executed iteratively in increasing detail at each successive organizational level. In this manner, the overall organizational strategy is translated systematically into ever more specific plans at each organizational level.

The level of detail at which the translation takes place depends on the organizational typology and the business size. Each department selects those objectives and performance measures from the Corporate Balanced Scorecards (detailed in Chapter 3) that it influences, and then translates those measures into its own situation. When the objectives are linked in this way, local efforts are aligned with the overall organizational strategy.

As stated in Chapter 8, the process used to determine the overall corporate performance depends on the organizational or system structure. Before we proceed to detailing the process on how to assess and evaluate each department's performance and the overall corporate wellness, we need to revisit two types of corporate systems, series and parallel.

11.1.1 Series Systems

In the human body, the heart drives the circulatory system. A brief review of the functioning of the heart will demonstrate a basic series system. The heart is a muscle responsible for pumping blood through the blood vessels by repeated, rhythmic contractions. The right atrium of the heart collects deoxygenated blood from the body, and the right ventricle pumps it to the lungs to remove carbon dioxide and pick up oxygen. The left atrium collects oxygenated blood from the lungs. From there the blood moves to the left ventricle, which pumps it out to the body.

If the heart fails, the entire system shuts down and the person will die or require drastic intervention such as a transplant or serious operation. This is because it is a series system. In a series system, a failure of any unit results in the failure of the entire system (in an organization, this is the equivalent of a department failing to meet its objectives or goals, which results in the failure of the corporation). In most cases, when considering complete systems at their basic subsystem level, it is found that they

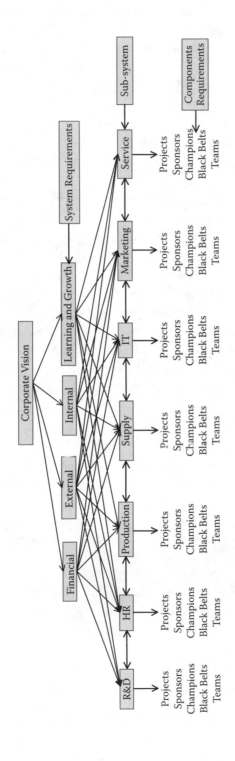

FIGURE 11.1

How corporate systems' requirements flow through the organization.

FIGURE 11.2
Subsystems in a series configuration.

are configured in a series. Figure 11.2 shows subsystems in a series con-figuration; a failure of any of these subsystems will cause a system failure (the failure of the entire corporation to meet its strategic objectives). In other words, all of the units in a series system must succeed for the system to succeed; therefore, all of the departments must meet their subsystems requirements for the entire company to succeed.

11.1.2 Parallel Systems

The circulatory system also contains an example of a parallel system; the two kidneys clean the blood in parallel. The primary role of the kidneys is to maintain balance in the blood by filtering and removing urea and minerals and excreting them, along with water, as urine.

If one kidney fails, the blood will be cleaned by the remaining kidney. There will be strain on the second kidney, but the body will be able to con-tinue functioning. This is a parallel (or a redundant) system.

In a parallel system, as shown in Figure 11.3, at least one of the units must succeed for the whole system to succeed. System failure occurs only when all of the units fail.

The human body has other parallel systems — two eyes, two ears, and so on. Assembly lines, each producing the same product or step in the assembly process, are an example of such systems. In some cases, there are parallel plants making the same product or providing the same ser-vice. In management, identifying alternative people with authority to make decisions is a parallel system. When the person who normally makes

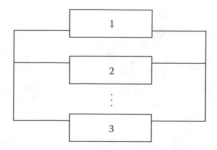

FIGURE 11.3
Simple parallel systems.

the decision is not available, the process continues with a decision by the backup person. When corporations make "risk assessments" of their business, they are looking at what breakdowns could happen (weather, electrical, terror, people, supply chain, and so on) to see what can be done before catastrophe strikes. Often they are identifying where a parallel system is needed as a standby to kick in during an emergency to ensure that the organization is able to continue functioning and meeting its customers' needs.

11.2 CORPORATE SYSTEMS

Just as the human body is composed of both series and parallel systems, corporations are also complex systems that involve both series and parallel configurations, although it is not always easy to recognize which units are in series and which are in parallel.

The system's success rate can be analyzed using the rolled-up DPMO process for systems consisting of parallel subsystems and serial subsystems by calculating the yield for the individual series and parallel sections and then combining them in the appropriate manner. The next sections provide examples of how to calculate the success rate for serial, parallel, and complex processes.

11.2.1 Scanning Serial Processes

The process of scanning the corporate functions is referred to as assessing the performance or the wellness of each department or subsystem by locating weaknesses and identifying opportunities for improvement. A system's requirements are cascaded to subsystem requirements and, for each requirement, a department sponsor, Champion, Black Belt, and teams are assigned to work on each of the subsystem requirements.

Each team then defines goals and the required measures for success. These measures usually are listed in the team charter (see Chapter 6). The DPMO metric is used to measure the team's success in meeting the subsystem requirements. We then roll up the DPMOs for each team to measure the department or subsystem's ability to meet its requirements.

Throughout this book, we have listed common measures for each of the corporate functions, which usually link to the subsystem requirements.

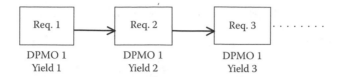

FIGURE 11.4
Production subsystem's requirements arranged in a series system.

To demonstrate this, we will calculate the performance of one department or subsystem, production. Assume that production's subsystem requirements are independent, that is, arranged in a series system (Figure 11.4).

In a pure series system, the subsystem's overall yield is equal to the product of the yield of each requirement in that subsystem.

$$Yield = \prod_{i=1}^{n} Yield_i$$

This means that the department overall yield is equal to $Yield_1 \cdot Yield_2 \cdot Yield_3$, and so on. Table 11.1 shows a simulation of the DPMO and the yield of each requirement in the production subsystem and the calculation of the overall department yield. Using the table in Appendix B, the yield can be converted to DPMO and then to a Sigma level. Note that each subsystem requirement is assigned to a team and we can assess the team capability or DPMO in the same way. These subsystem requirements become projects and assigned to sponsors, Champions, and Black Belts (Figure 11.5).

The same calculation is done for each of the corporation's subsystems, such as Human Resources, IT, R&D, and so forth. Again, using the table in

TABLE 11.1

Overall Production Subsystem Yield

Subsystem Production	DPMO	Yield
Requirement 1	54799	94.52%
Requirement 2	13903	98.61%
Requirement 3	8198	99.18%
Requirement 4	2555	99.74%
Requirement 5	1866	99.81%
	Department Yield	92.20%

Production Sub-System		
Requirement 1	Requirement 2	Requirement 3
Project 1	Project 2	Project 3
Sponsors 1	Sponsor 2	Sponsor 3
Champion 1	Champion 2	Champion 3
Black Belt 1	Black Belt 2	Black Belt 3
Team 1	Team 2	Team 3
DPMO 1	DPMO 2	DPMO 3
Yield 1	Yield 2	Yield 3

Production Subsystem Yield = Yield 1* Yield 2* Yield 3

FIGURE 11.5
Production subsystem requirements assigned to Black Belts.

Appendix B, we convert each department's yield to a Sigma level and use this measure of quality as a basis for any decision to improve any department's performance. Figure 11.6 shows the Sigma level for various departments (subsystems) using a radar chart, a graphical method for displaying multivariable data. It is apparent from the chart that the HR subsystem is performing poorly and needs improvement. We usually assign a Black Belt to address the situation, using the Sigma level as a guide for improvement opportunities. Using this process, management can set goals to improve the performance of their subsystems if needed.

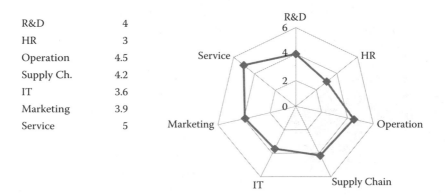

R&D	4
HR	3
Operation	4.5
Supply Ch.	4.2
IT	3.6
Marketing	3.9
Service	5

FIGURE 11.6
Radar chart demonstrating sigma level for various subsystems.

11.2.2 Scanning Parallel Systems

In a simple parallel system (see Figure 11.3), at least one of the units must succeed for the system to succeed. Therefore, in a parallel system, all n units must fail for the system to fail. Put another way, if unit 1 succeeds or unit 2 succeeds or any of the n units succeeds, then the system succeeds. The success rate for subsystem performance, measured using the yield as metric, is given in the following formula:

$$\text{Yield}_{sub} = 1 - [(1 - \text{Yield}_1) \cdot (1 - \text{Yield}_2) \cdot \ldots \cdot (1 - \text{Yield}_n)]$$

or

$$\text{Yield} = 1 - \prod_{i=1}^{n} (1 - \text{Yield}_i)$$

For example, consider a subsystem with three units in parallel systems with yields of 50.00%, 78.80%, and 97.13% respectively; the overall subsystem yield is equal to:

$$\text{Yield}_{sub} = 1 - [(1 - 0.5000) \cdot (1 - 0.7880) \cdot (1 - 0.9713)] = 99.70\%$$

We then convert the subsystem yield to Sigma level using the table in Appendix B. The overall subsystem Sigma level is equal to 4.3. Note that the subsystem's overall yield is greater than any unit yields because they are arranged in a parallel system. Therefore, to improve subsystem performance, use parallel systems as much as possible. In parallel configuration, the unit with the highest yield has the largest influence on subsystem performance.

11.2.3 Combination of Series and Parallel Systems

In order to calculate the yield for a combination of series and parallel systems, we calculate the individual yield for the series and parallel sections and combine them in the appropriate manner. Consider a system with three units. Units 1 and 2 are connected in a series and unit 3 is connected in parallel (Figure 11.7).

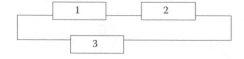

FIGURE 11.7
Combinations of series and parallel systems.

Assume that unit 1 has yield of 99.38%, unit 2 has a yield of 97.72%, and unit 3 has a yield of 90.30%.

First, we calculate the yield of the series, which consists of units 1 and 2.

$$\text{Yield}_{series} = \text{Yield}_1 \cdot \text{Yield}_2$$

This gives $0.9938 \cdot 0.9772 = 0.971141$ or the $\text{Yield}_{series} = 97.11\%$.

The yield of the overall subsystem is then calculated by treating units 1 and 2 as one unit with a yield of 97.11% connected in parallel with unit 3.

Using the equation for parallel systems, the overall subsystem yield is calculated using the following equation:

$$\text{Yield}_{sub} = 1 - [(1-0.9711) \cdot (1-0.9030)] = 99.7\%$$

As indicated, a corporation is comprised of complex systems that sometimes cannot be broken down into a group of series and parallel systems. This is due primarily to the fact that some units might have two paths leading away from it. Several methods are available that calculate the subsystem yield or performance of complex systems. These methods include the decomposition method, the event space method, and the path-tracing method. They are beyond the scope of this book, but for more information on these methods, we suggest you consult books on system reliability. A few software programs on the market are intended for reliability calculations that can also be used to calculate subsystem performance since they use the same methods to determine system reliability and can easily be modified to calculate the performance of the corporate systems. An example of such software is BlockSim (available through ReliaSoft), which provides a comprehensive program for complete system reliability.

11.3 CORPORATE SIGMA INDEX

To calculate the Corporate Sigma Index (CSI), the quality level of the overall corporation, we use a "bottom-up" approach (Figure 11.8). It starts by calculating the DPMO and the yield of each team in each department, then calculating the DPMO and the yield of each department or subsystem.

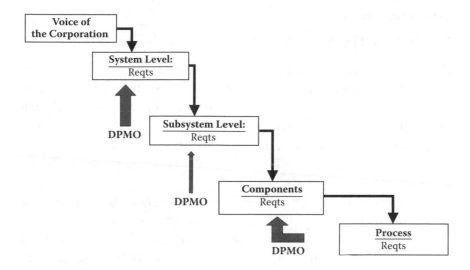

FIGURE 11.8
Roll-up DPMOs.

The final step is calculating the system's yield for the entire corporation or system. The system's yield is equal to the product of each subsystem yield. Assuming we have series systems, $Yield_{sys} = Yield_{R\&D} \cdot Yield_{HR} \cdot Yield_{Op} \cdot Yield_{IT}$. Again, using the table in Appendix B, we convert the corporate yield into DPMO and then Sigma level. The final Sigma level is called the Corporate Sigma Index (CSI). It is a measure of the ability of the corporation to meet its business objectives. We can use this measure to set corporate goals and improve the overall corporate performance (see Table 11.2).

TABLE 11.2

Sigma Level for Various Corporate Subsystems

R&D	HR	Production	Supply Chain	IT	Marketing	Service	System
$DPMO_{R\&D}$	$DPMO_{HR}$	$DPMO_{Pro.}$	$DPMO_{SC}$	$DPMO_{IT}$	$DPMO_{Mar.}$	$DPMO_{Ser.}$	
$Yield_{R\&D}$	$Yield_{HR}$	$Yield_{Pro.}$	$Yield_{SC}$	$Yield_{IT}$	$Yield_{Mar.}$	$Yield_{Ser.}$	System's Yield
$Sigma_{R\&D}$	$Sigma_{HR}$	$Sigma_{Pro.}$	$Sigma_{SC}$	$Sigma_{IT}$	$Sigma_{Mar.}$	$Sigma_{Ser.}$	CSI

11.4 OBJECTIVES OF A CORPORATE CHECKUP

The overall objective of the Corporate Sigma process is to enable the corporation to perform its mission and meet its vision. It translates the corporate vision into actions. The process described is a holistic approach that applies systems engineering methods, which allows you to evaluate the performance or the health of the corporation. It uses a single number that reflects the overall capability of an organization, the Corporate Sigma Index (CSI).

The use of CSI allows corporate leaders to make better decisions regarding improvement opportunities and identifies where to concentrate efforts and resources. Just as in system engineering, the initial CSI calculation will most likely be below the desirable value or the overall system's requirement that is the corporate vision. In order to improve it, management needs to identify improvement opportunities and initiate projects. As subsystems improve, the CSI value improves or grows, and as the CSI value improves, the corporation gets closer and closer to reaching its vision. When the corporation reaches its vision, it is important for management to define a new vision to build on the momentum they built up.

11.5 CORPORATE 911: TRAUMA

> The measure of success is not whether you have a tough problem to deal with, but whether it's the same problem you had last year
>
> **John Foster Dulles**
> *Secretary of state, 1953–1959*

Corporate Sigma is a concrete methodology used to define measure, analyze, improve, and control a company's health. We hope we have been successful in opening your eyes to a new way of thinking about the health of your organization and structuring a system to enhance, support, and sustain its well-being.

Thus far, we have explained in detail a new way of thinking about a corporation by comparing it to the human body. When a person's vital signs turn negative, the person along with the medical profession takes action to bring the person back to normal. The same is true for corporations. In the preceding sections, we have shown you how to assess the health of your organization, and what tools to use to cure your corporate ills. However, as with humans, there are always unforeseen catastrophes, unpredictable events that can significantly alter our well-being in an instant; a car accident, power outage, or a slip on an icy walkway are all examples of such life-threatening emergencies. Unpredictable events such as natural disasters disrupting production, logistics, or workforce; economic recessions; or new products or technologies can affect corporations as well. Some recent examples include Hurricane Katrina, which affected oil and gas availability and diverted construction resources; the credit freeze of 2009; and the emergence of digital photography.

We all know that no matter how well we care for ourselves, emergencies arise, and the need for diet, exercise, and balance are superseded by the need for special and immediate care. At such moments, first responders assess the situation and quickly determine the patient's primary complaint through observation or questioning. They also ascertain if they can handle the situation or if they need to call an ambulance. Their first step is to ensure that the ABCs (Airway, Breathing, and Circulation) are functioning and start containment/corrective actions as they identify problems. While one responder is doing this, another will collect basic information on the patient's medical history, including any special considerations such as allergies, medications, known medical conditions, and, in some cases, religious requirements.

If the decision is to call an ambulance, the information about the patient's condition is relayed to the 911 operator to ensure that the proper level of response is sent. This initial information helps responders determine if additional support such as police or fire departments is needed, for example, to deal with any environmental factors such as crowds, fights, fire, and chemicals that may be contributing to the patient's problem. If the first responders, EMTs, or paramedics are unable to solve the problem through basic first aid, they will either recommend a visit to the doctor or transport the patient to a hospital for additional care.

When a corporation faces an emergency, the Six Sigma DMAIC approach still works, but its focus is now on containment of the problem followed by accelerated corrective action. Even with smooth, well-defined processes that have been optimized through a Six Sigma program (diet, exercise, and balance between bureaucratic and individual decision making), traumas to the corporation do occur. Situations like these can make or break a corporation and its reputation with its clients. (If your experience is anything like ours, the trauma usually seems to come on a Friday afternoon when all of the specialists are out of the office.) This is where the practice that comes from implementing DMAIC can help achieve fast execution:

Define: First responder on the scene does a quick assessment of complaint/problem. Identifies what departments needs are to help resolve the problem —the police, fire fighters, environmental experts, and others needed to contain the situation.

Measure: Check the vital signs for this process.

Analyze: What is the likely scope of the problem? How many departments, offices, or products are affected? What is its impact? Can this situation be managed by the first responders or do you need to pull in others to help manage the problem? Who should be in charge — first responders (people who find the problem), EMT (local experts/Green Belts), or ER (senior management, Black Belts, cross-functional team)?

Improve/Contain/Control: Just as these measures often occur almost simultaneously in medical emergencies, they need to be taken quickly during corporate emergencies. What steps are needed to contain the problem, that is, to restore vital functions? What blocks, whether technological or physical, are needed to keep the problem from spreading? What resources (people, product, information, etc.) are needed?

Repeat cycle as many times as needed.

Like a response to a medical emergency, a corporation's first response to trauma needs to be fast and systematic repetition of, in this case, the DMAIC steps. This allows responders to adjust to any changes in the "patient's" vitals to ensure survival. There is one difference, which is the patient often cannot be transported, and therefore the experts need to be brought to the problem either physically or technologically via the Internet, phone, videoconferencing, and so on to deal with the situation quickly and effectively.

In any emergency, someone must be in charge; therefore, it is best to have an emergency process in place and clearly understood before the problem arises. Usually, the process owner or a designated Six Sigma belt is in charge, depending on the severity of the problem. In this fashion, resolving problems goes more smoothly because everyone knows the expectations and process ahead of time.

Let us consider the following scenario, which illustrates how trauma to a corporation could occur. A client calls/e-mails with a problem. You have been providing them with essentially the same product for years. Your company has even worked jointly with them to develop reusable packaging that not only works for shipping the product but also fits into their production process, saving both companies money while greatly reducing waste.

The lift mechanism has failed, resulting in a near miss for employees in the area, shutting down the customer's production line for several hours and causing lost productivity. They are understandably angry and want a fast response. You know that if you do not resolve this problem quickly, it could happen again or, even worse, the client might decide to make a competitor their primary supplier of this product. A nonperforming, unhealthy company might take the stance that it is time to "CYA" and try to shift the blame to how the product was handled at the customer's site. However, your company decides to recognize the potential damage to the company — it could be a black eye or a knockout depending on the response — and kicks into high gear going using the Rapid DMAIC approach.

> *Define:* E-mail received from client. Problem: Packaging failure at company, which led to a near accident and lost production.
> *Measure:* Customer angry, possible loss of business and reputation.
> *Analyze:* Broken packaging. Need to involve production and maintenance personnel, who work on this product; best to have everyone talking at once.
> *Improve:* Sound the alarm. Contact people involved and set up impromptu conference call.
> *Contain/Control:* Discuss situation. Determine what information is needed.

Repeat:

> *Define:* Describe situation to assembled team.
> *Measure:* What information is available? Perhaps inventory or shipping, but the person responsible for inspection and maintenance data has gone home.
> *Analyze:* List what information is needed. Use five whys or fishbone diagram to seek potential causes. Inventory logs and shipment history shows locations.

Improve: Assign someone to retrieve missing information and others to collect information. Contact production about problem. Contact customer, show concern, and request serial number and photographs of broken package.

Contain/Control: Stop production and shipments until the issue is resolved. Collect data. Define how communication will occur between team members (e-mails, share drive, phone calls, all of the above).

Repeat. At this point, DMAIC should be operating on parallel paths. In this case, we will follow the path that might happen in production with maintenance and inspection.

Define: Packaging failure resulting in potential safety issues.

Measure: How many units are in production? Where are they? Is additional information available from the customer yet?

Analyze: Have units inspected. Document findings (cracks in welds, bends, damage, etc.). Review inspection/maintenance logs. Review failure mode and effect analysis (FMEA) for packaging design and update (create one if none exists).

Improve: Implement improvement opportunities identified in FMEA exercise.

Contain/Control: Green-label all inspected/OK packages. Red-label potential problem packages and move to containment area. 100% inspection of all packages.

Repeat Parallel — Customer Service.

Define: Contact customer. Confirm description of problem. Ask if more details are available.

Measure: Request serial number of package involved. Request photographs.

Analyze: What steps is the customer taking to ensure no repeat of the problem?

Improve: Show concern over problem. Describe briefly what your company is doing to investigate the problem.

Contain/Control: Share with client how inspection should be done. Offer to send someone to help with inspections.

And so on.

As you can see from this brief example, we go through the DMAIC process repeatedly, and on each round, we get closer to a solution. With traumas, you need to contain the problem to ensure that the situation doesn't escalate and worsen the problem.

Now think about a time that you faced a serious problem or trauma at work and you felt good about the resolution of that problem. Think back to how the problem was resolved. Likely, you were following these steps without realizing it. The team was focused on the problem since it was well defined, and everyone was working to resolve it. Now think about a time when everything went wrong. Likely, none of these steps were followed or the assembled group could not get past the define/measure stages because they were too busy assigning blame.

Using the DMAIC process routinely to improve processes should become second nature to everyone. Should a crisis occur, all of the personnel involved are then able to follow a process with which they are familiar and to which they are accustomed, which will lead to a good outcome. The discipline you have instilled in the corporation pays off. People feel valued and energized about their work; instinct kicks in for all the systems, leading to the best possible outcome.

11.6 A HOLISTIC APPROACH: THE VALUE OF DISCIPLINE

Like the human body, where a disciplined approach to diet, exercise, and relaxation wards off illness and injury, the corporation that practices disciplined approaches can ward off illness and injury, making it more resilient to changing environments.

However, it is also important to remember that a corporation is more than the sum of its parts. A holistic approach is needed to ensure the health of the entire corporation. We have all heard of someone dying of a heart attack at a young age, although the person was thought to be vigorous and healthy. Yet an unsuspected problem brought the person down in the prime of life.

The same can occur to a corporation. A failure in one of the subsystems can bring down the entire corporation. Consider a company that makes the best product in their industry. They have the best and brightest employees, innovation is high, and the products in the pipeline look very promising. Everyone wants this product, and the closest competitor is still months or years away from developing something similar. Yet the corporation's accounting system is not working properly. Suppliers are paid late. Management is focused on selling the new product and doesn't consider the issue in accounting to be very important. Occasional late payments become routine. Suppliers start refusing to ship unless they are paid up front. They are calling everyone in the company they know to try to resolve the problem. Employee morale starts falling — who wants to work for a company that cannot pay its bills? Rumors start flying about why the bills have not been paid. The best and brightest employees start leaving; new talent is not interested because the company's credit rating has slipped. During this time, the competition has caught up; they are able to meet demand because they pay their suppliers on time.

A failure in one subsystem brought down the whole corporation, which is why it is important to view all the vital subsystems as part of the whole. If one fails, they all fail, and, in today's economy, it is vital for your corporation to become/remain healthy and resilient to the change. Therefore, should a crisis occur, you will be able to resolve it quickly and prevent a larger catastrophe.

We wish you good luck on your journey toward developing a healthy corporation, and encourage you to remember that although good resolutions sometimes fail on the first try, over time, by changing one habit at a time, you will move your corporation closer to a healthy and sustainable lifestyle.

Appendix A:
CLD Simulation in Excel

CLD SIM

CLD SIM is a Microsoft Excel macro for simulating CLDs and is available from ROI Creations, LLC. To obtain a copy or to schedule a workshop, contact John Dubuc at john@roicreations.com.

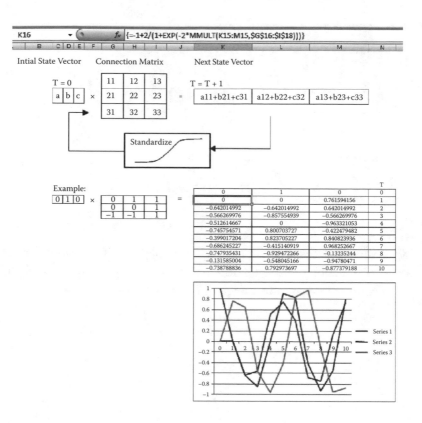

Intial State Vector   Connection Matrix   Next State Vector

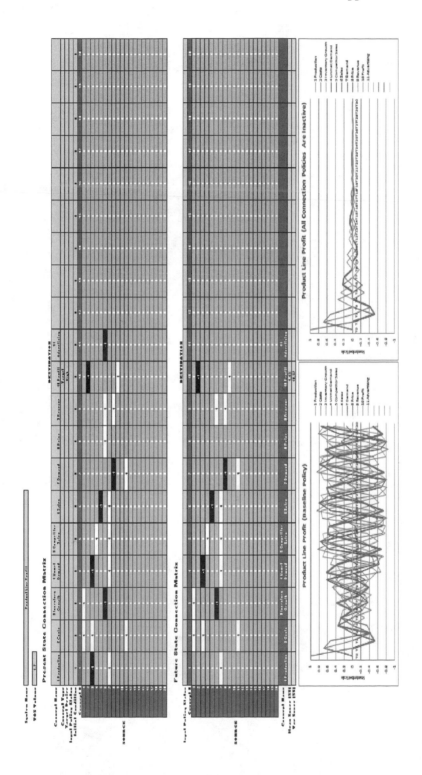

Appendix B:
Relationship between Sigma Level (Short Term), DPMO, and Yield

Sigma Level	DPMO	Yield
1.0	691462	30.9%
1.1	655422	34.5%
1.2	617911	38.2%
1.3	579260	42.1%
1.4	539828	46.0%
1.5	500000	50.0%
1.6	460172	54.0%
1.7	420740	57.9%
1.8	382089	61.8%
1.9	344578	65.5%
2.0	308538	69.1%
2.1	274253	72.6%
2.2	241964	75.8%
2.3	211855	78.8%
2.4	184060	81.6%
2.5	158655	84.1%
2.6	135666	86.4%
2.7	115070	88.5%
2.8	96801	90.3%
2.9	80757	91.9%
3.0	66807	93.32%
3.1	54799	94.52%
3.2	44565	95.54%
3.3	35930	96.41%
3.4	28716	97.13%
3.5	22750	97.72%
3.6	17864	98.21%
3.7	13903	98.61%

(*continued*)

Sigma Level	DPMO	Yield
3.8	10724	98.93%
3.9	8198	99.18%
4.0	6210	99.38%
4.1	4661	99.53%
4.2	3467	99.65%
4.3	2555	99.74%
4.4	1866	99.81%
4.5	1350	99.87%
4.6	968	99.90%
4.7	687	99.93%
4.8	483	99.95%
4.9	337	99.97%
5.0	233	99.98%
5.1	159	99.9841%
5.2	108	99.9892%
5.3	72	99.9928%
5.4	48	99.9952%
5.5	32	99.9968%
5.6	21	99.9979%
5.7	13	99.9987%
5.8	9	99.9991%
5.9	5	99.9995%
6.0	3	99.9997%

Selected Bibliography

A Guide to the Project Management Body of Knowledge (PMBOK Guide), 4th ed. Newtown Square, PA: Project Management Institute, 2008. Available from www.pmi.org.

Abrahams, Jeffrey. *101 Mission Statements from Top Companies: Plus Guidelines for Writing Your Own Mission Statement*. Berkeley, CA: Ten Speed Press, 2007.

American Productivity and Quality Center (APQC). *Aligning Information Technology with Corporate Strategy*. Houston, TX: Consortium Benchmarking Study, 1999.

Anderson, Virginia, and Lauren Johnson. *Systems Thinking Basics, from Concepts to Causal Loops*. Waltham: Pegasus Communications, 1997.

Armstrong, James. "A Systems Approach to Process Infrastructure." International Council on Systems Engineering Symposium, 2005.

Bennis, Warren G. *On Becoming a Leader*. New York: Perseus Books, 1989.

Bennis, Warren G., Rowan Gibson, Alvin Toffler, and Heidi Toffler. *Rethinking the Future*. London: Nicholas Brealey, 1996.

Bloem, Japp, Menno Van Doorn, and Piyush Mittal. *Making IT Governance Work in a Sarbanes–Oxley World*. Hoboken, NJ: John Wiley & Sons, 2005.

Brassard, Michael, and Diane Ritter. *Coach's Guide to the Memory Jogger II*. Salem, NH: Goal/QPC, 1995.

Cater-Steel, Aileen, Wui-Gee Tan, and Mark Toleman. "Challenge of Adopting Multiple Process Improvement Frameworks." 14th European conference on Information Systems, 12–14 June 2006, Goteborg, Sweden.

———. "Transforming IT Service Management—The ITIL Impact." 17th Australasian conference on Information Systems, 6–8 December 2006, Adelaide, Australia.

Clausing, Don P. *Total Quality Development: A Step-by-Step Guide to World Class Concurrent Engineering*. New York: ASME, 1994.

CMMI Product Team. (2007). *Capability Maturity Model Integration (CMMI), Version 1.2.*, 2nd ed. Pittsburgh PA: Software Engineering Institute, Carnegie Mellon University. Available from www.sei.cmu.edu.

Collins J., and J. Porras. *Built to Last: Successful Habits of Visionary Companies*. New York: Collins Business, 2004.

Covey, Stephen R. *Principle Centered Leadership*. New York: Free Press, 1992.

———. *Seven Habits of Highly Effective People*. New York: Free Press, 2004.

———. *The 8th Habit*. New York: Simon & Schuster, 2004.

Creveling, Clyde M., Jeff Slutsky, and Dave Antis. *Design for Six Sigma in Technology and Product Development*. Upper Saddle River, NJ: Prentice Hall, 2002.

Drucker, Peter F. *The Essential Drucker: The Best of Sixty Years of Peter Drucker's Essential Writings on Management*. New York: Collins Business, 2007.

Deming, W. E. *Out of the Crisis*. Cambridge, MA: M.I.T. Press, 1985.

Ferguson, Douglas. "Lean and Six Sigma: The Same or Different?" *Management Services* 51, no. 3 (Autumn 2007): 12–13.

Garvin, David A. *Managing Quality: The Strategic and Competitive Edge.* Tampa, FL: Free Press, 1988.

Gupta, Praveen. *Six Sigma Business Scorecard.* New York: McGraw-Hill Professional, 2006.

Hamel, Gary, and C. K. Prahalad. *Competing for the Future.* Cambridge, MA: Harvard Business School Press, 1996.

Harry, M. J., and R. Schroeder. *Six Sigma: The Breakthrough Management Strategy Revolutionizing the World's Top Corporations.* New York: Bantam Dell, 2005.

Hiekkanen, Kari. "IT Governance: T-76.5762 Legal Aspects of Service Management." Lecture/Presentation, Helsinki University of Technology, SoberIT Software Business and Engineering Institute, 25 November 2008.

Information Technology Infrastructure Library (ITIL) Official Website. www.itit-officialwebsite.com.

Judge, William Q. *The Leader's Shadow: Exploring and Developing Executive Character.* Thousand Oaks, CA: Sage, 1999.

Kaplan, Robert S., and David P. Norton. *The Balanced Scorecard: Translating Strategy into Action.* Boston: Harvard Business School Press, 1996.

———. *The Strategy-Focused Organization.* Boston: Harvard Business School Press, 2001.

Kirwan, K., A. Urs, H. Sassenburg, and Andre Heijstek. *A Unified Process Improvement Approach for Multi-Model Improvement Environments.* Pittsburgh: Software Engineering Institute, Carnegie Mellon University, 2006.

Kosko, Bart. *Fuzzy Thinking: The New Science of Fuzzy Logic.* London: Flamingo, 1994.

———. "Hidden Patterns in Combined and Adaptive Knowledge Networks." *International Journal of Approximate Reasoning* 2 (1988).

Matufelija, B., and H. Stromberg. *Systemic Process Improvement Using ISO 9001:2000 and CMMI.* Boston, MA: Artech House, 2003.

Maxwell, John C. *Developing the Leader within You.* Nashville: Thomas Nelson, 2005.

———. *The 21 Irrefutable Laws of Leadership: Follow Them and People Will Follow You.* Nashville, TN: Thomas Nelson, 1998.

Mayor, Tracy. "Six Sigma for Better IT Operations and Customer Satisfaction." *CIO Magazine* (December 1, 2003).

McAfee, Andrew. "Mastering the Three Worlds of Information Technology." *Harvard Business Review* (November 2007).

OPM3 Product Team. *Organizational Project Management Maturity Model (OPM3),* 4th ed. Newtown Square, PA., Project Management Institute, 2008. Available from www.pmi.org.

———. *Organizational Project Management Maturity Model (OPM3) Knowledge Foundation.* Newtown Square, PA.: Project Management Institute, 2003. Available from www.pmi.org.

Pande, P., R. Neuman, and R. Cavanagh. *The Six Sigma Way.* New York: McGraw-Hill, 1980.

Peterson, Steve, and Barry Richmond. System Dynamics and Public Policy. Undated white paper by the Peterson Group.

Process Classification Framework, Version 4.0. Houston, TX: APQC, 2006. Available from www.apqc.org.

Pyzdek, T. *The Six Sigma Handbook.* New York: McGraw-Hill, 2001.

Rampersad, H. *Personal Balanced Scorecard: The Way to Individual Happiness, Personal Integrity, and Organizational Effectiveness.* Charlotte, NC: Information Age, 2006.

Rampersad, H., and A. El-Homsi. *TPS Lean Six Sigma: A New Print for Creating High-Performance Companies.* Charlotte, NC: Information Age, 2007.

ReliaSoft. *System Analysis Reference, Reliability, Availability and Optimization,* 2007. Available from http://www.weibull.com/systemrelwebcontents.htm.

Richmond, Barry. "System Thinking: Critical Thinking Skills for the 1990s and Beyond." *Systems Dynamics Review* 9, no. 2 (1993).

Rother, Mike, and J. Shook. *Learning to See: Value Stream Mapping to Add Value and Eliminate Muda.* Cambridge, MA: Lean Enterprise Institute, 2003.

Schonberger, Richard J. *World Class Manufacturing.* New York: Free Press, 2008.

Scott, D. Cynthia, Dennis T. Jaffe, and Glenn R. Tobe. *Organizational Vision, Values and Mission.* Mississauga, ON: Crisp Learning, 1993.

Scott, Mark N. "Complementary or Competing? Achieving Synergy with OPM3, CMMI, and ISO 9001–2000," Presentation at the National Defense Industrial Association (NDIA) seventh annual CMMI Technology Conference and User Group, November 2007, Denver, CO.

Senge, P. M. *The Fifth Discipline: The Art and Practice of the Learning Organization.* New York: Doubleday, 1990.

Siviy, J., P. Kirwan, L. Marino, and John Morley. "Strategic Technology Selection and Classification in Multimodel Environments." White paper, Part 2 of five part series, May 2008, Pittsburgh, PA: Software Engineering Institute, Carnegie Mellon University.

Taber, Rod. "Knowledge Processing with Fuzzy Cognitive Maps." *Expert Systems with Applications* 2 (1991).

Womack, J. P., and D. T. Jones. *Lean Thinking: Banish Waste and Create Wealth in Your Corporation.* New York: Simon & Schuster, 1996.

Womack, J. P., and D. Roos. *The Machine That Changed the World.* New York: Scribner, 1990.

Index

About the Authors

Anwar El-Homsi has over 19 years of quality and statistics experience in a variety of industries. He has held engineering and management positions at Becton Dickinson, Eastman Kodak Company, Heidelberg, Xerox Corporation, and Corning Corporation. He is currently the president of Transformation Partners Company. His areas of expertise are Six Sigma methodologies, including Design for Six Sigma (DFSS), design of experiments, statistical process control, and reliability engineering. Mr. El-Homsi is considered  an expert in Six Sigma deployment and philosophy. An outstanding coach and trainer, he has trained more than one thousand engineers and scientists, and mentored many Black Belts who documented millions of dollars in direct savings. He received his M.S. in applied statistics from the Rochester Institute of Technology and his B.S. in engineering from Alfred University. Mr. El-Homsi is a Master Black Belt and certified quality engineer; he teaches Lean and Six Sigma philosophy, tools, and concepts at Bucks County Community College and Erie County Community College. He was a member of the Advisory Council for Rochester Institute of Technology's Center for Quality and Applied Statistics. He is an originator and served as president of the Society of Reliability Engineers, Rochester Chapter. Mr. El-Homsi is the coauthor of the revolutionary book, *TPS-Lean Six Sigma: Linking Human Capital to Lean Six Sigma*.

Jeff Slutsky is worldwide director of Design for Six Sigma at Bausch & Lomb Inc., located in Rochester, New York. He has spent 25 years in medical product development, including 15 years at Eastman Kodak's clinical products division and five years at Johnson & Johnson's Ortho-Clinical Diagnostics. He was CEO of Product Development Systems and Solutions (PDSS), Inc., and served as a worldwide DFSS/product development consultant for Sigma Breakthrough Technologies Inc.

Mr. Slutsky has worked in South Korea, Germany, France, England, the United States, and Malaysia with dozens of companies including 3M, Samsung, Maytag, Hoover, Westinghouse Air Brake, Trane Air Conditioning, Becton-Dickinson, Cummins Engine, and StorageTek. He has trained and certified over 1200 DFSS Green, Black, and Master Black Belts.

His expertise includes corporate deployment of DFSS, new product development process re-engineering and its integration with DFSS product, systems engineering, FDA/ISO design control, gate keeping, and the DFSS tools including stakeholder analysis, quality function deployment, concept creation/selection, measurement system analysis, design of experiments, and robust design.

Mr. Slutsky is an adjunct professor at the Rochester Institute of Technology where he teaches graduate and undergraduate courses in systems engineering, robust design, and product and production systems development. He has guest lectured at Rensselaer Polytechnic Institute and is coauthor of the Prentice Hall text *Design for Six Sigma in Technology and Product Development.*

Mr. Slutsky enjoys cross-country skiing, boating, canoeing, camping, and hiking. He has two children, Jason and Alison, the loves of his life.

Feedback is welcome at ael-homsi@TPcompany.com or nsig@aol.com.